Copyright
Al

No part of this book may be reproduced, stored in a retrieval system, or transmitted by any other means, including photocopying, mechanical, or recording without written permission from the publisher or author except reviewers who may quote brief passages for reviews in newspapers, magazines, journals, or Internet web pages. Permission can be arranged by writing to the publisher.

Published by Shining Tramp Press
2114 Harbor View Drive, Rocky Hill, CT 06067

ISBN 978-0-9749352-1-8

Library of Congress Cataloguing-in-Publication Data

Murphy, Kevin J., 1949-

Lydia Sherman: American Borgia
Kevin Murphy, - 1st ed.

265 p.; 23.5 cm.
Includes author's notes and index.

Murphy, Kevin J., 1949-

1. Sherman, Lydia (1824-1878)
2. Murphy, Kevin; 2013
3. Serial murder investigation - Connecticut, Derby, New Haven, Wethersfield – case study
4. Serial murder, Connecticut - psychology

Printed by Amazon.
First Edition: March 2013

Dedicated to

BRENDAN J. MURPHY
1952-2012

When we were young, he turned me into a reader just by giving me a copy of *The Great Escape*.

Table of Contents

Danbury Genealogy

Preface

Chapter 1   Lydia

Chapter 2   Childhood

Chapter 3   Marriage to Edward W. Struck

Chapter 4   Lydia's Children

Chapter 5   Maria Curtis & Dennis Hurlbut

Chapter 6   Horatio Nelson Sherman

Chapter 7   Arrest & Preliminary Hearing

Chapter 8   Trial in New Haven

Chapter 9   Wethersfield Prison & Lydia's Passing

Appendix A   Lydia's Confession

Author's Notes

Bibliography

Map & Photographic Credits

Acknowledgements

Index

Danbury Genealogy

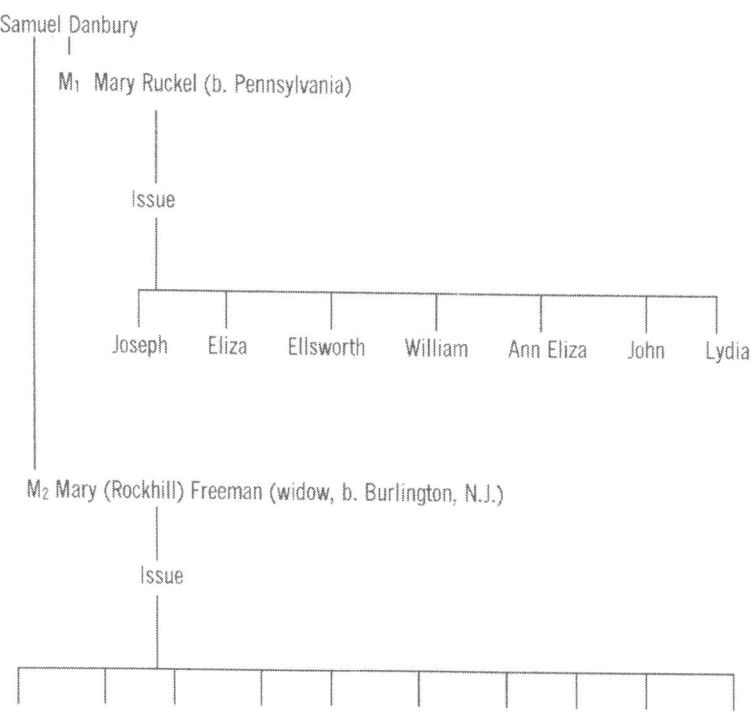

Note: By the time Lydia was arrested for murder in June 1871, her siblings Eliza, Ellsworth, and William had already passed away. Attending her preliminary hearing and trial were Joseph, Ann Eliza, and John, all of whom had since relocated to New Brunswick, New Jersey, from Trenton.

PREFACE

Lydia Sherman began her killing spree in 1864, when she was thirty-nine years old. Her first victim was her husband, Officer Edward W. Struck, who had been dismissed by New York City's Metropolitan Police force for Failure to Obey Rules. In the months ahead, he became despondent and eventually slipped into lunacy. Lydia's solution was to put arsenic in his gruel. Thanks to the poor medical training of nineteenth century physicians, she was able to repeat the process with two subsequent husbands and seven children before she was caught.

The term "serial killer" was first coined in the 1970s by former FBI profiler Robert Ressler. While Ressler worked as a behavior profiler, the concept of the "signature killer" was also developed. Los Angeles's "Lonely Hearts Killer" Harvey Murray Glatman first earned the designation. Though Glatman killed at least three women in California, he was tried and found guilty of first-degree murder in just two cases and put to death in San Quentin's gas chamber in September 1959.

Even after a ten-victim killing spree, Lydia Sherman was just another Gilded Age murderess. At the end of her homicidal spree, Lydia was sentenced to prison for the remainder of her natural life and died behind bars when she was only fifty-three years old.

Even before New Haven Superior Court's Judge David Sanford sentenced Lydia Sherman on January 11, 1873, she was persuaded by personnel at the New Haven County jail to give a confession of her horrific past. (See Appendix A.)

Lydia Sherman's confession of December 28, 1872 was about as close to the truth as she ever ventured, but she was so cunning and deceitful that every word demanded careful examination. Lydia's poor memory for names and dates created a document with many unintentional errors. Beyond that, Lydia changed other items to spare the large Danbury clan of Trenton, New Jersey and her uncle, John Clayton—and his wife and children—of the New Egypt area, near the Pine Barrens of the Garden State.

Lydia Sherman was essentially illiterate and dictated her confession to Warden Charles Webster and his wife Jennette. (An exemplar of her signature, scratched out when she was forty-five, can be seen in Chapter 5.) The confessor thought if she explained everything to God and the world, she would receive forgiveness.

Truth told, Lydia had another reason to make this confession. Authorities in Connecticut were prepared to dump three more arsenic-saturated bodies at her feet—murders she could never have sidestepped. Moreover, if New York authorities ever exhumed her first husband, Edward Struck, and the couple's children from Manhattan's Trinity Cemetery, Lydia's position would become even more untenable. The woman was a consummate dissembler, but she could never have explained away ten arsenical poisonings. With just one count of second-degree murder, Lydia knew that she would die in prison. For once, Lydia Sherman and the truth came together seamlessly. She died in 1878 while incarcerated at the Wethersfield prison and was interred in the Ancient Burying Ground behind the First Church on Main Street. As readers will see, Lydia Sherman's life was improbable and bizarre—from the smallest episodes right up to the ten ghastly murders. However, it's a tale that deserved to be told.

KM

Rocky Hill, CT – March 2013

CHAPTER 1
Lydia

Records from the old Connecticut State Prison at Wethersfield indicate that the murderess Lydia Sherman transferred from New Haven County jail on January 11, 1873, the same day that Judge David C. Sanford handed her a life sentence. This notation concluded a paperwork chain-of-custody protocol, but it wasn't until 4:45 in the afternoon of February 3, 1873 that prison guards ushered Mrs. Sherman to the Wethersfield prison block.

Five shackled men were loaded onto the sleigh outside the New Haven County jail and rode with the murderess to the Elm City's train depot. A crowd gathered to get a glimpse of Lydia, but she "drew a thick veil over her eyes." From Union Station in New Haven, the train, on its normal route, carried the criminals thirty-five miles to Hartford's Union Station. From there, the six were shuffled over to the Park Church (Asylum and High Streets, overlooking Bushnell Park) where another sled waited. Onlookers stared, but Lydia again retreated behind her veil. Only one *Courant* reporter was lucky enough to get a peek. He noted: "she had a sharp, hard face, with a terribly cold eye." Twenty minutes later, the sleigh deposited its sorry cargo at the state prison grounds, a seventeen-acre compound starkly plunked in the farming town of Wethersfield, Connecticut.[1]

When Matron Sarah Waterhouse processed Lydia Sherman into the Connecticut State Prison system, she recorded Lydia's height as five-foot-two-and-three-quarter inches. Waterhouse's account and all existing records describe Lydia's eye color as black, though black irises are extremely rare.[2]

Always thin, Lydia weighed only about 100 pounds. Accounts of Lydia's glamour vary widely. The *New York Herald* referred to her in her early twenties as "a beautiful maiden." A Sunday edition of the same paper labeled her "the infamous and beautiful Lydia Sherman" and later babbled about her "sheer viciousness and beauty."[3] While Lydia was effectively under house arrest awaiting her preliminary hearing in July 1871, a reporter for *The Sun (New York)* declared—

"In appearance, Mrs. Sherman is very striking. . . . Once started on a subject, she rattles away for ten minutes without interruption, smiling sweetly as her eye meets yours. Generally while conversing, she looks you square in the face."[4] On the first day of Lydia's murder trial a *Hartford Courant* journalist wrote, "The prisoner was brought in at 10 o'clock, looking worn by her long confinement, but calm and handsome as ever."

Later, the same newspaper characterized her as "pretty but vicious." The stories go on and on. Lost in the grubby exactitude of these comments is the element of charm. A reporter for London's *Spectator* incisively remarked, "she seems to have had a calm, kindly manner, popular with men."[5] Sex appeal, as always, sold papers.

Before the mid-1830s, newspapers cost six cents and were the province of the wealthy. Just as crime began to rise wildly, new technology allowed New York entrepreneurs to launch papers that sold for only a penny. Benjamin Day first printed *The Sun* in 1833 and a half dozen imitators quickly took up the gauntlet. In 1835, just when readers thought that the bottom of the journalistic barrel had been plumbed, a small, cross-eyed Scottish immigrant, James Gordon Bennett, perfected the art form with his *New York Herald*. Bennett's true genius lay in his obsession with crime, and he soon became the biggest guttersnipe publisher in New York history. These papers thumbed their noses at society, as street urchins aggressively hawked penny dailies full of police news and sensational murder stories.[6]

As Bennett emblazoned his family's coat of arms on the lowest form of journalism, fate handed him the crime of the century—the hatchet murder of a beautiful young prostitute. The object d'art of the *Herald's* little gold mine was Helen Jewett (née Dorcas Doyen), born in rural Maine. Her career as a soiled dove began in Portland, wound its way through Boston, and climaxed in Manhattan, where she became a top earner at an upscale Thomas Street brothel run by a woman with the pseudonym Rosina Townsend. About three o'clock in the morning of April 10, 1836, a regular patron viciously attacked Helen Jewett with a hatchet until her lifeless body lay in an ugly pool of blood. In an effort to hide evidence, the killer then set Helen Jewett's body ablaze. The police soon brought in a suspect, Richard Robinson, the son of a prominent New Haven County, Connecticut farmer. (Robinson was eventually acquitted of the murder.)[7]

Though it hadn't been done before, Bennett went directly to the place of attack. With a little money placed in the right hands, Bennett was given unfettered access to the crime scene. A police officer pulled back the covering from the dead girl's corpse, and Bennett went to work. The scene was so ghastly, reported Bennett that "he could scarcely look at it for a second or two."[8]

Day after day, the *Herald* saturated the streets of New York with details of the butchered prostitute and the farm boy suspect from the respectable family. It was a new type of journalism, featuring close observation and salacious, titillating reportage. His readership couldn't get enough. Lost on no one was the fact that the penny dailies benefited mightily when the killers and their victims were attractive people.

Regardless of the many different variations on the theme of Lydia Sherman's looks, it must be believed that she projected a certain amount of magnetism and charm, and not surprisingly, men sought her out. This appeal, allure or *je ne c'est quoi* is very common among female sequential killers, particularly black widows who specialize in wealthy spouses. True, Lydia was only semi-literate, but she hid it well, and managed to fascinate new acquaintances.[9]

After she was convicted of murder in New Haven Superior Court, Lydia found obscurity at the Wethersfield prison from February 1873 until May 1878. The women inmates were of course separated from the male prisoners, and during the five-years Lydia spent behind bars, the number of women housed in the female quarters fluctuated between one and nine. In September 1873—seven months after her arrival—Lydia was the only woman prisoner. She spent a great deal of her time "sewing on garments" in the prison's huge unisex laundry room.[10] Her siblings, who had all settled in New Brunswick, New Jersey, never visited.

Matron Sarah Waterhouse, who ran the women's quarters, wasn't overly consumed with watching Lydia even though a murderess with ten victims was unheard of in the 1870s. Still, Lydia Sherman's presence must have caused prison officials to ponder their means of confinement. Was Lydia more cunning and devious than other prisoners? Not to Sarah Waterhouse. For her, Sherman was just another callous inmate and she had seen a number of them.[11] Without arsenic, Sarah presumed, Lydia posed little threat to her keepers.

Historically, female murderesses show a preference for poison—especially arsenic—and there were a number of cases throughout the United States by 1873. Laura Fair of San Francisco, Phoebe Westlake of Chester, New York, and Elizabeth Wharton of Baltimore all killed with venom, and buried two to four victims apiece. With the blood of ten people on her hands, Lydia Sherman earned the sobriquet, "Queen

Poisoner".[12] The fact that she looked more like a belle and less like a monster peaked the public's curiosity.[13]

Sometimes newspaper reporters—who as a rule love gallows humor—couldn't help but poke fun at this modern day "Borgia".[14] The *Boston Post* once printed, "Lydia is allowed to take care of the plants in the Connecticut State Prison, and she poisons the bugs beautifully."[15]

Given Lydia's apparent good behavior, Matron Waterhouse's job was dull. When the number of female prisoners climbed to fifteen during the 1860s, two matrons were required, but since 1873 Sarah Waterhouse, forty-five years old, worked the women's quarters by herself. She wore her dark brown hair pinned up in a bun, and—bun included—she stood about five feet tall. Like Lydia, she didn't weigh much more than a hundred pounds. She dressed conservatively, usually adding a light-colored scarf, which she knotted at her neck. Earning an annual salary of only $208, Sarah Waterhouse brought home about half of what the guards on the men's side made.[16]

Lydia fell quietly into the routine of the prison, and eventually became no more to Matron Waterhouse than a spectral shadow appearing and disappearing quietly in the small women's quarters of the penitentiary. However, while the matron was lulled to sleep by the monotony, Lydia schemed.

Only a couple of women had escaped from the Wethersfield prison since it opened in 1831. Also, some male prisoners had wandered off from their jobs in the fields or slipped away from a coal gang or group of inmates shoveling snow. Beyond that, there had been numerous calculated escapes. In just the handful of years since Warden Edward "E. B." Hewes had been in charge, five men had absconded, including one inmate who managed to go over the wall in 1876 while helping to repair cornices on the main building. The first four were not caught, but the inmate fixing the moldings was recaptured on a nearby road shortly after the alarm sounded. In sum, escape was possible for the truly motivated. It was Lydia's turn to try.[17]

Thanks to the quietude, Matron Waterhouse settled into some rather sloppy habits—including visiting friends in Wethersfield during the quiet evening hours after supper and before slumber roll call. Lydia recognized this absence as an opportunity.

Regardless of her mode of escape, Lydia sensed that she needed some leeway. Because it afforded her reduced duties, greater freedom and less scrutiny, illness became her companion. Oddly enough, playing the part of the terminally ill woman proved somewhat difficult for Lydia. Her sister, Ann Nafey, once observed that Lydia was "remarkably good natured, always pleasant, laughing, and full of fun. Nothing ever seemed to trouble her."[18]

Lydia rose to the challenge and feigned malady beautifully—complete with convincingly executed fainting spells. Through the usual prison channels, she got hold of some yellow crayons and routinely massaged her face and hands with this waxy substance until her skin took on the jaundiced color of a deathly ill patient. It worked. Her solo performances netted long periods of time in her cell. There wasn't much anyone could do, so they left poor Lydia alone with her indisposition. (The Connecticut State Prison at Wethersfield always kept a small infirmary, but did not have a full time medical officer until 1898 when a new "bughouse" was built and thirty-three prisoners were transferred in from the insane unit of the Middletown Hospital.)[19]

After renovations were completed at the end of 1876, four tiers comprised the Wethersfield woman's cellblock—with ten cells per floor. The basement pens and those on the fourth floor were seldom used. During the "lights out" bed check at 10 o'clock, Matron Waterhouse shouted a "good night" to each prisoner. She waited for a response, and then locked the inmate's cell door, otherwise open to the hallway during the day. Typically, she locked the pens on the main floor first and then walked up the stairs to lock the doors on the upper level.[20]

Lydia's disguise as a terminally ill patient bought her exactly the autonomy she needed to perfect her escape. The jaundiced color of Lydia's flesh, along with wooziness and the feeble bearing of a very sick woman, persuaded Matron Waterhouse to bend the rules. Lydia was allowed to spend more and more time in her cell and to skip the 10 o'clock "good night." Waterhouse even exempted Lydia from the tedious work of cleaning the cellblock.

On February 4, 1876, when a Rhode Island prison reformer, Henry Dorsey, hosted a dinner for the Wethersfield convicts, a reporter wrote, "Mrs. Lydia Sherman, the Derby murderess, [is] unable to attend the service; her health is very poor, and she is failing fast."[21] Lydia's plan was working magnificently.

As the guard performed her duties day after day, the increasingly yellowed Lydia surreptitiously watched and listened. One Tuesday night, May 29, 1877, Lydia heard Matron Waterhouse speak of going to a church caucus in Wethersfield. Warden E. B. Hewes—not a particularly tough keeper—frowned on such plans, but the officers at the prison worked long hours and Hewes occasionally showed some flexibility. Besides, the few inmates in the female cells would be of no concern as long as Matron Waterhouse securely locked the complex.

When Sarah left, Lydia immediately convinced one of the younger inmates to lower the wicks of the gas wall sconces in the hallway, claiming the light hurt her eyes. She then went over to the sink, where she spent an unusual amount of time, "getting rid of the artificial, in order to secure a natural complexion, and thus make detection more difficult."[22]

When Sarah Waterhouse did not return to the prison at bedtime, Lydia decided to make her move. She quickly got out of bed, arranged the covers to look like she was sleeping soundly, undressed, and then deftly donned a white muslin dress with purple polka-dots and a brown veil—both stolen from the laundry and squirreled away for months. The soon-to-be free woman threw some keepsakes into a sack, tucked some money into her stocking, smoothed her garments, and was ready. Her bankroll consisted of thirty dollars—ten dollars from the sale of homemade articles to other inmates, plus another twenty given to her by New London burglar, George Minor, released a few weeks earlier. Lydia had sewn some shirts for Minor in addition to other favors. No, not intimate favors. Truth told, Lydia's fellow inmates considered her as a prim, proper religious woman.[23]

Sarah Waterhouse finally dashed back into the complex at 10:30 p. m., and she forgot, as she often did, to lock the gate just inside the outer door. Upon hearing the matron's footfall, Lydia quickly exited her cell and secreted herself in a storage chamber—the first pen on her block. She was now only fifty feet from the front door of the prison.

The women's penitentiary was quiet. With very little light, the matron rushed around and locked the cells on the first floor and then quickly ascended the stairs to lock the units on the second tier. Lydia waited patiently in the storage cell, afraid to draw a breath.

Luck was with Lydia. One of the inmates on the second floor conveniently shouted, "Rat! . . .I saw a rat!" This horror turned the whole place into a madhouse. Inmates screamed and carried on like banshees. While Sarah Waterhouse raced back to the kitchen looking for a brighter lamp and some kind of blunt instrument, Lydia advanced just a little bit and crept into the small office next to the kitchen. After that, she was able to slip behind a jutting partition next to the stairs. As soon as Matron Waterhouse found the right implements, she passed right by the frozen-still Lydia, and ascended the stairs a second time. As she did, Lydia tiptoed down a short hallway and out the front door. She slinked across

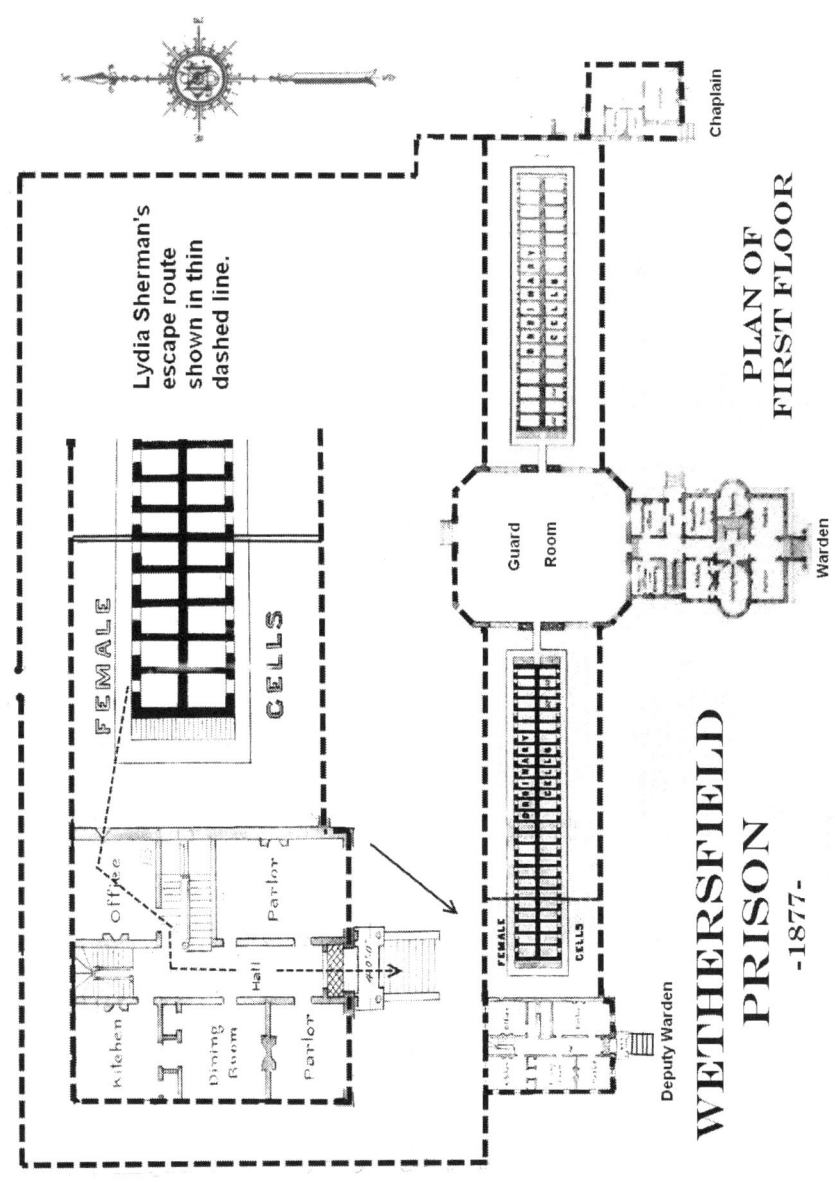

the small stoop, down a few steps, and with confidence waltzed down the prison's bluestone walkway.[24]

One of the prison attendants noticed a pedestrian, but mistook the form in the polka-dot dress for the warden's wife, who might have ventured out to meet her daughters coming from a concert at the Baptist Church. Lydia walked west on Prison Street and then north on the main road toward the city. Hartford Avenue was one of the widest boulevards in the old village and sported an eccentric collection of well-spaced houses. Some of them predated George Washington's presidency, while more recently, wealthy Hartford retailers built a number of stately homes. Some of these newer properties used gaslights, but that night, nothing illuminated Hartford Avenue.

She wanted to catch the last horse car into Hartford, which usually trundled by around 11 o'clock. However, when it finally arrived, Lydia spotted Dan Hayden, the former post office clerk who had served a stretch in the state prison for robbing the mails.[25] Lydia didn't feel she could trust Hayden, so she let the car go. Instead, she walked along the Hartford & Wethersfield Horse Railroad lanes until she reached the Valley Railroad tracks at the north end of Hartford Avenue (still in Wethersfield). It was so pitch black that Lydia got completely confused and mistakenly followed the Valley Railroad line all the way to the massive Colt Patent Fire-Arms manufactory on the banks of the Connecticut River in Hartford. There, she glimpsed a gaslight at the corner of Charter Oak Avenue. She turned into the street. Eventually, Lydia found a man and asked for directions to the train depot. The man tried to direct her, but couldn't seem to make himself understood. Finally, he gave up and escorted the lost out-of-towner across Bushnell Park and left her outside Union Station. When Lydia got to the platform, the 1:07 a.m. "owl train" to Springfield, Massachusetts sat patiently on the tracks. She got on board without buying a ticket.

Lydia's escape featured an enviable start. Not until 7:45 the following morning did anyone at the prison notice her absence. Josephine Hewes, the warden's daughter, happened to wander over to the female sector, and not seeing Lydia, asked questions. A search ensued. Law enforcement officers of every city, town and county scoured the state—particularly the environs of Wethersfield. The *New York Times* described the runaway as having "black hair, and a dark sallow complexion, almost approaching a saffron color."[26] Lydia's illness gambit had triumphed.

Spurious sightings were reported. Some people felt Mrs. Sherman found refuge in Wethersfield, while others insisted she secured a good hiding place in Hartford. On June 2, New Britain's police chief issued a dispatch claiming Lydia had been seen on the New Hartford road, going west.

CHAPTER 2
Childhood

Lydia Sherman was born in Trenton, New Jersey on Christmas Eve 1824, the youngest of her mother's seven children. Her father, Samuel Danbury, was a butcher with his own shop in the city's small business district. He also rented a stall in Trenton's successive public markets near the base of King (Warren) and Queen (Broad) Streets. With the help of two wives—both named Mary—Samuel Danbury ran this business for more than fifty years and fathered at least fifteen children. (Samuel had seven children by his first wife, eight by his second wife, and acted as guardian for two stepchildren.)[27]

Samuel Danbury's father, also named Samuel, owned a farm in East Amwell Township, just north of Trenton, where Lydia's father and his siblings grew up. Samuel Danbury the junior, born in 1790, had little time for school and the resulting illiteracy made business life difficult and denied him a part in the governance of his adopted hometown.[28]

Sometime around 1811, Lydia's father moved to Trenton to open his own butcher shop. In the same year, Samuel Danbury met and married Mary Ruckel, who was originally from Pennsylvania. Mary handled correspondences, billing and bookkeeping. When Samuel Danbury's signature was required, he signed with an X.[29]

At the time of their nuptials, Samuel was twenty-one and Mary was seventeen. In a little over one decade, Samuel and Mary Danbury birthed seven children, built up Samuel's butcher shop, and became reasonably successful as they took their place in the life of Trenton. Sadly, everything fell apart when Mary Danbury suddenly died in the fall of 1825.

In an effort to lighten his load, two of the smaller children—and more likely three—were sent to live with relatives. Ann Eliza was placed with an aunt in Burlington, New Jersey. Lydia, the youngest, was put in the care of a grandmother, Widow J. Clayton, "and taken to the territory in New Jersey known as 'New Egypt,' where she resided for some years."[30] Clayton was a fairly common name in New Egypt. By 1840, there were eleven separate Clayton households.[31]

Samuel married Mary (Rockhill) Freeman—widowed with two children—and eventually became the patriarch of a large blended family. Eight more children were born between 1826 and 1839.[32]

Without stretching the point, it could be stated that Samuel Danbury's life was completely built around the women who enabled him to function in a city that, year by year, became more sophisticated and more important in the judicial, legislative and executive life of New Jersey. In the early 1800s, Trenton blossomed as an industrial center with manufacturing plants producing iron, steel and textiles. Later, European immigrants moved into Trenton to work in its growing pottery businesses and the wire rope manufactory of the bridge builder John Roebling, who opened his first facility in 1848.[33]

When Samuel Danbury first started his butcher shop, Trenton had been the state capital (since 1790), but the legislature met there even before that date. The town (north of the Assunpink Creek) was built primarily along two north-south parallel streets, King and Queen, with Front Street (now State Street), the connector on the south. Trenton was an important city. Sitting at the head of navigation on the Delaware River, a major route from New York to Philadelphia, it was also one of the few post towns in New Jersey. Still, in the early/mid 1800s, Trenton served as home to only about 1,500 people.[34]

Like all of the slowly blossoming towns of early-nineteenth century America, Trenton was a dusty little place with dirt streets, poor firefighting capabilities, and no sewage system worthy of the name. Since 1804, a wooden log-pipe aqueduct delivered drinking water thanks to Stephen Scales who capitalized on a robust stream moving through his farm in the Fifth Ward.[35]

Merchants had small shops, but the town created public "markets" (much like today's farmers' markets) where venders from all over the city and countryside could sell fresh produce, fish and meat. There were a number of different locations over the years, but Samuel Danbury rented first a stall in the State Street market and moved to the Greene Street market in 1845, a large open space with 32 stalls each renting for 20 shillings.[36]

Housewives and servants plied the market all day long, as butchers and farmers laid out their very best meat, fish and produce for public consumption. Samuel maintained his brick and mortar shop where he packed the large orders of steaks and chops for his commercial customers, but also rented the public market stall and battled head-to-head with his competitors for the retail dollar.[37]

The atmosphere between the different merchants was not always cheerful. At one point, for example, one of Samuel Danbury's competitors was brought up on charges for offering, "for sale the flesh of a sheep, and selling part of the same, knowing it to be unwholesome." Indeed, in court, Samuel Danbury was forced to testify that he and Jacob Baumgartner "were both butchers, their stalls opposite to each other; that he had seen in May a sheep at Baumgartner's stall which he told witness [Danbury] died without being slaughtered; and that witness [Danbury] saw him sell a leg to a lady."[38]

Later that same day, Baumgartner was brought before the bar and charged with "exposing for sale the flesh of a hog slaughtered while diseased, and for selling the same, knowing it to be diseased." Once again, Samuel Danbury was forced to testify to the selling of the pork,

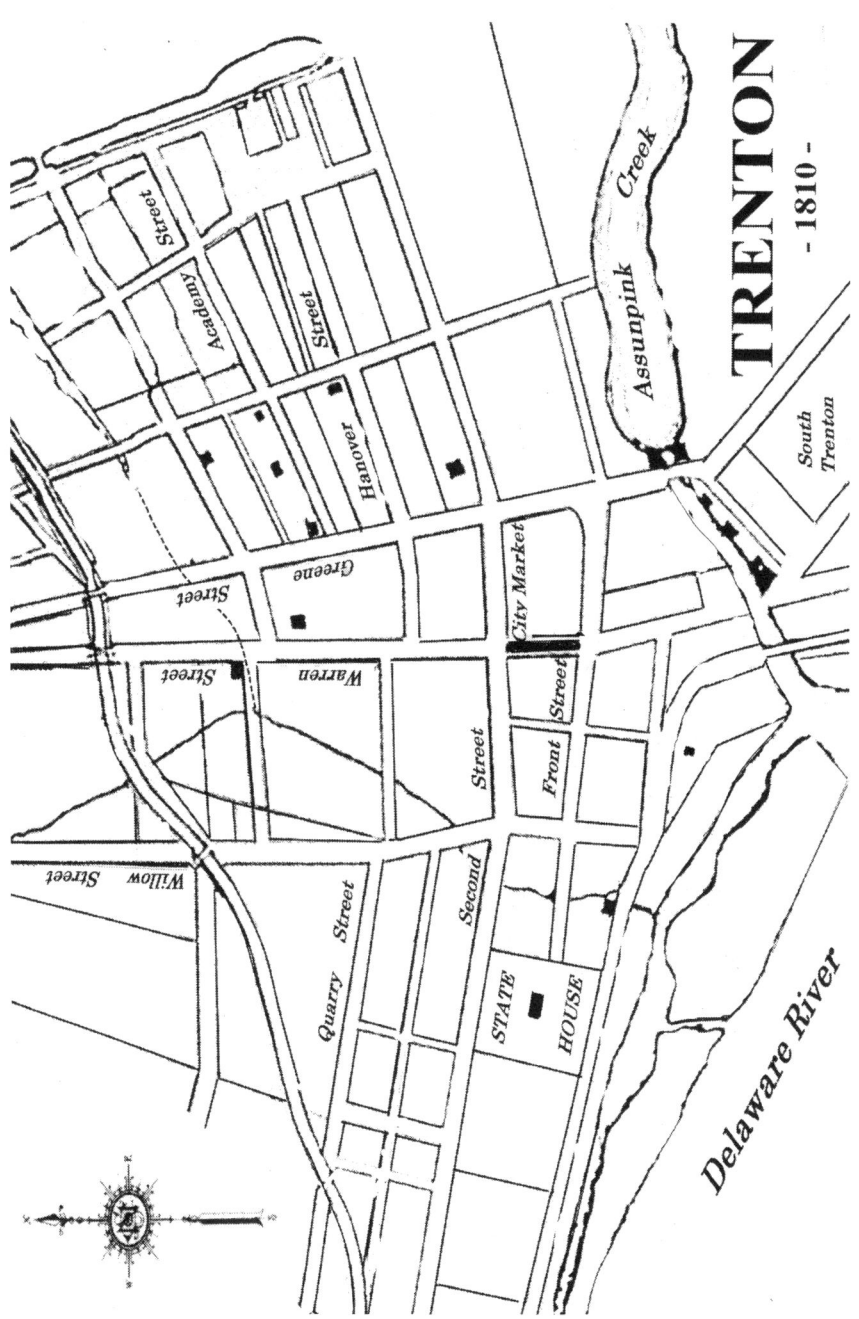

and was satisfied that it was diseased. He testified, " 'I told Baumgartner that I should not like to eat such pork.' His answer was that, 'If people didn't know it, it made no difference.' He [Baumgartner] told me it came from the still house; he had bought it for six or seven dollars, and it weighed over 300 lbs., and that he had made more money off it than all the meat that was in the market that day." The courts fined Baumgartner for these misdeeds and the two butchers left the courthouse to return to work as usual.[39]

Still, Lydia's father's business practices weren't really a part of her life. Within days of losing her mother, Lydia's father cast her from his life as he would a calf carcass. Could this abrupt separation have played a part in her adult psychosis?

The British psychoanalyst John Bowlby, building on Freud's work,[40] concedes that most children who have undergone experiences such as Lydia's, often recover and resume normal development. But, some don't.

Why some individuals should recover, largely or completely, from experiences of separation and loss while others seem not to is a central question, but one not easily answered. . . . Conditions likely to play a part [in differential response] can be considered under two main headings: [1] those intrinsically to or closely associated with the separation itself, notably the conditions in which a child is cared for while away from the mother, and [2] those present in the child's life over a long period, notably his relations with parents during the months or years before and after the event.[41]

In Lydia's case, "her grandmother" in Hornerstown became her primary caregiver.[42] As far as Bowlby's second concern—after Lydia was removed to Hornerstown, she had little or nothing to do with her father. In fact, Lydia gave many interviews to reporters and jailors following her arrest and conviction for murder. She always mentioned the death of her mother, but never talked about her father. Samuel Danbury died in 1868, just three years before Lydia was taken into custody in New Brunswick, New Jersey. Since Lydia knew some of her siblings during that period, she no doubt had heard of her father's passing and possibly more.

Hornerstown, Lydia's new home from roughly 1825 to 1840, was only one of about a dozen small crossroads that were lumped together with New Egypt—an unincorporated village until 1845—for census purposes. A family that lived in a tiny village like Hornerstown, usually simplified matters by telling outsiders they lived in "the New Egypt area." New Egypt was the biggest village and had the largest mill. Allentown, Cream Ridge, Arneystown, Imlaystown, Prosper, Goshen and Hornerstown were a few of the other hamlets of far western Monmouth County, New Jersey, that were thrown together with New Egypt in Upper Freehold Township at census time.[43]

During Lydia's childhood, there were only 675 families—about 4,500 people—including 14 slaves and 105 freed slaves in the forty-seven square miles of Upper Freehold Township. Very few Native American families remained in the area, because the three different branches of the indigenous Delaware (Lenni Lenape) tribe and the local Lahway Indians had already been uprooted and driven to reservations west of the Mississippi River. Now, in 1825, Hornerstown contained "several dwellings, a gristmill, a saw mill, and a fulling mill."[44] In truth, the village was just two narrow dirt roads crossing amid a few shacks, dwarf pitch pine, scrub oak and white cedar trees.

Lydia grew up in her grandmother's home until she was about seven or eight years old.[45] When Lydia was strong enough to work on a farm, she moved in with her Aunt Elizabeth and Uncle John next door to Widow Clayton. As Lydia later recounted, "We all worked hard, and I was able to go to school about three months in the year. I never attended school much when a girl."[46]

The Claytons were a family that Lydia always praised extravagantly. Of her Uncle John she submitted, "In his family, I was always treated with the same kindness as the other members."[47] Lydia helped on John Clayton's farm until she was fifteen and a half.

Hornerstown was a typical South Jersey-Pine Barrens settlement. In the early 1800s, there was little difference between the people who actually lived in the Pine Barrens and the farm folks who grubbed a living on its margins.

The Pine Barrens encompassed about six hundred and fifty thousand acres of South Jersey, and huge sections have always been uninhabited. Twenty thousand and thirty thousand acre tracts with nary a soul living there—even today. The earliest European settlers of the area found the acidic, sandy soil worthless as farmland and refused to clear it. Today's "Pinelands National Reserve" is actually much larger than the original hundreds of thousands of acres that nineteenth-century neighbors called the Pine Barrens. So said, New Egypt is among the towns that today form the northwestern boundary line of the Pinelands National Reserve.[48] During the 1800s, the few people who lived in the Pine Barrens, the "pineys," were accused of being illiterate, criticized for supposedly working sporadically, vilified for alcoholism and at least some incestuous behavior. After the impure bog iron and blast furnace business of the 1830s and 1840s collapsed, most of the pineys depended on simple moss, berry, and wood gathering for their livelihood. In the spring, the pineys went into the lowlands to gather sphagnum moss; come summer, they shook blueberry bushes to coax the ripe fruit into boxes; cranberries followed in the fall. The seasonal berries

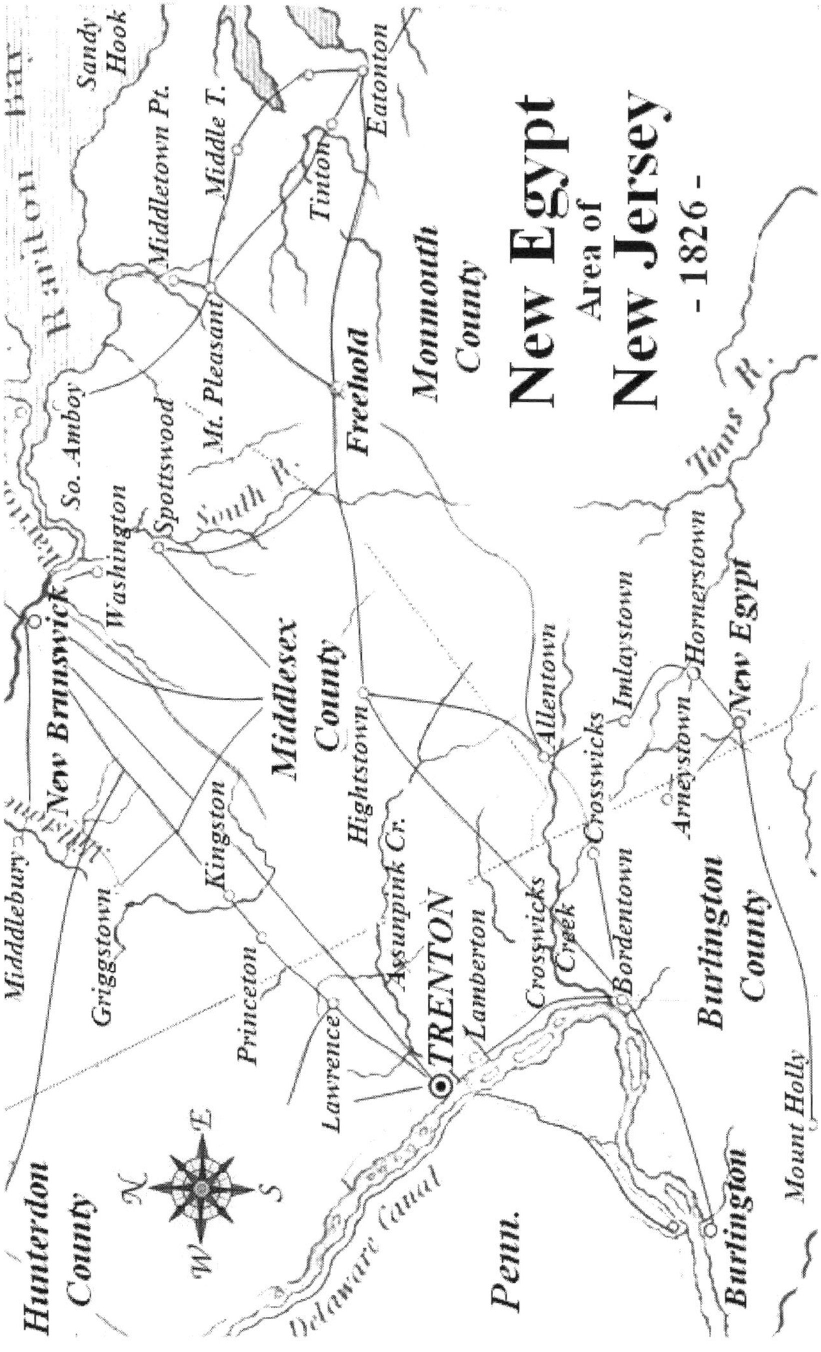
New Egypt
Area of
New Jersey
- 1826 -
Hunterdon County
Middlesex County
Monmouth County
Burlington County
Penn.
Sandy Hook
Middletown Pt.
Middle T.
Eatonton
Tinton
Mt. Pleasant
Freehold
So. Amboy
Spottswood
South R.
Washington
New Brunswick
Middlebury
Griggstown
Kingston
Princeton
Lawrence
TRENTON
Lamberton
Assunpink Cr.
Hightstown
Allentown
Crosswicks
Crosswicks Creek
Bordentown
Imlaystown
Arneystown
Hornerstown
New Egypt
Toms R.
Mount Holly
Burlington
Delaware Canal
N
E
S
W

were trucked to towns with canneries—including neighboring New Egypt—for processing. In the winter, they relied on rudimentary cordwood and charcoal businesses.[49]

Just beyond the Pine Barrens, in the small farming communities, clusters of modest houses sheltered plenty of day laborers, farmers, sawyers, millers, and a profusion of basketmakers who improvised beautifully with the available resources. New Egypt had as many as eighteen basketmaking businesses. Using corn shucks, grass, pine needles, reeds, roots, vines and tree splints, locals created and sold a vast array of baskets. Descendents of the early settlers of Hornerstown, like Harry and Ward Horner, made white-oak splint baskets. These hand-fashioned works of art were used to carry oysters, fish, clams, berries and other fruits. Other styles toted clothes and household items around homesteads and farms.

Mormons settled New Jersey in 1832 and arrived at Hornerstown shortly thereafter. During Lydia's stay, there were about 100 members of the Hornerstown Mormon Church. Of interest here though is the Methodist faith. Preachers traveled on horseback and were encouraged to "work a circuit." Joseph Cromwell introduced Methodism to Hornerstown Protestants in the late 1700s. Originally, meetings were held in private homes. Then a farmer, Job Horner, donated an acre of land for the construction of the Zion Methodist Episcopal Church completed around 1800.[50]

Lydia named two of her children after icons of the Methodist religion—John Wesley and George Whitfield—and insisted on a Methodist Episcopal service before she was laid to rest in 1878. She most likely attended Hornertown's Zion Methodist Episcopal church with her grandmother, aunt, uncle and cousins.

Later we shall see that at the age of thirty-nine, Lydia became a murderess. Why? The many different forces that brought Lydia to her abysmal end will all come to light as her story unfolds, but it is well to keep in mind that the poorly educated medical doctors of the 1800s actually facilitated her killing. For this reason, it is important to examine very carefully the different types of medical practitioners and their educations during Lydia's lifetime. While this knowledge does not justify or excuse Lydia's behavior, it does give us a level of understanding that is crucial.

When it came to medical doctors of the New Egypt area between 1825 and 1840, the residents were like the denizens of the most rural communities all over America, which is to say there were few allopathic physicians (the forebears of today's medical doctors). In the first half of the nineteenth century, a doctor could succeed only under two conditions. Firstly, a physician needed to locate in an area where there were enough wealthy people to support his practice. This definitely was not the case in Hornerstown. Secondly, a physician had to offer services that were demonstrably better than what the locals could provide for themselves. This also was not the case in Lydia's hamlet.[51]

A few of the larger villages near Hornerstown—Allentown, Imlaystown and Cream Ridge—supported a single practitioner, but these doctors made only a meager living and were often involved in other businesses. For example, Dr. George F. Fort went to the University of Pennsylvania Medical School and set up practice in Imlaystown in 1830. Fort quickly got involved in politics—later railroads—and first participated in New Jersey's government in 1844. He followed that with terms in both chambers of the legislature and then served as governor of the state from 1851 to 1854. Afterwards, Dr. Fort returned to Imlaystown to practice medicine once again, but finally retired to New Egypt He died on April 22, 1872. (Dr. Fort passed away during Lydia's eight-day murder trial in New Haven, Connecticut.)[52]

In the early ninetieth century, physicians spent hours on horseback or in a carriage moving from one sick patient to another. It was a hard way to make a living. Obviously, if patients lived in a village, a doctor might be able to see a great many of them in a ten- or twelve-hour day. However, in the countryside, men of medicine spent far more time trundling along rocky, rutted roads in their buggies than they did seeing patients. The dearth of medical practitioners in rural areas was just a fact of life that doctors and country folks accepted.[53]

In the countryside—places like Hornerstown—lay practitioners were trained in the arts of healing with native herbs, spices, nostrums, and plasters. Even a highly competent doctor could not compete with village practitioners who treated the practice of medicine as a birthright. The poor, rural people of America developed an unerring confidence in their own common sense. Farm families would nurse their own back to health and were quick to rely on the help of a village elder recognized for competence based on experience and inherited knowledge.

It was a shaky time for American allopathic medicine. Doctors wanted desperately to form societies and gain recognition for unique skills. Their potential patients demurred, choosing instead to handle the problems of daily medical care themselves. The distrust of physicians in rural areas like Hornerstown went even deeper because physicians—allopaths—still practiced "heroic" medicine, a great deal of which included bloodletting, and cleaning out the stomach and bowels with powerful emetics and cathartics, like calomel (mercurous chloride).[54]

While Lydia was growing up in her grandmother's home, farm wives were expected to deal with illness and to maintain an assortment of remedies. They kept a wide variety of herbal medicines on hand—as they would a sewing kit or a button box. In the late fall, women put up medicinal herbs just as they did culinary specimens. Self-help medicinal books, like Buchan's *Domestic Medicine*, published in Philadelphia in 1771, offered detailed advice.[55] John C. Gunn's *Domestic Medicine*—which appeared in 1830 and by mid-century replaced Buchan's work as a popular favorite—was written "In Plain Language, Free from Doctors Terms."[56] Most of these remedies worked for the people who chose to use them.

Remembering Lydia's affiliation with the Methodist church, it is worth mentioning that a popular text, *Primitive Physic*, preached that most folks were fully competent to treat disease. This book of remedies was compiled in 1747—in England—by John Wesley, one of the most important figures in the founding of Methodism.

These medical books differed considerably from allopathic medicine because they instructed readers to use as little medicine as possible. Under most circumstances, the body would heal itself. The use of powerful drugs, espoused by the newer medical doctors, was not necessary.

Just as an example of the type of folks who have lived in New Egypt over the decades, a descendant of the Claytons of Hornerstown, farmer Paul Clayton, died in 1991 at the age of 107. Clayton never drove a car or tractor, but managed to till his 176-acres of potatoes, tomatoes, grain and corn with his five horses. In 1978, he and his daughter Thelma sold their land to the Monmouth County Park System at a price that was below market value. The result is Clayton Park.[57]

What Lydia didn't know while she was working on the Claytons' farm was that two of her brothers, John and Ellsworth—who now made their homes in New Brunswick, New Jersey—had put out feelers in 1838 to locate their long lost sister.

As a result, when Lydia was fifteen and a half, John and Ellsworth Danbury journeyed to the Clayton farm to see her. When they returned to

New Brunswick, Lydia accompanied them for a visit. After three weeks, Ellsworth brought her back to the farm. He stayed on to work with the Claytons for the winter. In May of 1840—when the poor country roads were dry enough so that a simple rainstorm wouldn't sink a buckboard up to its axles in mud—Ellsworth brought Lydia back to New Brunswick where she moved in with his family—three toddlers and his wife Mary.

According to Lydia's sister, Ann, Lydia also spent time with their oldest brother Joseph Danbury.[58] Joseph Danbury started as a grocer, became a machinist and eventually was a partner in New Brunswick's Middlesex Machine Works on Dennis Street, doing business under the name Danbury & Pasco.[59] Joseph Danbury was an extremely able businessman, amassing a fortune in the machine parts business.[60] That said, Joseph—only eleven years older than Lydia—emerges as a shadowy figure in Lydia's life. As painful as it must have been for Lydia's brother John and sister Ann to give interviews to the press after Lydia's murder spree was exposed, Joseph Danbury offered little. He would not discuss the details of Lydia's past, saying only that he believed strongly in her innocence. Interestingly enough, Lydia never mentioned her brother Joseph, even though he attended her trial.[61]

Ellsworth Danbury, about six years older than Lydia, was "a pioneer in the pony express business. He was a short, nervous man and was daily loaded with bundles." And, evidentially, he was hot tempered.[62] When the pony express trade morphed into the railroad freight business around 1840, Ellsworth became an agent of the New Jersey Express Company. On a run from Uniontown to New Brunswick, a peddler named Fisher refused to pay an extra shilling for his bag. Ellsworth assaulted the man and the blow blossomed into an all out fight. Fisher got an indictment of Ellsworth Danbury and a jury found in favor of Fisher.[63]

The move to New Brunswick in 1840 wasn't meant as a permanent solution to Lydia's insecure existence, but she did enroll in public school and at least partially made up for her lack of education.[64]

At that time, New Brunswick supported only 8,200 citizens, but its central location between New York and Philadelphia, along with its position on the southern bank of the Raritan River, made the city a natural center for traders, travelers and a diverse group of manufacturers.[65]

New Brunswick gradually became a center for the transport of grain. The Delaware & Raritan Canal reached New Brunswick in 1834, making way for the transport of coal east from Pennsylvania and other goods through to the west. Eventually the Raritan River carried the third largest tonnage of any river in the country. Railroad growth, in combination with waterpower, created an explosion in industry. New factories sprung up, producing wallpaper, rubber, clay, firebrick, and terra cotta products. In addition, New Brunswick nurtured shipbuilding on the banks of the Raritan.

Rutgers (originally Queen's College) moved to New Brunswick in 1766 and the New Brunswick Theological Seminary took up residence in 1784, originally sharing space with Queen's College. This relationship was a difficult one and the seminary was forced to relocate a quarter mile away. Rutgers grew so fast over the next few decades that the seminary again wound up in the middle of the Rutgers campus.

When she was seventeen, Lydia entered domestic service as a housekeeper for an alumnus of Rutgers College and New Brunswick Theological Seminary—Rev. Robert Van Amburgh. He and his wife Margaret lived in tiny Lebanon, New Jersey—twenty-five miles west of New Brunswick.

As stated earlier, just before her sentencing in January 1873, Lydia was quick to praise those who had been good to her when she was growing up, giving high marks to a number of different people, but she had nothing at all to say about Rev. Robert Van Amburgh. Though Lydia never came right out with it, her reticence suggests that something was amiss in his home. Lydia stayed three years, but left like a sudden breeze when the opportunity presented itself.

Robert Van Amburgh was of French and Hollander decent, born in 1809, six miles south of Poughkeepsie, New York. His father, also named Robert, had a large farm and was a slave-owner as late as 1810. New York's principal manumission law was passed in 1799, making all slaves free by 1827, but the minister's father was clearly a man who wasn't troubled by the iniquity of slavery. He seems to have complied with the law only when noncompliance would hurt his own name.[66]

A bit of a braggart, Rev. Van Amburgh once wrote, "even at ten years old [I] could handle a scythe with the same ease and agility as any older laborer." It is of course utter nonsense that a fifth grader could work a scythe as well as a seasoned farm hand, but this type of autobiographical boast betrays Robert Van Amburgh's egotistical nature better than any biographer's remarks could.[67]

Van Amburgh worked on his father's farm until he was he was about twenty-four, although in his early twenties, he claimed to have fallen under the religious tutelage of two different ministers in the nearby towns of Hughsonville and Whitesboro, New York. Van Amburgh entered Rutgers College in the Class of 1837 and then graduated from the New Brunswick Theological Seminary in 1840.

To hear him tell it, when Van Amburgh entered the public ministry, "[My] preaching was so popular and so significantly successful that [I] was tendered a call in almost every vacant church where [I] ministered."[68] His first assignment was in the Reformed Dutch Church in Lebanon, New Jersey (the village Lydia called Jacksonville).[69] It was here in Lebanon that Van Amburgh started a pattern of agitating for new churches that the parishioners didn't need and couldn't afford. He wielded his religious authority with immense skill and built a number of new churches and rectories, but was forced out with great regularity.

Rev. Robert Van Amburgh

After seven years in Lebanon, he resigned his post to become the rector of an old church at Fordham, New York. Once again, he used his powerful personality to push through a new church that was dedicated in 1848. Five years later, he was called back to Lebanon, where he immediately replaced the old brick church with a new frame structure. In 1869, he moved to High Bridge, New Jersey, where he again insisted on a new church. A structure went up, but ill feelings toward the cleric and his dreams were so widespread that some elders resigned and parishioners forced Van Amburgh out without decorum. His next two stops were the

Lower German Valley and Annandale, where he continued to build bigger and more luxurious shines to himself.[70]

Rev. Van Amburgh and his wife Margaret eventually had four children. However, unlike other men who paid $25 to have their life stories published in the popular biographical encyclopedias of the day, Van Amburgh chose to make no mention of his wife Margaret or their children.[71]

Lydia's three brothers and Robert Van Amburgh almost certainly knew each another in New Brunswick. Van Amburgh was in the city for six years and there were fewer than 8,000 residents when he first arrived. Too, the New Brunswick Theological Seminary was only a few blocks north of the Bayard-Liberty-New Streets neighborhood—near the Raritan River—where the Danbury siblings had taken up residence. This connection between Joseph, Ellsworth and John Danbury may well have secured Lydia's employment with the Van Amburghs and thus her relocation in early 1842.[72]

There are several nagging questions about this chapter in Lydia's life. First, after Lydia's brothers spent so much time and trouble reuniting Lydia with the rest of her siblings in New Brunswick, why did she enter domestic service twenty-five miles away in Lebanon, New Jersey?

Lydia exhibited some troublesome habits later in life that might allude to her childhood. Multiple murders aside, Lydia was irritatingly secretive. She was a dissembler, lying about matters that were not worth the trouble. She was cunning, a feature that in and of itself requires no contrition, but is unattractive nonetheless. When Lydia's brothers came to know her well, were they sorry they had brought her to New Brunswick? Were there incidents that caused problems among the Danbury siblings and their families in New Brunswick? Was the job with the Van Amburghs in Lebanon, New Jersey just a convenient way to get Lydia out of town?

Another troubling question regards the position Lydia took with the Van Amburghs: Why would a married couple—with no children yet—need an attractive seventeen-year-old, live-in female domestic servant? Of course, Margaret Van Amburgh could have envisioned a life without housework, or Robert Van Amburgh—for his own selfish reasons—may have convinced his wife of the merits of the arrangement. Regardless of the details, unless there existed some crying need for constant help—such as an invalid in the family—a young middle class married couple without children usually did not hire a live-in domestic servant in 1840. The Van Amburghs' arrangement was unusual for a small village in Hunterdon County, New Jersey, and in fifty years of marriage, Lydia was the only live-in servant the Van Amburghs ever hired.

After three years service, Ellsworth Danbury visited Lydia—a friendly call that turned into Lydia's goodbye to the Van Amburghs forever. She got in Ellsworth's carriage and never looked back.[73]

Ellsworth Danbury's wife, Mary, had a sister who knew the tailoring business and she took Lydia under her wing. In three months time, Lydia landed a job as a tailoress for Mr. William Owens and perfected her craft partly at his shop in New Brunswick and partly at her brother Ellsworth's house. When business slacked off, Lydia acted as a domestic servant for William and Ida Owens in their New Brunswick home. William Owens was a class leader in the Methodist Church, and as Lydia admitted, "a very fine man, and his wife was an excellent lady."[74]

Lydia joined their Methodist Church and remained with the Owens family as a domestic servant for the next four months, ultimately returning to Owens's tailoring shop for another year. During this period, her new class leader at the church, Jacob Edmonds, a well-to-do retired industrial ball manufacturer, introduced her to another member, Edward W. Struck. The couple first met "at a love-fest in the Liberty-street [Methodist] church in New Brunswick."[75] Though Struck "was a widower with six children—the youngest only four"—he was also a devout Christian.[76]

CHAPTER 3
Marriage to Edward W. Struck

After the usual dating-betrothal interlude, Lydia married Edward Struck at Ellsworth and Mary Danbury's New Brunswick home in 1846.[77] When a twenty-one-year-old woman marries a widower twice her age—with six children—it raises some questions. Did Lydia fall in love with Edward Struck and his children? Was her marriage to Edward Struck occasioned by an inner yearning for the father she barely knew? Did Lydia accept the first man who asked her to marry, bringing up concerns about her self-image? Lastly, as we will see, Lydia was drawn to needy men—just as her father Samuel was a needy man. Did this parallel have anything to do with Lydia's attraction to Edward W. Struck? History hides the complete answers from us, but the questions tell their own story.

In the initial months of their marriage, Edward Struck commuted to Yorkville in New York City where he extended his trade as a carriage blacksmith. He returned to New Brunswick on Saturday nights, but by Monday morning he was back at work in Yorkville. After a while, he got a blacksmith business up and running on the corner of Church and George Streets in New Brunswick.[78] Building his own business sounds like a huge step forward for Edward Struck—and he deserves a lot of credit for the effort—but he could not earn the kind of money the big coach companies in New York paid while blacksmithing in New Brunswick. So, the Strucks moved to Yorkville, where Edward Struck took a job with Brewster & Company, one of the biggest coach makers in the United States.

James Brewster Sr. began his carriage business in New Haven in 1809 after visiting the shop of John Cook, often considered the Elm City's first carriage maker inasmuch as he began fabricating two-wheeled carriages as early as 1794.[79] Brewster built his factory on the corner of Elm and High Streets, hired the best tradesmen available, and paid the highest wages—always in cash. Brewster recognized the benefits of investing in his workers and always sought to raise their intellectual horizons and influence beneficially their moral compasses. Though his factory originally catered to the average buyer, James Brewster quickly adopted the richly appointed English carriages as his touchstone. Year by year, his horse-drawn vehicles fetched the highest prices and ultimately his sons, James, Jr. and Henry, opened showrooms and new manufactories in New York. By 1860, New York had eclipsed New Haven as a carriage-manufacturing center.[80]

Edward Struck worked for James Brewster Jr., drawing perhaps one of the highest paychecks of any blacksmith in the city. James Brewster, Jr. lived on Long Island, but oversaw his assembly facility in Broome Street and his showroom on Fifth Avenue at the corner of 14th Street. Brewster made road wagons for as little as $300 and fancy coaches for up to $475.[81] Though the work was desirable, Struck stayed for only a year. It was during this time that Edward and Lydia Struck's first child, Lydia, was born.

For unknown reasons, Edward Struck couldn't stand the prosperity. In 1847, the Struck family moved to lower Manhattan where Edward found a job with a much smaller coach maker, the English immigrant, John Butler, at the corner of Prince and Crosby streets. This shop sat diagonally across the street from the Metropolitan Hotel. Struck moved his family into a tenement at 244 Elizabeth Street—just south of Houston Street—only three blocks from John Butler's shop. Lydia birthed two more babies, John Wesley and George Whitfield.[82]

While the Struck family's new rental was close to Edward Struck's work, Manhattan's Sixth Ward wasn't exactly the perfect place to raise children. The Strucks' rooms lay a short distance north of New York's infamous Five Points slum. The Sixth, Seventh and Thirteenth Wards were abysmally crowded sections of Manhattan where gangs ruled. When the Potato Famine devastated Ireland—beginning in 1845—the number of Irish immigrants passing through Castle Garden into New York's lower East Side exploded beyond the ability of the city to absorb them. As a result, year-by-year, the poorest parts of Manhattan—a list continuously headed by Five Points—turned into violent and disease-infested ghettoes.[83]

The near-constant violence of Five Points showcased the brutal gangs inherent in working-class neighborhoods and provided New York's city government with street toughs as operatives. When William Marcy "Boss" Tweed became the head of the New York County Board of Supervisors in 1858, he also became the grand Sachem of Tammany Hall. Tweed saw these impoverished Irish youths and the many gangs of Five Points as resources to be exploited. In them, Tammany Hall found the muscle it needed to rule New York.

Five Points was built over a soupy landfill that had once been the "Collect," a disgusting pond—some would say swamp—the main source of New York's water supply before Aaron Burr's Manhattan (water) Company won a charter from the legislature in 1800. The repugnant landscape coupled with the impoverished immigrants and the ever-increasing gang activity, and Five Points quickly became a desperate pool of filth and brutality. Not surprisingly, respectable families wanted out. To escape the rabble and grime of Lower Manhattan, merchants and their families moved farther uptown.

By the middle of the 1840s, John Butler was making plans to move his coach business to a quieter and safer part of New York. Ultimately, Butler moved to Carmensville (upper West Side) in the late 1840s. The Strucks followed and Edward continued to work for Butler over the next decade. It was during this time that Lydia had four more children—Ann Eliza (named after Lydia's older sister), Josephine (possibly named after Lydia's oldest brother), Martha Ann and Edward W. (after her husband). As the Struck family grew, once again a regular paycheck as a carriage blacksmith in a small shop showed itself to be inadequate, and turmoil within the New York City Police Department presented a great opportunity for Edward Struck.

The New York City Police Department was established in 1844. At the time, New York City's population of 320,000 was served by an archaic force consisting of 1 night watchman, 100 city marshals, 31 constables, and 51 municipal police officers.[84] In 1844, the state legislature at Albany approved a proposal by New York's Common Council that created a new Municipal Police force of 1,200. Unfortuantely, this force didn't last long.

By the early 1850s, the city's police squad was a mess. Beat cops smoked cigars, chewed tobacco and drank alcohol on duty. It was common practice for policemen to set up their own rackets. They expected citizens to make payoffs for the return of stolen property. Protection rackets for storeowners—run by the police—were common.

In 1854, New York elected the Tammany Hall Mayor, Fernando Wood. Reasonably well-liked and charismatic, Wood organized an annual police parade, kept street walkers out of sight and closed the saloons on Sunday. However, on the other side of the ledger, Wood stuffed ballot boxes and used the police as instruments of graft. When the total count at election time was 100,000 ballots, control of the policemen guaranteed 10,000 of those votes.[85]

During Woods's reign, an increasing number of Irishman got police jobs. In 1855, only 17 percent of the city's policemen were Irish-born when the city-at-large was more than 28 percent Irish-born.[86] A year later, Wood had lost public support and Governor John Alsop King took control of the city by organizing a Metropolitan Police force—controlled from Albany. King's idea was to create a New York force that included the city and three other boroughs—although New York's outer boroughs did not become a part of New York City until 1898.[87]

King's plan went into effect in 1857, with the new Metrpolitan Police supplanting the Municipal Police. For a short time, the city suffered under a completely unworkable system—300 state-controlled Metropolitans and 800 Municipals. The Municipals resisted the governor's move, but King called out New York's Seventh Regiment and made it a fait accompli in short order.[88]

In an effort to improve his large family's finances, Edward Struck took a job on the new Metropolitan Police force of New York. At forty-nine-years, for a new recruit, Struck was old.

Only 851 men, including 563 patrolmen, 196 special duty officers, 64 roundsmen, 21 sergeants and 7 captains empowered the newly created Metropolitan Police force. Patrolman Edward Struck was given badge #510 and originally worked at a precinct in southern Manhattan.[89] Thanks to the New York Draft Riots of July 13-15, 1863, the ranks of the Metropolitan Police expanded more rapidly than could be imagined. In its first decade, the Metropolitan Police force more than tripled to 2,566 men—1 superintendent, 4 inspectors, 18 surgeons, 45 captains, 177 sergeants, 91 roundsmen, 2,137 patrolmen, and 93 doormen.[90]

No matter where the power rested in New York, a patrolman's work depended on his assigned precinct. The Bronx and the northern end of Manhattan were rural areas where livestock, including goats, grazed. (Thus the pejorative nickname "Goatsville.") Older cops liked the precincts in upper Manhattan because they were quiet. One downside was that Goatsville offered few opportunities for "sugar" or graft. There were better parts of the city for payoffs, like Five Points and the Bowery. However, the granddaddy of them all was the Tenderloin, which stretched from Fourth (Park) to Seventh Avenue, between the twenties and thirties. In this grid, a patrolman never paid for meals and accepted all sorts of sweeteners.[91]

The owners of the Tenderloin dives did not usually pay off the beat cops, though they might toss them some change now and then. A visitor who drank too much and got into a fight or some other trouble would reward the police with money though. That said, the "heavy sugar" went to the captain via his wardman, or collector, who would keep a portion—usually 20 percent—for himself, and then reward his patrol.[92]

The extra cash mattered, because when it came time for a promotion, a cop had to pay. An officer promoted to roundsman might be charged $300; from roundsman to sergeant, $1,600; sergeant to captain cost $12,000 to $15,000. These requirements could, of course, be modified in special situations.[93]

In Edward Struck's time, New York's police payroll was small, but it was still the city's largest workforce, and the policemen were expected to perform a number of supplementary duties. They supervised the election machinery, bird-dogged street cleaning, and the precinct houses doubled as homeless shelters. Since these stationhouses had green lights at their entrances, they were called "green light hotels."[94]

Not long after he became a policeman, Edward Struck was transferred to the Thirtieth Precinct in Manhattanville—on the Upper West Side of Manhattan above Central Park—and the family moved to 125th Street (Manhattan Street), just off Broadway. Manhattanville was a lovely little village in New York's Twelfth Ward, a sleepy backwater in an otherwise churning, chuffing engine of human and commercial commerce.

Manhattanville, technically, was an outlying section of New Harlem. The Village of New Harlem originally encompassed the territory from 74th and 129th Streets, between the Harlem and Hudson Rivers. The earliest non-native settlers of Manhattanville were the people who first planted the fields of Harlem's western valley. This was a diverse lot of Quakers, Old Yankees, Dutch and German immigrants.[95]

Based on earliest maps of the area, Manhattanville appeared as an amphitheater, with highlands separating it from New Harlem, and with the hills of Washington and Morningside Heights on the north and south, respectively.[96] The valley was almost barren. Around the crossroads of the Bloomingdale road and 125th Street, this rural village grew. During the American Revolution, Washington's army seems to have crossed "Hollow Way"—Manhattanville—from the northern hills of Washington Heights to the southern highlands of Morningside Heights and engaged the British near the Hudson River. Evidently, George Washington watched the fighting from Convent Hill at 126th Street.[97]

In 1806, Jacob Schieffelin—one of the largest property owners of the land between Morningside Heights and Washington Heights—opened the new village's first school, the Academy, described as "an excellent school . . . constantly kept up, under the superintendence of trustees." In 1819, a stage line was established from Chambers Street to Manhattanville. Later a depot and post office were added. At the time, there were only fifteen houses on a few streets. The brick houses were only two stories tall and an occasional single family home sat back, harkening to a simpler streetscape. There were open spaces where ledge cropped out, plenty of undeveloped building lots and cabins of the "squatter" type. Manhattanville was a throwback to earlier, simpler times. The 45-degree bias of Lawrence and Manhattan Streets mocked New York City's new grid system.[98]

In the late 1840s, the Croton Aqueduct Committee was directed by New York's Common Council to provide Croton water to the inhabitants of Harlem and its vicinity by "constructing a suitable reservoir on the hill between Manhattanville and Harlem."[99] By 1845, Manhattanville had 500 residents. Except for the primitive stagecoaches, these folks weren't even

connected to the lower, busier parts of the city until the Hudson River Railroad was completed in 1851.[100] Manhattanville offered the Strucks a pleasant change from the madness of the lower wards of the city.

The uppermost ward of New York was known for its great estates. However, as the decades rolled by, the ambience of Manhattanville changed as factories emerged on Manhattan Street thanks to its ready access to the Hudson River ferry, and the completion of the Hudson River Railroad.[101] Nevertheless, for most of the 1800s, Manhattanville included the small village at 125th St. and the Bloomingdale road, but also numerous educational, social, and religious institutions, long before they became the province of Morningside Heights to the south.[102]

In 1857, Edward and Lydia Struck settled into second-floor rented rooms of a tenement and joined the First Presbyterian Church at Ninth Avenue and 126th Street.[103] By the end of the Civil War, this congregation languished and the church was rudderless for a time. In an effort to help out, Rev. Payson of the Harlem Presbyterian Church journeyed eight blocks to Manhattanville and held Sunday services. The Struck children—particularly Lydia and Martha Ann—formed a close bond with their new pastor, Rev. Mr. Edward Payson of the infamous Payson clan of clerics.[104]

When fifty-two-year-old Edward Struck was re-assigned to Manhattanville, there were forty-seven policemen living in the Third District—the western third of the Twelfth Ward. They were all younger than Struck.[105]

A second consideration cries out for attention. The police officers in their twenties, thirties and forties couldn't rub two nickels together. Patrolman Edward Struck had a houseful of kids, no real estate and very little money. Contrarily, there were many sergeants and captains who had shocking amounts of money.[106]

Consider the difference between the wealthiest residents and the members of the police force around Manhattanville in 1860. The owner and publisher of the *New York Herald*, James Gordon Bennett, had $300,000 in real estate and another $250,000 in personal property and cash. Meanwhile, editor and publisher, Conrad Shwackhamer, had a rolling estate worth $60,000 and $5,000 in personal property. There were many other men of wealth in all three districts of the Twelfth Ward; they all had real estate and showed something in personal property.

Contrarily, there were 47 policemen in the Third District of the Twelfth Ward and 14 owned real estate. However, only 2 of these homeowners showed any personal property at all! Struck's superior, Capt. James Hartt had $5,000 in real estate, yet he declared no cash to census takers. Sgt. Isaac Potter was in the same boat as Capt. Hartt—$5,000 in real estate, but—we are led to believe—no cash. Where did they hide their hauls? Meanwhile, in the same section of Manhattanville, there were thirteen physicians and the vast majority of them had barely enough to live on.[107]

These strands woven together suggests the policemen in the Thirtieth Precinct were as corrupt as ever, but Edward Struck wasn't one of them. He may have been too old to be a patrolman but he was honest—just the kind of person that cops on the take would not want around.[108] Perhaps an even meatier matter is whether or not the younger men on the force thought Struck too old for a beat-walking patrolman. As we shall see, an event at the St. Nicholas Hotel in late 1863 hurtles these considerations into an unwelcome light.

A short time after their 1857 arrival in Manhattanville, the Strucks' twenty-two months-old daughter Josephine contracted a case of the measles.[109] The illness hit her particularly hard. She caught cold and this produced an inflammation of the bowels, a nasty turn that caused her death two weeks later. To put Josephine Struck's death in perspective: In

1860, there were 3.8 million people living in the State of New York and 46,941 died from accidents and disease (1.2 percent). Carried one step further, measles accounted for only 746 of these deaths.[110]

Given Lydia's future proclivities, Josephine's death is troublesome. If we choose to believe Lydia's confession—first published in the *New York Herald* on January 13, 1873—then we must conclude that Josephine did indeed die of complications from measles. We must also believe that Lydia did not begin her diabolical killing spree until 1864—seven years later. Lastly, death from all causes in young children was extraordinarily high at mid-century, which should offer enough grounds to reluctantly give Lydia the benefit of the doubt in Josephine's case.

Josephine Struck's attending physician was Dr. John W. Mitchell, "a distinguished practitioner of the homeopathic school." Dr. Mitchell was also the medical officer of the new Women's Infirmary—dedicated to patients with diseases exclusive to women—on Washington Heights between Tenth Avenue and the Bloomington road. Thirty-six-year-old John Mitchell lived in a rooming house in Manhattanville and had neither a wife nor children.[111]

In the two preceding decades, the dominance of scientific medicine—allopathy—was in doubt, as homeopaths, botanical, and Eclectic doctors formed professional groups, opened their own medical schools and attended patients. The largest of these factions—the homeopaths—followed the teachings of the German physician Samuel Hahnemann, the man who oddly enough coined the term allopathy. When Hahnemann first graduated from medical school in the early 1800s, the fields of chemistry, physiology and anatomy were alive with scientific energy. The practice of medicine, however, was crippled by superstition, poor medical education of its practitioners and fierce competition between the many different disciplines, from the autodidacts to the "regular" doctors.

Homeopathic physicians often had better outcomes compared to their allopathic counterparts, because the allopathic remedies were so harmful compared to the non-toxic nature of homeopathic remedies. Not surprisingly, patients preferred the more gentle treatment they received at the hands of the homeopaths. (John D. Rockefeller, the richest man in America, engaged a homeopath as his personal physician.)

Indeed, homeopathy had its proponents, but during the Civil War, it experienced a serious setback. "Regular" doctors refused to serve with homeopaths on hospital staffs. For decades, homeopaths were excluded from hospitals in major U. S. cities. The War of the Rebellion proved more of the same. Regular doctors controlled the military medical boards where they openly excluded homeopaths from service. Despite the backing of Congress, homeopaths were powerless to gain approval for serious military duties. [112]

It makes sense that Lydia would trust a homeopath over an allopath for illnesses she couldn't help heal on her own. Most likely, Lydia trusted and needed Mitchell's expertise.

New York was a hotbed of public dissent during the Civil War. In 1862, Lincoln's new Secretary of War, Edwin Stanton, designated New York's Metropolitan Police as provost marshals, and encouraged them to arrest deserters. New York detectives ranged all over the eastern US to arrest Southern sympathizers. The following year, the police became full-fledged soldiers in what could fairly be considered one of the significant battles of the war—the New York Draft Riots. It was precipitated by the enactment of a draft law—the country's first—which took effect in July 1863. Conscription was bad enough, but the law allowed wealthy people to buy exclusions for $300.

The Irish immigrants saw freed slaves as unwanted competition for scarce jobs. The Draft Riots caused unrest on an order never seen before in America. In three days of rioting, 120 men were killed including 11 freed slaves who were lynched. Property damage was estimated as high as $5 million. It took New York City a long time to get back to normal after such a brutal and scarring incident.[113]

While New York's wounds festered in the aftermath of the Draft Riots, Manhattanville began to experience trouble with undesirables from the lower wards of Manhattan. Part of the attraction for these shiftless thugs was the Bloomingdale road. From the foot of Convent Hill to Manhattanville it was one of the best roads in the city, and acted as a magnet for anyone who wanted to race horses, carriages and sleighs. Unfortunately, these intruders were completely without interest in the local people and threatened the lives and health of anyone on the Bloomingdale road when they chose to use it.[114]

In the ensuing years, this racing on the Bloomingdale road morphed into trouble at election time. Edward Struck's Captain, James Hartt, reported at the Thirtieth Precinct headquarters that at 4 o'clock in the afternoon on Tuesday, November 3, 1863—"A band of men, numbering about 80, came into our Precinct. They were desperate looking men, and arranged themselves along the street opposite where the polls were held. From their maneuvering, it soon became evident that serious mischief was intended. One of the roughs, named Collins, dealt a powerful blow in the face of a bystander, without provocation."[115]

All hell broke loose. The conflict was fierce. Officers were hit with stones, and a pistol ball felled one patrolman as he suffered a long gash on his cheek. Many were arrested as the troublemakers seemed intent on the destruction of the ballot boxes at a local polling station. They were eventually chased from Manhattanville and into the northern section of Central Park. The bucolic nature of Manhattanville was changing.[116]

All over Manhattan, but particularly in a quiet place like the Twelfth Ward, murders were a rarity. Citywide, most policemen spent their careers on uniformed street patrol, where their daily concerns were fairly mundane—rousting drunks, loiterers and rowdies. Decisions were made quickly. A disorderly drunk would go to the precinct house, and twenty-four hours later, a judge would sentence him to ninety days in jail. Edward Struck did well during his first seven years on the force, but in late November 1863, serious trouble came calling.[117]

At about 1 o'clock on Friday afternoon, November 20, 1863, a longshoreman entered the mammoth St. Nicholas Hotel, at 515 Broadway (116th Street; across from the Bloomingdale Insane Asylum) and made his way to the barroom at the back of the first floor. In no time at all, he got into an altercation with the barkeeper Henry Allen. The stevedore seized Henry Allen and cut him severely in a number of places with a rigger's knife. Cries of "Murder!" rippled through the first floor of the hotel and out the door onto Broadway.

By chance, Deputy Sheriff James E. Merriam was riding by the St. Nicholas Hotel on a stage and heard the commotion. Merriam sprang from the vehicle and went directly to the barroom where he found Henry Allen down on the floor with the longshoremen on top of him, ready to end the bartender's life. As Merriam broke up the two combatants, the unidentified longshoreman focused his rage on Merriam and launched a new attack. Completely out of options, Merriam drew his pistol and shot the deranged man dead.[118] (Some cops had been carrying firearms on an informal basis for several years, though New York City policemen were not officially fitted with revolvers until 1896 when Teddy Roosevelt was a police commissioner.)[119]

As the madness at the St. Nicholas Hotel reached a climax, Edward Struck was patrolling his beat, several blocks to the south. The stage driver soon met Patrolman Struck and explained the situation to him. Struck went immediately to the St. Nicholas Hotel as word flashed to the Thirtieth Precinct Station House on 131st Street and doctors were called in to examine the dead man's body.

Soon an ugly rumor surfaced that Patrolman Struck could have prevented the whole situation except that he refused to confront the longshoreman because the man had a pistol, and Struck did not. A jury of inquest was held and doctors rendered the opinion that the longshoreman was deranged. Unfortunately for Struck, the inquiry took a dreadful turn. The employees of the St. Nicholas testified that Struck was at the hotel, but afraid to go inside.

To accept this version, one would have to believe that Deputy Sheriff James Merriam strode right past a uniformed New York City policeman without seeing him, or that Edward Struck took cover at the first sign of trouble. The first theory is ridiculous on its face and the second does not take into account the stage driver's conversation with Edward Struck several blocks south of the St. Nicholas Hotel after the murder. Struck was clearly innocent of any wrongdoing, raising the revolting possibility that he was set up by fellow officers. Regardless of the truth concerning the shooting at the St. Nicholas, in December 1863, Edward Struck was released from his job for Failure to Obey Rules—based almost exclusively on the testimony of the employees of the St. Nicholas Hotel.[120]

After his discharge from the police force, Edward Struck plummeted into a deep depression. For three months, he did nothing. Captain Hartt worked hard to get Struck reinstated, but to no avail. As Edward Struck's mood refused to improve, Lydia went to see her husband's former employer, John Butler, to ask if her husband could go back to work as a carriage blacksmith. Butler held Edward Struck's work in high regard and vowed to take him back at any time, but Struck was so depressed that he refused to take the job. At long last, Lydia brought her husband to John Butler's shop, where Butler remarked, "I am glad you have come back to work. You can do the best you can, and I will pay you well."[121]

Struck returned to John Butler's carriage shop, but only stayed a few days. Butler, a thoroughly decent man, understood the situation intimately and finally visited his old employee at home. Apparently the rumors of cowardice had so unhinged Struck that each day it became harder for him to leave the house. Butler didn't give up on Struck though, coaxing him back to work a second time. Lydia even accompanied him and kept him company for hours at a time. It was no use. One evening, Struck came home and snarled, "He would not work anymore, because everybody in the street looked at him is if he was a coward."[122]

The following morning, Struck wouldn't even get out of bed, vowing never to leave the house again. Even an old friend and fellow blacksmith, John Olmstead, a man whom Struck respected greatly, couldn't reach the deeply depressed Struck, who wouldn't even talk to Olmstead. For months, Struck just lay in bed. His muscles began to atrophy and "he could hardly use his hands or feet."[123] He refused to see a doctor, although finally he agreed to see his daughter Gertrude, one of his children by his first wife. Lydia's son John "went down to New York and brought her up to see him."[124] While visiting, Gertrude ran across a doctor who was visiting someone else in the neighborhood and convinced the physician to look at her father. The doctor tried to help the former policeman, but was rebuffed. Unable to get Edward Struck to speak, the physician left some medicine with Lydia and departed.[125]

The doctor's visit changed nothing though and Edward Struck continued to deteriorate. One day, he staggered to his dresser, took out a pistol, put it in his mouth and taunted, "Mammy, if I should fire this off, it would blow my head off." Lydia took the gun away from him and put it back in the drawer. Then he went for a razor, and Lydia was forced to lock up both suicide weapons.[126]

At this point, Struck began to imagine things. He became convinced that he was about to be arrested. Lydia sent for Captain Hartt, in the hopes that his former boss could shock him back to reality. When Captain Hartt arrived, Struck would neither look at him nor talk to him. Captain Hartt finally told Lydia that her husband was out of his mind, and should be confined to a lunatic asylum. Apparently, others had told Lydia the same thing, implying in the process, that Struck may do harm to her and the children. Day after day, Struck got worse. One night, he woke Lydia and told her to bring him his clothes and shoes because "they" were coming to get him in the morning.

Struck's next move was to ask Lydia to get places for the children, because she would not be able to care for them. Struck was acting so badly that Lydia summoned a policeman—possibly Officer Watson Wagner who lived downstairs. According to Lydia, Wagner advised her "to put him [Struck] out of the way" as he would never be any good to Lydia or the children again. After further prodding, the policeman explained that Lydia should get a certain quantity of arsenic, even telling her where to get it and how much to give her husband.[127]

As Edward Struck continued his tailspin, Lydia mulled this over. In a jailhouse confession much later, Lydia claimed to have been "a poor weak woman who had not finally the strength to resist a great temptation, which came to her when burdened with the care of a sick and complaining husband, and with poverty."[128]

At her wit's end, Lydia traveled to Harlem and purchased about one ounce of arsenic for ten cents at a druggist's shop. Arsenic was sold freely in the nineteenth century, without any type of license, permit or paperwork; the signature of the buyer was not requested or required. However, arsenic's inherent danger was never out of mind. Typically, druggists would not even put the white powder on their scales. They estimated the desired amount as closely as possible and wrapped it carefully in paper before giving it to customers.

The Harlem druggist's shop that Lydia chose was on Third Avenue—near the Harlem Savings Bank and Post Office—the busiest section of Harlem. Lydia exercised great caution in buying the arsenic (falsifying her later claims that she never thought she was doing anything wrong by poisoning her husbands and children).[129] There were several druggists in Manhattanville where Lydia could have purchased the arsenic, but by traveling eleven blocks to Harlem, she wouldn't run into any policemen or neighbors that she knew. Also, the druggist might not remember one unfamiliar face among the many customers he waited on during the usual course of business.[130]

When Lydia returned from Harlem, she made some oatmeal gruel, and dumped in a thimble full of arsenic. Lydia gave the mush to her husband. He took several helpings that afternoon. Almost immediately, he turned sick. The early symptoms of arsenic ingestion are similar to those of food poisoning—stomach and head pains, cramps, vomiting, and diarrhea. In advanced cases, the aforementioned symptoms are followed by headaches, hair loss, delirium, confusion, drowsiness and convulsions.

The instant her husband begun vomiting, Lydia sent for Dr. Jackson of Carmansville—the tiny hamlet just north of Manhattanville—and he was at the Strucks' tenement house later that evening.

Dr. George F. Jackson, a typical "regular doctor" (allopath) at the time of the American Civil War, was originally from Pittston, Maine. Dr. Jackson practiced medicine in Boothbay, Maine for four years before he and his wife Rachel relocated to Washington Heights, New York where he remained in practice for the next thirty-eight years.[131]

Dr. Jackson's education was barely acceptable by contemporary standards although his stint at Jefferson Medical College in Philadelphia gave him a preferable bent toward science. In the middle of the nineteenth century, there were forty-two medical schools in the United States, while in France only three schools served the whole country. At the time, the population of France was 50 percent larger than that of the United States.[132]

Virtually all medical schools were self-supporting in the 1800s, with a few notable exceptions. The driving force behind the founding of so many medical schools lay in the body of physicians who would ultimately teach at these new institutions. By linking to a local college, these new med schools achieved instant credibility, while the college achieved additional prestige without any financial risk. A new medical school derived nearly all of its income from tuitions—which were split equally among the instructors—so the organization of these schools proved a lucrative pursuit for many practitioners from a wide gamut of medical disciplines.[133]

The competition between medical schools led to reduced graduation requirements and shorter terms. The course of study ranged from mere lectures to a combination of lectures, dissection and clinical study, but seldom did the course of study extend beyond the four month minimum mandated by the average state legislature. In truth, most of these schools—particularly the ones springing up like neighborhood clinics in the Midwest—were mere diploma mills.

Often medical schools buttressed their limited programs by insisting that students engage in an apprenticeship with an established physician after they had their M.D. degrees. However, these same medical schools had no financial incentive to follow the progress of their graduates and this requirement became nothing more than window-dressing. Around mid-century, the four-year-old American Medical Association surveyed 30 medical schools and found that only 4 required certification of apprenticeship for a full three-year period, 19 others required certification of some apprenticeship without any specification of time, and 7 did not require any certification of apprenticeship at all. While a graduate of one of America's medical school may have understood the value of the postgraduate apprenticeship requirement, arranging one proved difficult because of the surfeit of physicians and the reluctance of older practitioners to jeopardize their own livelihoods. The burgeoning number of medical schools heightened competition to the point where older doctors helping younger physicians-to-be was a very difficult arrangement.

Soon after mid-century, the *New York Times* scolded, "Quackery flourishes in this country to an alarming extent, because it is indisputably true that intelligent persons are, at times, unable to decide between the plausible quack and a hot-pressed practitioner fresh from some irresponsible licensing shop—called into existence by corrupt legislatures. . . . In France, England, Germany and Russia, a degree in science or arts is essential before matriculation in a medical college, and at the expiration of the usual term of study, covering from four to seven years, the candidates are examined by gentlemen of acknowledged attainments, appointed by the state—men who have no interest in this or that school, and who are beyond the bribe of the paltry price of a diploma fee."[134]

Without much imagination, one can see that the months Dr. Jackson amassed actually studying medicine were woefully inadequate. When the thirty-three year old physician came face-to-face with Edward Struck, he couldn't get his patient to answer a few simple questions much less aid in formulating a diagnosis. Frustrated, Dr. Jackson handed Lydia two different containers of sedative powders to give to her husband during the night. Dr. Jackson may not have known what was wrong with Edward Struck, but he still thought Struck was so sick he might not recover. Lydia claims to have been up all night with her husband, while his internal organs disintegrated under the arsenic's abrasive power.

A heavy fog had blown in the night before and the weather was unsettled as the sun came up on May 26, 1864. General. Grant bore in on

Petersburg; the fashionable ladies of New York swore off all foreign luxuries to help the war effort; smallpox was found in lower Manhattan; and the newspapers hawked patent medicines like Dr. Ricord's Essence of Life and Blair's Gout and Rheumatic Pills. And, at 8 o'clock in the morning, Edward Struck breathed his last.[135]

A second doctor, Nathaniel C. Husted, was involved in Edward Struck's case, and his name appears on the coroner's record as the attending physician.[136] While Husted was "from the city"—living on W. 42nd Street—a six-mile buggy ride to Manhattanville was not unusual when one considers how hard doctors worked in the 1860s to fill their days. Between the number of young men off at war and the financial struggles of the average family, physicians inevitably had time on their hands.

Born in Connecticut, Husted taught school for a few years before sitting through the required four months of lectures to receive his M.D. degree from the New York University Medical School in 1858. The "University" had enormous classes. In fact, "it stood second to only one school in the U. S. in graduations." Jefferson Medical College in Philadelphia always prided itself on the record number of M.D. degrees it conferred since 1824.[137] However, as the *New York Times* lavished praise on Manhattan's three medical schools—the dignified College of Physicians and Surgeons on Crosby Street (five months of lectures required); the staid New York Medical School on 13th Street (five month of lectures as well); and the brand new diploma-mill-style New York University Medical College on 14th Street (only four months of lectures stipulated)—it taunted America's medical school cradle, "Philadelphia long monopolized a majority of 'this numerous class of our population,' but she needs now to keep a bright look-out or Gotham will snatch her laurels and demand of the coming World's Fair a premium for manufacturing more and better doctors per annum than any other trans-Atlantic city."[138]

At the outbreak of the Civil War, Dr. Husted volunteered as a surgeon and was sent to attend the wounded at Fortress Monroe and in the field with the Army of the Potomac.[139] Husted had a fairly average education and had served nobly in the war. He had seen plenty of amputations and undoubtedly plenty of typhoid fever, cholera and dysentery, but probably not a single case of arsenical poisoning. Therefore, as attending physician at Edward Struck's bedside, Husted had nothing to offer beyond what Dr. George Jackson had already diagnosed.

With regard to the newly deceased Edward Struck, Dr. Husted and Dr. Jackson mutually agreed to a diagnosis: consumption (tuberculosis).

Physicians of every discipline loathed post mortem examinations (autopsies). The wisest course was to sign a death certificate quickly, and issue a burial permit the same day. Except in rare cases, the internment of the deceased would cement the physician's diagnosis—and safeguard his reputation.

In New York—during the period when Edward Struck expired—practitioners not only decided whether or not an autopsy was to be performed (although the family or the coroner could have overruled them) physicians controlled burial permits. Lydia, questioned the skill of doctors in 1872, stating "It seemed strange to me that the doctors, who were considered very talented, and who were allowed to give burial permits in New York, did not discover anything."[140]

Edward Struck's funeral was held at the First Presbyterian Church, and he was interred in Trinity Cemetery, overlooking the Hudson River at 153rd Street.

Lydia's behavior at the time of her husband demise was mesmerizing. By all accounts cunning, deceitful, and secretive, she could also play the part of the anxious, troubled spouse with alacrity. While the doctors were there, she frittered about her husband with cold compresses and the devotion one would expect from a trained nurse.[141]

As the wife of a policeman and the natural mother of six children, Lydia had taken her place in society—a far better place than the spouses of the tens of thousands of laborers, shoemakers, hack drivers, bartenders, painters, carpenters, and porters all over Manhattan. At least in her mind, it would have been far better for her if her husband just died suddenly.

Lydia would never have thought of herself as a statistic, or a woman who behaved the same as so many other female killers down through the years, but in many ways she was a textbook murderess. While the crimes of male multiple killers are extremely involved affairs almost always with a sexual component—whereby they often kidnap, rape and torture their victims—they also leave some type of a "signature," at the crime scene and routinely take "souvenirs." Female multiple killers are quite different. "If it can be said this way, the one signature they leave is the murder itself. The murder is seen as a method to attain other goals—profit usually the most often cited motive. . . . Often there is no crime scene to analyze. There is no scene because nobody knows a crime has occurred."[142] As Lydia worked assiduously to fool the small army of physicians she encountered over the years, she was in effect deconstructing crime scenes by reducing them to sickrooms. When Lydia completed her work, the practitioners involved never would have considered that they were practicing medicine in the middle of a crime scene. As we shall see, the treachery of a run-of-the-mill female multiple murderess is beyond frightening.

When Lydia gave Edward Struck a thimble full of arsenic, she was acting as a typical woman killer. "At least 45 percent of females used poison sometimes, and 35 percent only poison."[143]

Lydia inadvertently gave her husband almost a perfect lethal dose of arsenic. One level teaspoon of arsenic contains approximately five grains, which, depending on circumstances usually constitutes a fatal dose. A larger issue: arsenic—most commonly "white arsenic" or arsenic trioxide (As_2O_3)—is colorless, odorless, and tasteless. Common white arsenic is actually tiny octahedral crystals, but white arsenic has the consistency of white flour. It even looks harmless. Moreover, arsenic can be administered in one big dose or given over time in small doses, making it generally harder to detect. The slow accumulation of arsenic in the human body generally leads to Aldrich-Mees lines—horizontal lines of discoloration on the fingernails and toenails.

The English chemist Joseph Mellor believed that as far as public records were concerned, preparations of arsenic were more frequently used for criminal purposes than any other poison.[144] Arsenic was an ingredient in Victorian wallpapers. Arsenic was also popular due to its easy availability for use as a rat poison.

How is it that so many killers—particularly women—were able to rack up such appalling body counts with impunity? Were there no forensic tests for arsenic?

As late as 1836, there was no satisfactory way to test for small amounts of arsenic. Up to the early 1940s, arsenic was successfully used to treat syphilis as it was a key ingredient in Salvarsan. It was also given to victims of leprosy and other contagious tropical skin diseases. Still, most of the tests for arsenic were time consuming and required large amounts of the material for identification.

James Marsh, a British chemist at the Woolwich Arsenal in London became the assistant to Michael Faraday upon the latter's appointment to the Royal Military Academy in December 1829. Marsh was an inventor, but now devoted his time to the study of poisons and their effects.

As a result of the frequent need of arsenic analysis, he began a concentrated study of the element and possible tests for it about 1832. Marsh's scientific abilities came to the fore in 1836 when the townspeople of Plumstead asked his advice on the arsenical poisoning of a local politician. As a qualified chemist, who was familiar with the German Reinsch test—the gold standard of the time—Marsh applied yellow precipitates, ammonia solvents, and various other laboratory materials to the decedent's tissues. He also introduced these same substances to the coffee, the alleged vehicle of transmission for the arsenic. Unfortunately, when Marsh presented his evidence at the inquest, the jurors were confused by the chemistry. Marsh cursed himself for overestimating the abilities of the average juror and determined to simplify the matter by developing a test that could prove the presence of even the smallest amounts of arsenic in the human body.

Marsh's breakthrough came in 1840 when he perfected a novel test that depended on the fact that when tissue or body fluid containing arsenic came into contact with hydrogen—freshly liberated by the action of zinc and dilute acid—hydrogen gas containing a small amount of arsine gas was released.

This arsine gas was deadly stuff and actually killed a number of researchers over the years. Nonetheless, the arsine gas fumed off to deposit a silvery-black film—that is, metallic arsenic—on a porcelain bowl. Marsh was able to produce visible stains on the bowl when only very small amounts of arsenic were present.

Marsh wrote a report based on his pioneering research and revolutionary test that was published in the *Edinburgh Philosophical Journal* in October 1836. Others articles followed in 1837 and 1840. Upon publication of his articles on arsenical poisoning, toxicologists and other scientists around the world experimented with the information that Marsh provided, and were even able to added small improvements of their own.[145]

The Marsh test gave experts an accurate way to detect small amounts of arsenic; and his testing method helped vastly in closing poison investigations.

The first documented court use of the Marsh test was in 1840, when Marie Lafarge was found guilty of poisoning her husband in Paris. Madame Lafarge's husband died suddenly of a gastric ailment in January 1840, after eating a slice of cake baked by his wife. Charles Lafarge's maid claimed to have seen Mrs. Lafarge pouring a white powder into her husband's drink. Of course Marie Lafarge claimed it was the harmless gum Arabic used to build up Charles' strength, but when it was shown in court that Madame Lafarge had twice purchased arsenic from the local chemist, the jury turned against her.

It was in the Lafarge trial that Joseph Bonaventure Orfila—considered the father of forensic toxicology—appeared for the defense and was asked by the judge to demonstrate the new Marsh Test. Unfortunately for Marie Lafarge, Orfila found arsenic in her husband's stomach, liver, thorax, heart and brain.

Arsenic was also used in Paris Green, a compound developed around 1775 by Carl Scheele. Paris Green was used as a pigment in paints, wallpaper, fabrics, as well as rat poison and pesticides. Though Paris Green was not recognized as a health hazard until the end of the Gilded Age, medical professionals knew of its dangers early on. Victorian wits called it "inheritance powder."[146]

Although arsenic probably reached its greatest popularity in the pages of murder-mysteries, it has always enjoyed practical uses. From the Civil War to 1910, it was the main ingredient in embalming fluids. (This attribute will come in handy later.)[147] From the late 1800s to the 1960s, it was heavily used in pesticides. Indeed, pesticides accounted for the greatest use of arsenic in the first half of the twentieth century.[148]

During Victorian times women took orally an arsenic product, Fowlers Solution, which was especially popular with prostitutes because it provided a nice blush to the cheeks. Fowler's Solution actually ruptured the blood vessels in the skin—hence, the rosy complexion.[149]

Poisons of all sorts go back to the ancient Greeks, but fifteenth and sixteenth century Europeans claimed their own popular place in poison history. Lucrezia Borgia was the illegitimate daughter of Rodrigo Borgia—who later became Pope Alexander VI—and Vannoza dei Cattanei. Lucrezia and her brothers Cesare, Giovanni and Gioffre constituted a power hungry clan, deeply mired in the political and sexual intrigue of the Renaissance. They arranged a number of marriages for Lucrezia to advance their own political aspirations. Though no proof exists, it is generally accepted that some of Lucrezia's husbands were poisoned to death. Though little is actually known about Lucrezia, much less how much she had to do with the political machinations of her father and brothers, she will forever be associated with poisonings.

From Italy, the excitement moved to France. During the reign of Louis XIV, fatal lacing was quite prevalent. Princess Henrietta of Orleans, daughter of Charles I and sister-in-law of the King, was poisoned. Catherine de Medici, the fourteen-year-old bride to the throne of France—through her marriage to fourteen-year-old Henry II—has always been credited with the poisoning of a number of her political enemies. However, like Lucrezia Borgia, no one ever saw Catherine actually poison anyone.

Both in the eighteenth and nineteenth centuries, arsenic reigned as the undetected agent supreme in countless murders in the United States, thanks to its perfect properties as a poison and the dismal level of medical knowledge among physicians. While giving a lecture in New York in 1895, Charles Pellew of Columbia College proffered, "it is hard to tell how many are poisoned every year," and he asserted further, "embalmers who use arsenic were unwittingly the confederates of poisoners. Still, by accident, several wholesale poisoners have been detected."[150] (Lydia Sherman among them.)

But what was Lydia thinking? Aside from the chemical, criminal, social, and toxicological merits and demerits of arsenic, she had options. The Bloomingdale Insane Asylum had been founded in 1806 as a branch of New York Hospital. A decade and a half later, the governors of Bloomingdale wanted a quiet place in the country that would be more suited to their charges, so they bought land at 117th Street between 10th and 12th Avenues. By 1821, their new facility began accepting patients. Nine years later, a separate building for more violent males came into use and a similar facility for violent females opened its doors in 1837. The Bloomingdale institution sat on forty-six acres in Manhattanville and was the very last word in the humane treatment of the mentally ill. The Bloomingdale Insane Asylum was only eight blocks south of where the Strucks lived on 125th Street. Without much effort, Lydia could have placed her husband in this facility, and since she didn't have any income, it wouldn't have cost her a dime. But Lydia chose to poison him instead. Why?[151]

One of the most curious personal quirks about Lydia was that she started life on the lowest rung of the ladder, yet was almost always able to pass herself off as someone of a much higher station. She dressed very well and spoke excellent English. The husbands, lawyers, judges and jailers who dealt with her always overestimated her station in life and treated her accordingly. Based on her assumed self-importance, perhaps Lydia did not want the stigma of having her husband confined to the Bloomingdale Insane Asylum or the Lunatic Asylum on Blackwell's Island.[152]

With that in mind, Lydia successfully put her husband out of the way, but her household finances were worse than ever. She secured a less expensive rent in the village (Norfolk Street), and moved in with her six children. However, she was broke. And so, as Lydia preferred to say, she "became discouraged." In this miasma of dire and unremitting poverty, her thoughts took an unnatural turn.

CHAPTER 4
Lydia's Children

Manhattanville, like every other spot in New York, changed markedly through the years. When the Strucks first arrived in the late 1850s, less than a thousand people lived in the village, and the neighborhood maintained a distinctive rural atmosphere. But as the central part of New York—west of Central Park—became more and more developed, the areas to the north, including Manhattanville, evolved too. Some property owners in Manhattanville tried to pass off the village as a summer resort. From the *New York Tribune*— "Manhattanville on the Hudson. . . . A Lady, having an old-fashioned mansion in the above location, would accommodate a few first-class Boarders for the Summer. The house contains large and airy rooms. The Hudson River Railroad is within five minutes walk of the house."[153] The completion of the Hudson River Railroad in 1851 made the village easily accessible and helped to attract commercial enterprises of all sorts.

However, the evolution of life in Manhattanville wasn't a concern in Lydia's mind, as the lack of money dominated her thoughts. Lydia's solution—the lèse majesté of motherhood—turns the stomach. Her two youngest children—Martha Ann, six years old, and Edward, four years old—would be "better off out of the way." She thought the matter over for several days, all the while feeling "much discouraged and downhearted."[154] Besides, the summer heat just wouldn't relent.

On July 4, 1864, New York City made every effort to celebrate the anniversary of America's Independence, even though the Union Army was hopelessly bogged down outside Petersburg, Virginia, and Gen. Sherman was slogging his way through Georgia. Organizers conducted a military parade and bells rang throughout the city. Fireworks displays and cannon salutes were among the usual demonstrations of enthusiasm as people by the thousands took excursions by railroad and riverboat, gladly gathering in the fresh air and green woods of the country in exchange for the hot and noisy neighborhoods of lower Manhattan. In Central Park, a military band played music as red, white, and blue buntings flew from the masts of ships at the docks and moorings surrounding the island city.

At some deep level though, it was a melancholy time, for the War of the Rebellion was going badly. The Union Army had only begun the siege of Petersburg a month before, but the Confederate trenches and breastworks in front of the town were so extensive, the battle promised to be a long one. Meanwhile Gen. William Tecumseh Sherman had only entered Georgia two months before to begin his scorched earth plan to Atlanta and then on to the sea. Beyond these contemporary trials, most people had a hard time dislodging from their memories the grisly fighting at Gettysburg during the Independence Day holiday the year before. While the news of war took most of the headlines, markets were moribund, as commodity prices—from grain and rye to molasses and whiskey—remained low. One paper observed wryly, "ill bred boys will undoubtedly take delight and flinging firecrackers under the feet of horses, and . . . endanger the lives and property of others."[155]

In the Struck household, melancholy morphed to despair for the children born to a mother with no moral sense. Though Lydia had poisoned her husband with one massive dose of arsenic, she decided smaller doses might be more appropriate for Martha Ann and little Edward. After sprinkling a pinch of powder into their oatmeal and feeding them, she evidently experienced pangs of conscience and sent for Dr. Elliott. In so doing, Lydia took an enormous risk. Dr. Augustus G. Elliott was a well-respected Manhattanville obstetrician who graduated from the Columbia College of Physicians and Surgeons in 1843, followed by a yearlong internship at New York City Hospital. Elliott was also one of the founders of the New York Academy of Medicine (a Manhattan medical society) in 1847. A forty-three-year-old physician with a superb education, and almost two decades of medical practice, might have ended Lydia's career as an arsenical poisoner before she built up an insuperable head of steam. Sadly, Elliott missed the diagnosis.

Instead of suspecting foul play, Dr. Elliott explained to Lydia that the children both "had gastric fever."[156] After Dr. Elliott did what he could, Lydia sent again for Dr. George Jackson, who told her that the two children were very sick. He went so far as to say that they might not live. The older of the two children, Martha Ann, was particularly affected by the arsenic and vomited almost continuously until she died on the morning of July 5, 1864—the day after the dose was administered. Dr. Jackson was completely deluded by Lydia's attentive mother routine and labeled the cause of death "gastric fever."

Four-year-old Edward was affected in much the same manner as his sister. He was sick to his stomach and vomited frequently. In the evening of the same day, he too died. Lydia later recalled, "He was a beautiful boy, and did not complain during his illness. He was very patient. The afternoon before he died . . . [his stepsister] Gertrude Thompson, came to see the children and she said, 'Eddy, why are you sick?' The boy mumbled something and Gertrude continued, 'Eddy, you will get better,' and he said, 'No, I shall never get well.'"[157]

Again the attending physicians, Drs. Elliott and Jackson, had no suspicions of poisonings and sadly clung to the gastric fever diagnosis. As with their father, the word "arsenic" did not appear anywhere on the children's death certificates.[158]

There was a certain level of distrust of America's physicians as demonstrated by the licensing practices of the first half of the nineteenth century. State legislators had been licensing doctors from about 1800 to well into the 1820s, but public opprobrium forced states to begin rescinding these licenses. Illinois, for example, empowered medical societies to issue licenses in 1817, but abolished licensing in 1826. Ohio behaved the same way in 1811 and 1833, respectively. "Licensing laws were repealed in Alabama in 1832, Mississippi in 1836, South Carolina, Maryland, and Vermont in 1838, Georgia in 1839, New York in 1844, and in Louisiana by 1852. Several states, including Pennsylvania—where the very first medical school in America was founded in 1765—never had any licensing."[159]

Licensing failed because constituents suspected that "license to practice" was tantamount to a favor to doctors rather than a guarantee of an unassailable level of competence. A license would only be of value to the typical physician if the public accepted it as evidence of superior knowledge. In sum, licensure failed because the public didn't think much of the skills of doctors.

It took almost a half-century for the pendulum to swing back. Slowly medical education expanded, competence increased, quackery was exposed, and the public accepted an entirely new posture toward licensure. Connecticut, for example, did not again begin to license medical doctors until 1893, more than two decades after Lydia (Danbury) Sherman deceived enough unlicensed physicians that she was able to poison ten people during a seven-year killing spree that ended in 1871.[160]

With enablers like the medical practitioners of the 1800s, Lydia could have poisoned half of Manhattan before suspicions were aroused. After burying her two youngest children next to their father in Trinity Cemetery, Lydia found work as a seamstress. Meanwhile, Lydia's son George Whitfield was fourteen and learned coach painting from his stepbrother William Thompson. The miserable $2.50 per week that the boy contributed to running the household was a godsend. However, in late August 1865, George became sick as a result of the paint fumes. Lydia sent for Dr. Elliott. The etiology of the disease seemed obvious, so Elliott diagnosed the problem as "painter's colic." Adding to Lydia's burden, Dr. Elliott cautioned that George could no longer work as a painter. Unfortunately, after the doctor's visit, the boy got worse. As Lydia became more and more discouraged, her mind once again took an ugly turn. Convinced George Whitfield would become a burden, she mixed arsenic in his tea and gave it to him. He died the following day. Though George's symptoms were the same as his two siblings, Dr. Elliott stuck to his original diagnosis: his young patient perished from painter's colic. He marked that on the death certificate. Lydia later recalled, "I gave him the arsenic because I was discouraged. I know now that is not much of an excuse, but I felt so much trouble then that I did not think about that."[161]

After the burial of George in Trinity Cemetery, Lydia visited Dr. Elliott to see if he would recommend her for nursing work. As bizarre as this sounds, Dr. Elliott cheerfully lined up Lydia with a number of visiting nursing jobs and she occasionally filled in at the office of Dr. Louis Rodenstein. Lydia's sister Ann told a reporter that Lydia also worked as a nurse in one of New York's hospitals.[162]

Did Lydia murder anyone in the course of her nursing duties? She was certainly capable, but studies on female multiple murderers suggests not. Killing strangers would not improve Lydia's lot in life.

In order to perform her duties as a nurse, Lydia had to leave her eleven-year-old daughter Ann Eliza home with the girl's older sister. The younger Lydia—now eighteen—worked in a dry goods store in Harlem, but there was no horse car railroad between Manhattanville and Harlem and the long walk to the dry goods store proved too much for the young lady. Besides, horse car lines throughout Manhattan cost six cents and there was never enough money in the Struck household budget for such luxuries. Eventually, the younger Lydia gave up the job. Miraculously, another job found its way up from the city, whereby the two Lydias could work on bonnet frames together at home. They did that for a couple of months. Lydia's daughter had a boyfriend named John Smith (though his name sounds like one of Lydia's ruses) who was a constant visitor during this period. The situation seemed workable, except that Lydia felt burdened by her younger daughter Ann Eliza. She thought, "If I could get rid of her, then Lydia and myself could make a living. This was in March [1866] . . . we had had a hard winter. I had no one to leave her with. I was discouraged. She had been unwell with the chills and fever, and was continually sick . . . I was downhearted and much discouraged."[163]

Lydia still had some arsenic left from the batch that she bought in Harlem to poison her husband in 1864. She visited a druggist in Manhattanville and bought some medicine for Ann Eliza. Into this medicine, she stirred some arsenic, and gave it to the girl. She followed up with a second dose.

At the beginning, Ann Eliza responded the same as her siblings. She became terribly ill immediately. But, little Ann Eliza had a stronger constitution than her brothers and sister. She clung to life for four days.

When Ann Eliza first got sick, Lydia sent for Dr. Louis Rodenstein and he attended the girl for the duration. In addition, Ann Eliza's pastor, Rev. Edward Payson of the Harlem Presbyterian Church, attended the girl's bedside until she died at noon of the fourth day—March 9, 1866.[164]

Although Lydia did a convincing job feigning devotion to her sick children—and seems not to have become physically ill by their suffering—it had to have been a gruesome ordeal. Arsenic kills by retarding the production of essential metabolic enzymes, leading to death from multi-system organ failure. Death by arsenical poisoning is an agony that tasks the imagination. While easy to administer, arsenic is a ruthless killer. From the tongue to the anus, all the organs of the alimentary canal burn like hellfire. There is steady vomiting and bloody diarrhea. The patient experiences agonizing stomach and bowel pains, while the poison literally burns the patient to death from the inside. There is an unquenchable thirst, the voice gets hoarse, and the skin is fiercely hot to the touch. Eventually, there is delirium, convulsions and death. Depending on the quantity of arsenic administered, a patient typically suffers through one to four days of unimaginable torture.

Nothing exposes the stone heart of Lydia better than to imagine her quietly nursing her children as their insides burned to uselessness before her eyes. She repeated this five times over a two year period and her children died thinking she loved them!

Once again, Lydia made the obligatory funeral parade to Trinity Cemetery to bury Ann Eliza. In the weeks that followed, she continued to keep house until May, leaving occasionally to do some nursing.

One Friday in May 1866, the younger Lydia took some work downtown and then spent the weekend with her stepsister Gertrude Thompson. Back in Manhattanville, her mother expected her to return on Saturday afternoon, and when the young lady didn't show up, telegraphed in an effort to reach her. Before a return telegraph could be sent, young Lydia arrived home. Unfortunately, she had contracted a fever and went directly to bed. Her mother walked to the druggist's and purchased more medicine. The older woman sat up all night with her daughter, and then sent for Dr. Rodenstein on Sunday morning. Rodenstein lived on Clinton Place only a few blocks north of 125th Street.[165]

Dr. Louis A. Rodenstein, a German immigrant, was another Manhattanville physician with a supposedly superb medical education. He graduated from the University of Pennsylvania School of Medicine in 1859, and interned among the patients on Blackwell's Island for a year thereafter. Rodenstein served in the Mexican war and answered the call

Dr. Louis H. Rodenstein

in the Civil War as well, arriving at the Antietam battlefield in Sharpsburg, Maryland two days after the fighting concluded. Antietam was the bloodiest single day of fighting in the Civil War (26,304 casualties) and allopaths like Rodenstein worked day and night amputating limbs in a Sisyphean effort to save the lives of those who did not perish in battle. (Two decades later, in 1885, Rodenstein was one of the founders of Manhattan General Hospital.)[166]

Dr. Rodenstein was of medium height with a thin face and a full dark beard. He made his house calls by riding a pony from house to tenement, and acted as visiting physician at the Sacred Heart convent and the Hebrew Orphan Asylum. Dr. Rodenstein was fondly remembered as "a fine man with a heart as big as a house."[167]

Rodenstein's problem wasn't education, bravery or diligence. It was age. After his work at the Battle of Antietam in late 1862, Dr. Rodenstein entered private practice. When he attended young Lydia, he had been in private practice for only a couple of years and simply did not have the experience to diagnose arsenical poisoning. When confronted with the real article, Dr. Rodenstein mistook it for typhoid fever.[168]

On Sunday afternoon, Rev. Edward Payson visited the younger Lydia, staying with her until late in the evening. According to Lydia, Rev. Mr. Payson gave her daughter all her medicines and took sole charge of her. Dr. Rodenstein came twice a day, but young Lydia's health continued to deteriorate. After two weeks, her mother sent down to the city for Dr. Francis Fleet, the English physician who had taken care of the Strucks when they lived on Elizabeth Street. (Young Lydia's stepbrother, William Thompson, brought the doctor up to Manhattanville from the city.) The two doctors—Rodenstein and Fleet—gathered in consultation.[169]

The rules of conduct among doctors arose from the medical societies. The American Institute of Homeopathy was founded in 1844, and more or less forced the organization of the American Medical Association two years later. One common mandate required doctors to refrain from speaking badly of other doctors, hospitals or medical schools. If two practitioners disagreed on a diagnosis, the final decision was to rest with the regular attending doctor, or if necessary, a third doctor could be brought in to render an opinion. All of this so the patient would never know that there had been uncertainty. Lastly, if the matter could still not be resolved, then and only then could the decision be placed in the hands of the patient. The obvious aim of medical societies was to build a level of authority and perceived competence that doctors had theretofore failed to establish.[170]

Unfortunately, the AMA proved impotent in it first fifty years. The lesser practitioners—members of questionable disciplines—felt the AMA was attempting to drive them out of medicine. In fact, the efforts of the AMA to marginalize the lesser practitioners backfired. The homeopaths, hydropaths, botanical healers, Eclectics, and assorted other practitioners actually grew in numbers. Also, the AMA's efforts to reform medical education failed due to insufficient membership and lack of money.[171]

The AMA's original code of conduct limited the organization's ability to assail poorly trained practitioners and force changes in medical education. Ironically, a half century later, in 1906, the AMA had collected enough data on deficient medical schools to shut them down, but their own code of ethics would not permit them to use the damaging information. The solution was to interest the Carnegie Foundation in the work of introducing excellence in medical schools. The Carnegie Foundation hired Abraham Flexner, the founder of a private secondary school in Louisville, Kentucky, to visit all of the medical schools in the United States (and Canada), rate them, and make recommendations as to closings and changes. Flexner completed this report in 1910 and it changed medical education forever. By 1880, there were 100 medical schools in the United States; by the turn of the century, the number blossomed to 160; and when Flexner released his famous report in 1910, there were 168. Thanks to the Flexner Report, by 1935 there were only 66 medical schools left in the United States.[172]

For the existing physicians, the increase in the number of practitioners was the unhappy side effect—11,826 doctors in 1880 increased to 25,171 by 1905. While the owners and professors of the medical schools were doing well, the average physician fell under intense competition.[173]

In the case of young Lydia's death, the older practitioner, Dr. Fleet, acquiesced to Dr. Rodenstein's diagnosis. It was Fleet's opinion that Dr. Rodenstein was doing everything in his power and the Lydia Struck should follow his advice. Twenty-one days later, on May 19, 1866, young Lydia died.[174]

Lydia contended that the Rev. Mr. Payson answered the door and accepted each parcel of medicine delivered by the druggist. In this way, Lydia could claim that her namesake died of natural causes. Lydia averred, "I never gave her anything but what the doctor ordered." Dr. Louis Rodenstein labeled young Lydia's cause of death typhoid fever, but in truth it remains a mystery because the girl's body has never been exhumed from Trinity Cemetery, nor were her organs tested for arsenical poisoning. All things considered, Lydia's killing spree does not earn her the benefit of the doubt in this case—even if twenty-one days seems like an appallingly long time to expire when Lydia was the person administering the arsenic![175]

Back when Lydia was advised to put her husband in a lunatic asylum, she rejected the idea, but one wonders if she considered placing her children out. In her confession and many interviews over the years, she never broached the subject, so we are led to believe she did not consider this option. Since Lydia knew first hand the pain of being given away, the possibility exists that she did not wish that choice for her children. Once again, Lydia leaves us with a puzzle—perhaps one that only another sociopath could understand.

When Lydia's namesake died, John Struck, Lydia's sole surviving child, was still working for the butcher, Henry Hall. Apparently, John helped with household finances, but now Lydia told him to keep his wages and try to support himself.[176] Chances are she didn't feel obliged to pay her doctor bills anyway.

For physicians like Dr. Louis Rodenstein, most services were provided on credit. Physicians collected fees quarterly or annually, but they lost a goodly portion, as bills went unpaid. Practitioners were vexed by the credit system, but they didn't have the leverage to force change. Physicians in New England only made about $500 annually and the doctors in rural Manhattanville did no better. Adding insult to injury, much of a doctor's annual compensation arrived in the form of apples or summer squash rather than cash.[177]

Lydia's ability to kill her husband and five of her six kids without raising suspicions sounds confounding, but she orchestrated enormous confidence in her ability as a mother and especially as a nurse. Moreover, she used the element of confusion to her advantage. She moved a number of times and changed doctors as often as she could. Without question, matters had reached the point where a close relationship with Lydia was, at the very least, poor judgment, and at the worst, tempting fate with reckless abandon.

Still, not everyone was oblivious to Lydia's trail of horror. Rumor had it that Cornelius Struck—Lydia's stepson—had long harbored suspicions about his stepmother. Struck served with the First Regiment, New Jersey Infantry for two years during the Civil War and was mustered out in 1865. Three years later, he married and fathered a little girl. Cornelius Struck and his young family lived at 125th Street and 9th Avenue in Manhattanville and he worked as a conductor on the Third Avenue railroad. According to the story, in the late 1860's, Cornelius Struck had requested that New York District Attorney Samuel Garvin exhume Edward Struck's body and those of his deceased stepsiblings. Garvin was an immigrant and an zealously ambitious political animal who in 1869 resigned a superior court judgeship to accept an appointment by Gov. John Hoffman as New York County district attorney, thereby filling a vacancy left by A. Oakley Hall—the new mayor of New York City. Obviously, Garvin was too busy with his own career to follow up on Cornelius Struck's suspicions of foul play.[178]

Lydia had several things going for her as an arsenic killer. Firstly, other than the ounce she bought before killing Edward Struck and the children, she didn't try to hide her purchases of arsenic and even asked pharmacists how much it would take to get rid of the rats in her home, how to set it out, and so forth. Secondly, Lydia was an attractive and charming woman who showed the concern of a distraught loving mother when caring for sick members of her family—whenever anyone was around. Thirdly, Lydia sensed clearly the madness of New York City during and after the Civil War. Everyone was preoccupied and services were strained to the breaking point. The last thing anyone wanted was time-consuming and costly post mortems. Fourthly, until the very end of her career when she possessed redoubtable skills as an arsenic killer, Lydia showed the cool nerves of a great gambler and the guile of an enthusiastic predator. Lastly, Lydia knew enough to pick doctors who would be slow to spot murder. Couple the wretched state of the medical arts with the dismal level of forensic pathology and Lydia was free to commit a long string of diabolical crimes without detection.

On the flip side, perhaps Lydia was becoming discomfited with the pile of dead bodies amassed at her feet, for she jumped at the chance to make a move out of New York. In April 1866, she found an opportunity to get out of the city with a good job in Pennsylvania. A Prussian immigrant and butcher in his middle thirties, John Maxon, harbored a dream of running a farm in Sailorsville, Pennsylvania (20 miles southeast of Wilkes-Barre and sometimes spelled Saylorsville). Maxon and his wife Christiana and their two children originally lived with John's parents, Jacob and Cattarina Maxon in Philadelphia's Nineteenth Ward, where the older man worked with horses in the stable business. Maxon hired Lydia as a housekeeper and offered her son John a position as a second farm hand and butcher.[179]

The farm worked out poorly, and Lydia and her son John left after only four months. Lydia convinced John Maxon to give her enough money to get back to New York and the Strucks left Pennsylvania early in September. They vacated in haste and left all personal possessions behind. Within a few years, John Maxon sold the farm and relocated to Philadelphia, near his parents. He promised to forward Lydia's furniture, but never did despite many letters from her.[180]

Back in New York, Lydia moved in with her stepdaughter, Gertrude Thompson, and John Struck returned to Henry Hall's butcher shop. Rather than go back to nursing, Lydia landed a position in a retail furniture business at 438 Canal Street. James Cochran, an entrepreneurial Irish immigrant—who spent very little time at the store—owned the firm. Lydia's principal job was to demonstrate sewing machines, and after one of these miraculous devices was purchased, teach the buyer how to use it. Under this arrangement, Lydia considered herself both "helper and clerk." Later she gushed, "I felt good and enjoyed my occupation. I had nothing to fret or trouble me."[181]

While working in Cochran's store on Canal Street, Lydia met James Langdon Curtis, an attorney and owner of the New Jersey Zinc Works. Curtis was an oddball with a massive ego that led him to run for the presidency of the United States in 1888 on the American Party of New York ticket. (Curtis received .01 percent of the popular vote.)[182] Curtis, his wife and three children lived in baronial splendor on E. 28th Street. His aged mother, Maria Fairweather Curtis—who lived in James' hometown of Stratford, Connecticut—needed a housekeeper. James sensed that Lydia was a neat and efficient woman, so he offered her the job. In addition to housekeeper, Lydia would be caretaker, companion— and whatever else was required—for Curtis's aged mother.[183]

Considering what the wake behind Lydia looked like, another move out of New York wasn't a bad idea. After the usual amount of haggling— including assurances from Curtis that his mother lived alone in the house—Lydia accepted the job at eight dollars a month. Since Curtis was too busy to take his mother's new housekeeper to Stratford, Lydia took the train alone and hired a hack to bring her to Maria Curtis's home.

Thanks to a letter of introduction from James Curtis, Lydia quickly took up residence with seventy-seven-year-old Maria Curtis.

From the start, Lydia and Maria get along swimmingly and the younger woman stayed for eight months. All the while, James Curtis came up from New York alone every Saturday night, spent the Sabbath with his mother, and returned to Manhattan on Monday mornings.

CHAPTER 5

Maria Curtis and Dennis Hurlbut

Maria Curtis could spot the spire of the old Episcopalian Church on the green and Stratford Academy from her front window. Her New Lane location in the center of the village was perfect for an elderly widow. Several times a week, Lydia bought groceries for Mrs. Curtis. She walked a block and a half up New Lane, south on Main a short distance, and then headed west on Broad just two doors to the grocery store of John Fairchild. In no time at all, Lydia had come to know John Fairchild fairly well. Fairchild, of course, was privileged to know nothing of Lydia's past.

Another of Fairchild's regular customers was a widower, Dennis Hurlbut. Fairchild realized that Hurlbut—known by everyone as "Ole Hurlbut" of Coram, Huntington (Shelton)—had just lost his wife, Almira, in September 1868. Fairchild also understood that it could not have been easy for seventy-two-year-old Dennis Hurlbut to take care of his homestead and himself in the wake of Almira's passing. In Huntington, Ole Hurlbut had many friends, but most townies thought he bordered on the edge of senility and consequently he didn't garner the respect he once did as a competent farmer and fisherman.[184]

In the mid-1600's, English settlers of Stratford found a thriving Indian culture at a place called Coram, along the western shore of the Housatonic River. By 1680, the European settlers had pushed the Native Americans out, and established farms in Coram. The town, called Huntington by the mid-1700s, wasn't officially incorporated as such until 1789. Huntington remained an agricultural town even as Derby's Birmingham borough thrived as a manufacturing center.[185] After the first

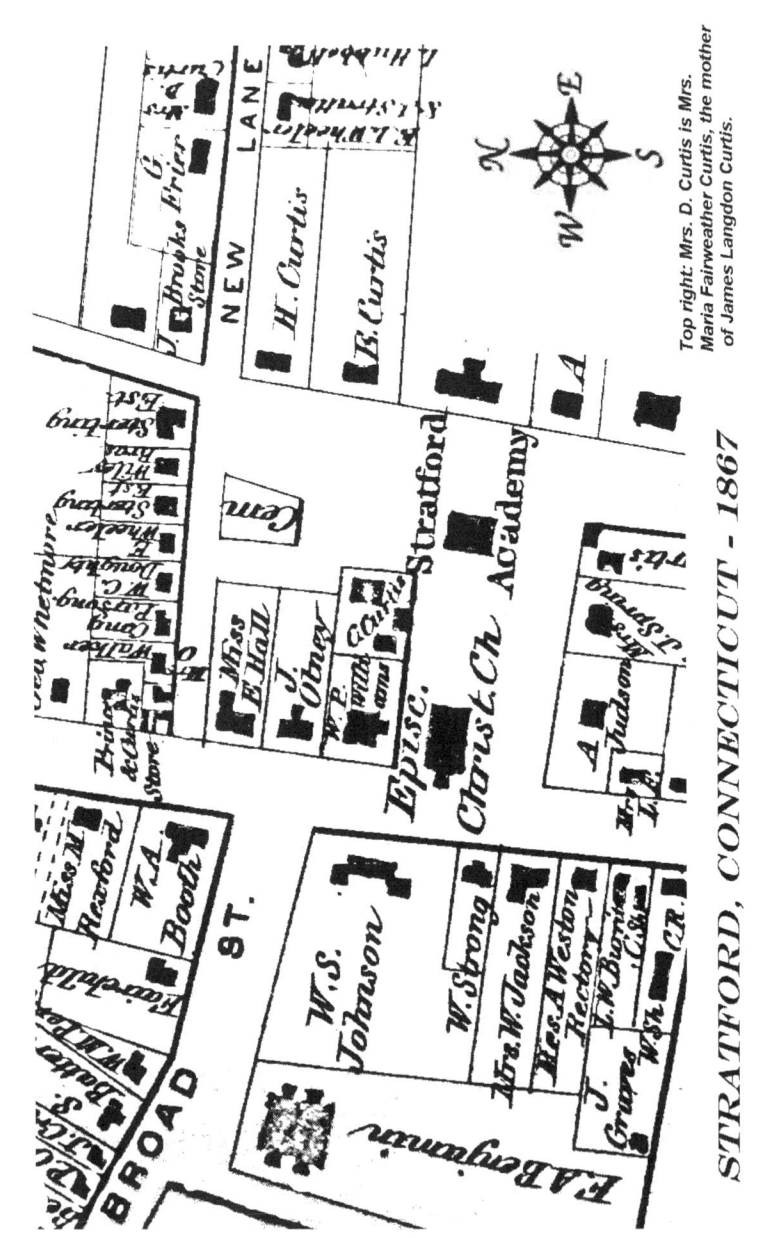

Top right: Mrs. D. Curtis is Mrs. Maria Fairweather Curtis, the mother of James Langdon Curtis.

STRATFORD, CONNECTICUT - 1867

wooden bridge was built across the Housatonic River in 1839, Huntington's industrial center started to play catch-up with Derby.

When it came to groceries and other supplies, Stratford was more than twice as far as Derby for Dennis Hurlbut, but Fairchild's grocery store offered a much larger selection and he came to prefer it over any of the grocery stores in Derby. On a recent trip down to Stratford to get supplies, Ole Hurlbut yapped at Fairchild, "John, I think I shall sell my place."

To that Fairchild replied, "No, Hurlbut, get some woman to keep house for you."

The old man yipped, "Sure, but where can I get a good woman?"

Fairchild answered, "I think I know one. I'll see."

With that, Fairchild waited for Lydia's next visit. When John Fairchild told Lydia that Ole Hurlbut of Coram was well off and would make her a good home, unwittingly he uttered the magic words. Lydia had spent so many years on the razor's edge of starvation that the promise of material comfort was an enticement of thrilling proportions.

A few days after that, Hurlbut returned to Fairchild's store and was greeted by the good news that Fairchild had recommended the position to a woman in the village. With that, Hurlbut called on Lydia at Maria Curtis's house. Following a short conversation, Dennis Hurlbut promised to stop to see Lydia again in a few days.

Lydia feigned misgivings. The next time she was in Fairchild's grocery store, she broached the subject. Though clearly she appeared undecided, Fairchild insisted that it presented a good opportunity for her and that she should take it. Still, since Dennis Hurlbut was a stranger, Lydia contended she would not go up to Coram permanently until after she'd seen the place.

On Hurlbut's next trip to Stratford, he drove Lydia out to his farm in a buggy. The farmhouse wasn't anything out of the ordinary, but neither was it a tarpaper shack. For example, the kitchen was big enough to accommodate all the cooking and still seat ten people at a big table. The farmhouse and spacious barn were surrounded by about a dozen acres of farmland. For a woman who lived most of her adult life in crowded tenements, Hurlbut's property must have seemed enormous and, of course, worth a small fortune.

During their time together, the two came close to agreeing on an arrangement. Lydia would cook and clean, while Dennis Hurlbut worked with the crops and animals. Hurlbut was so anxious for the deal to succeed that he constantly blabbed about having enough money to keep the two of them in fine style. He promised that if Lydia held up her part of their bargain, he would take care of her, no matter what. In spite of the desperate offers from Dennis Hurlbut, Lydia stayed with Maria Curtis for two more weeks—and Hurlbut returned to visit three more times.

Maria Curtis was in a difficult position because she didn't want to lose Lydia, but she liked her, and wanted what was best. At length though, she also realized she really had no say in the matter. Finally, Maria Curtis wished her friend well and assured her that if things didn't work out with Dennis Hurlbut, Lydia could always return to Maria's house in Stratford.

Maria Curtis's gracious words eased Lydia's exit. With that, the old farmer drove the six miles to Stratford one more time to collect Lydia. Still anxious to please this woman, Dennis Hurlbut topped all previous offers with one of marriage. He told Lydia that if she would be his wife, everything he owned would be hers. Just two months after he buried Almira, Ole Hurlbut took Lydia to Sunday services in Huntington; after the liturgy, the pastor, Rev. William Morton, married Dennis and Lydia in the rectory. The interest of a seventy-three-year old widower in marrying an attractive, forty-three year old woman doesn't overwork the

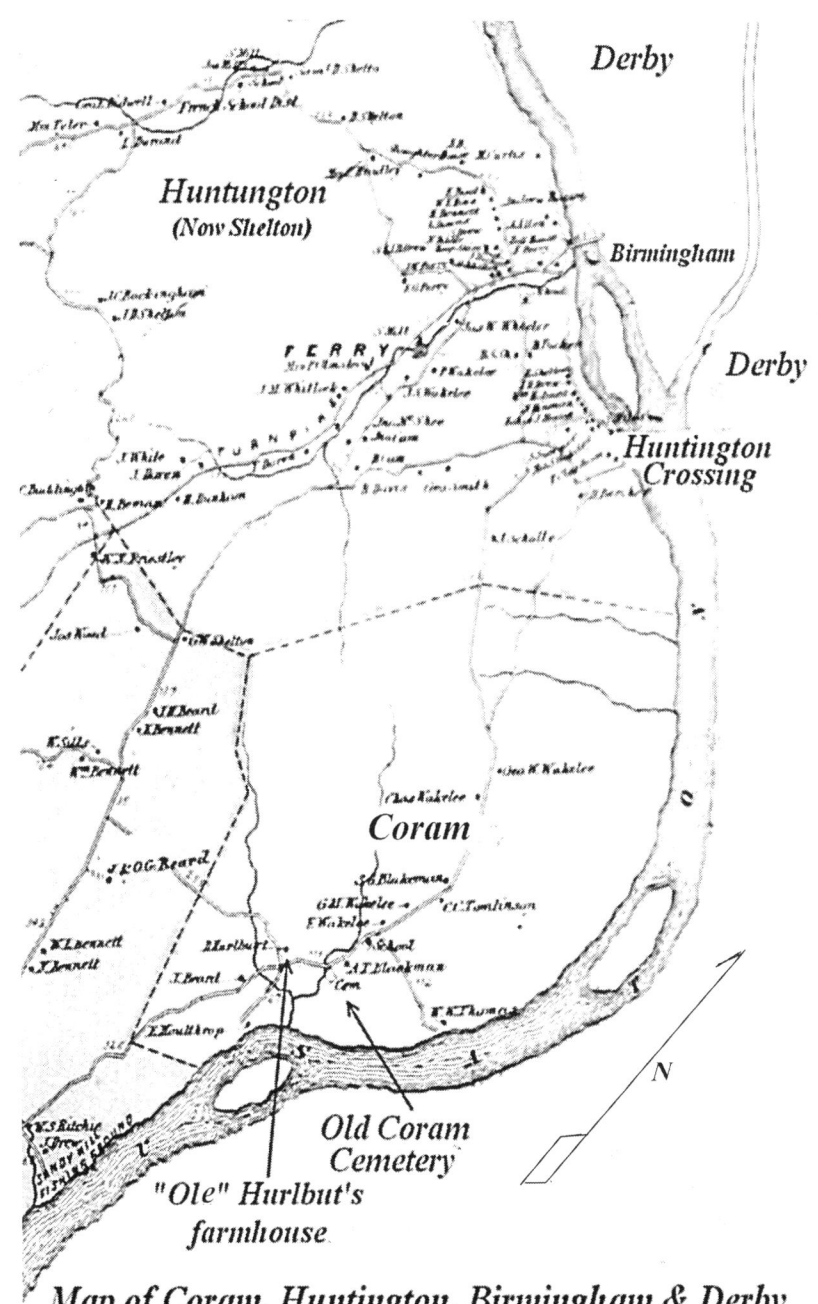

Map of Coram, Huntington, Birmingham & Derby

imagination, but examined in reverse, the situation is fraught with suspicion.

When Dennis Hurlbut of Roxbury, Connecticut traveled to Huntington with his late wife in the fall of 1828, they bought a small farmhouse on a quarter acre plot. For $120, it was Shangri-La by the Housatonic. About a year later, Dennis took ownership of a three-acre parcel nearby for $45. With just these two pieces of land, Dennis and Almira's dream farm was on its way. Over the next three decades, Dennis Hurlbut added to their estate. Eventually, he controlled in full or in part about 125 acres.[186]

But there wasn't a lonelier spot in all of Connecticut. The Derby-Shelton industrial boom had not yet begun and, absent a superb education, the average citizen fell back on farming the hardscrabble hilly lands of the area. Thanks to sound health and hard work of the most astounding sort, Dennis and Almira Hurlbut spent a lifetime piecing together their farm.[187]

They never had children, and the Hurlbuts downsized to the small acreage surrounding the farmhouse by the time of Almira's passing. Poor Dennis Hurlbut couldn't stand living alone, so finding Lydia was a godsend, literally.

Besides money, why would a woman like Lydia Struck marry a gnarly old farmer like Dennis Hurlbut? Huntington was such a tiny village that tongues wagged like cows' tails. Not that Lydia was ever affected in any way by peoples' gossip; she had the remarkable ability to completely ignore those around her when it served her purposes.

Ole Hurlbut, though, should have paid attention. The gossip might have served him well, if he had chosen to pay heed. Perhaps in all that claptrap, he would have learned a little something about Lydia's past. On the other hand, he had what he wanted, so why allow the idle talk of his neighbors to ruin his new life? Easy to say. Unbeknownst to him, Ole Hurlbut had only fourteen months to live.

Like almost every burg, the Town of Shelton, Connecticut, began as a small crossroads, in this case Coram (later Ripton). It split off from Stratford in 1789 and took the name Huntington after Connecticut's sitting governor Samuel Huntington. The final name change occurred in 1915, and represented a tribute to the Shelton family who owned the Shelton Company—the largest industry in this tiny manufacturing village of the 1860s. Compared to Derby, on the opposite bank of the Housatonic River, Huntington was tiny and out of the way. In fact, the first wooden covered bridge connecting the two manufacturing centers wasn't completed until 1839.[188]

Dennis Hurlbut—hard as a birch knot—couldn't care less. In his time, part of Derby sat in the nook of land where the Naugatuck met the Housatonic River. Just below the point where the two rivers joined, a ferry took passengers, wagons and teams from the base of the Old Coram Road across the river to Derby.[189] The Housatonic River was quite a bit more than just a dividing line for Dennis Hurlbut. In 1836, he paid Samuel Munson $50 for a one-tenth interest in the "Sandy Hill fishing place" on the western bank of the river. With nine other farmers—including one of his best friends, William Thomas, who lived right next to the Sandy Hill fishing place—Hurlbut stretched great seines across the usually fast-moving water to catch spring shad.

In the 1800s, farmers along the largest waterways of Connecticut put long nets across the rivers to trap American shad.[190] They dragged the catch up on shore with a team of horses. These little fish businesses required sizeable monetary outlays—nets, lines, floats, and boats, not to mention horses—and they also required a considerable amount of labor. Part-time and seasonal, these expeditions were typically run by a group of farmers working together. The farmer-fishermen built fish shacks by the banks of the river to dry nets and store equipment. They opened them up each spring when the shad were returning from the sea to spawn. Shad by the ton could be had this way. Small catches were sold to local fish markets, but a really good catch required a trip to New Haven.

These shad-fishing businesses added nicely to the meager incomes of local farmers including Dennis Hurlbut. He also had a knack for buying and selling land as opportunities arose. Over the years, his good business sense coupled with good fishing luck enhanced his financial position considerably.[191]

Despite long odds, the mésalliance between Lydia and Ole Hurlbut seemed from the first to achieve the optimum normalcy of a May-December marriage. Lydia did have a calm disposition and a kindly way about her. Whenever she was available, she seemed to attract men without much effort.[192]

Ole Hurlbut was a bit of a misfit, but he enjoyed an enviable bonhomie with the other farmers and fishermen of Huntington. His farm was often the meeting place for a curious mélange of characters. Undoubtedly, some of the neighbors laughed at the counterpoint of Ole Hurlbut's grubby habits and his newfound courtliness with Lydia. The marriage ambled along.

Dennis Hurlbut went happily about his business while Lydia made the meals and tidied the farmhouse. She even shaved her husband's beard two or three times a week when his hands got too unsteady to manage the straight razor. Ole Hurlbut was lovesick like a teenager and even referred to Lydia as his "darling." The neighbors were particularly impressed, for whenever Ole Hurlbut returned home, Lydia met him at the door with a kiss. Hurlbut was so enamored of Lydia that he gave her son John three thousand dollars to seed the Palace Gardens, a saloon on the corner of Prince Street and Broadway in New York. Sadly, John Struck was no more a saloonkeeper than his mother was a devoted wife, and the Palace Gardens flopped in short order. John Struck moved to Boston where he became an oyster dealer.[193]

One Sunday morning, the Hurlbuts got up and prepared for church. It was one of those days when Ole Hurlbut's hands trembled badly, and Lydia began to shave him. The simple act of sitting in the chair gave him a terrible case of dizziness, but he shrugged it off, insisting that if he busied himself with feeding his horses, all would be fine. When Hurlbut returned to the kitchen, he felt better. However, when Lydia tried again to shave him, the vertigo returned. Dennis's wooziness got so bad that they canceled their trip to church.

As Sunday wore on, Hurlbut had three more dizzy spells. (Lydia claimed later that Ole Hurlbut had an attack of these dizzy spells after three months of marriage, although at the time she told no one.) These attacks alarmed Hurlbut enough that he had his friend William Bennett make a few promised changes in his will. Since Dennis Hurlbut had brothers and sisters in Roxbury, Connecticut (Litchfield County) who were barely getting by, Hurlbut's decision—which hit the gossip mill straight away—to give everything to a woman he had only known for a few months caused a stir with his lifelong friends and neighbors.[194] As the day passed, Hurlbut became feebler, although he rallied himself to split a little wood on one occasion. His response to ill health was as it had always been—he would "try to work it off."[195]

On another Sunday, a neighbor gave the Hurlbuts some clams and Lydia cooked them for supper. Dennis Hurlbut's favorite drink was cider, and he kept a big hogshead of it in the basement. Lydia told him that he shouldn't have cider with the clams, but Hurlbut couldn't be dissuaded. He took a pitcher and went down into the cellar to draw a hefty measure of apple cider. As was his habit, when he returned to the kitchen, he ducked into the pantry to add a little saleratus (baking soda) to the cider.

Thanks to the clams and cider, Dennis Hurlbut was up all night with a bellyache that completely robbed him of sleep.

On Monday morning, he returned to the pantry for his daily dose of bitters. The bitters did little to alleviate his distress. Ole Hurlbut was sick. By mid-afternoon, Lydia finally broached the question of whether or not to send for the doctor. Hurlbut was not the type to send for the doctor for dizziness and stomach pains, so he declined and insisted that he would soon be better. That night he took another glass of cider.

On a previous occasion, John Struck, Lydia's sole remaining child, paid a visit to his mother at the Hurlbut farmhouse in Coram. Struck, Lydia and Dennis Hurlbut planned to spend the evening at Charles Tomlinson's farmhouse on the Coram Road, but before they got in the buckboard, Hurlbut and John Struck each took a swig of liquor. They offered some to Lydia, but she said, "No, I do not want any. I will take cider."[196] Her husband put some saleratus in the cider and handed it to her. She drank the amber mixture and then the three left for Tomlinson's farm. Presently, Lydia began vomiting and had to be taken home. She was very sick for about three hours, but eventually got to bed and slept well. John left early the next morning. (When this incident surfaced later, newspaper writers expressed the suspicion that Lydia had ingested "a taste of her own medicine" without realizing it.)[197]

By Monday night, however, Hurlbut was sick again. He was up all night and lost the whole day on Tuesday. By Wednesday he wanted a doctor. As Lydia and Dennis Hurlbut sat in the kitchen, Gideon Wakelee and Selah Blackman happened by with a team and wagon. When they saw how much their friend was suffering, they offered to go for the doctor. Hurlbut agreed. Since they had planned to take a load of firewood to Derby, they would rouse the doctor when they got there. With that, the two men left.

The first doctor Gideon and Selah approached was Dr. Samuel P. Church, the village physician of Ansonia (the northernmost section of Derby). Church was the son of Attorney Samuel Church, chief justice of the Connecticut Supreme Court of Errors from 1847 to 1854. After graduating from Trinity College in Hartford in 1841, young Samuel Church earned his M.D. degree at New York's Columbia College of Physicians and Surgeons in 1845.[198] (The College of Physicians and Surgeons and Columbia College merged in 1814.)

Church's education could not have been better. At the time, New York only has two medical schools, but Columbia's College of Physicians and Surgeons was the best of the two schools and its reputation as one of the finest medical schools in the nation wasn't lost on serious students of medicine. Columbia's College of Physicians and Surgeons was the medical school of choice for members of the most prominent families on the eastern seaboard. In just one year—from 1845 to 1846—the number of students jumped by 13 percent. Columbia used this success to maximum advantage. In 1846, the year after Dr. Church graduated, Columbia revamped its lecture schedule to include the four-month session required by law (November 1 – March 31), but also added two more sessions; a second session through the month of October, and a three-month session that would begin after the main four-month session ended.[199]

Columbia's standards for 1846 were exemplary: "Candidates for the degree of Doctor of Medicine, must have attended two full courses of lectures [two years]; they must also have studied medicine three years under the direction of a regular physician, and have attained the age of twenty-one. Each candidate was required to write a thesis on some subject connected with the science of medicine, and to deposit it with the secretary of the faculty. Previous to final examination, formal certificates of time and age were required. The examination of candidates took place semi-annually. Graduation was on or before the first of March; or for the alternate session, the second Tuesday of September."[200]

Ultimately, Dr. Charles Pinney was approached, but he was too busy for the long ride to Coram, so the men drove to Dr. Ambrose Beardsley's house on Elizabeth Street, near the village square. Unfortunately, Dr. Beardsley was not at home either, and he was not expected. At long last, they made contact with Dr. Gould Shelton of Huntington. Although he was not home when they stopped in, his wife offered to have him make the call as soon as he returned.

Dr. Shelton was away from home the whole day and wasn't able to get to the Hurlbut farm until midnight. After apologizing for the late hour, he attended to the sick farmer. He couldn't do much. Dr. Shelton had been up late the night before and had still more patients to see. After two hours, he simply had to be on his way. Lydia asked him to return the following day and he agreed.

Dr. Shelton came back about 10 o'clock the following morning, only to find his patient considerably worse. Ole Hurlbut looked bad enough that the doctor told Lydia to consider inviting Dennis's friends over to say their goodbyes. At this point, Dr. Shelton did an interesting thing—he told Lydia that he had done everything he could and if she wanted another doctor she had better send for one right away. She told him that she didn't know what doctor to send for inasmuch as they had attempted to contact two other doctors already—without success. With that, she asked Dr. Shelton to come back when he could.

At 2 o'clock in the afternoon on Thursday January 20, 1870, Hurlbut started to sink fast while Lydia bustled around in her well-practiced role as devoted caregiver. Then about five o'clock some of the neighbors— William Thomas and Cornelius Moulthrop—came in and Dr. Shelton returned. Dennis Hurlbut passed away soon thereafter.[201] Said one newspaper, "The physician who attended the deceased husband professed to be puzzled, but with the usual dilatoriness of country practitioners, nothing was attempted . . . in the way of a postmortem until . . . it was too late."

So Old Hurlbut was quietly buried, and Lydia inherited everything.[202] The most common estimates of Lydia's inheritance from Dennis Hurlbut

Dr. Gould A. Shelton

range from $10,000 to $20,000. There was even an article in the *New York Times* that set his final estate at $75,000. Little wonder the people of Derby and Huntington gossiped incessantly about Lydia and maintained hard-to-shake suspicions about the real cause of Ole Hurlbut's death. Actually, when his inventory was finally completed and submitted to the probate court in August 1870, Hurlbut's worldly goods started with 3 feather beds and 10 quilts, 2 tables, 8 cane chairs and 10 kitchen chairs,

2 rocking chairs, a cook stove, a buggy and a lumber wagon, tin ware, 2 axes, tools, and $30 worth of hay. Hurlbut's farm—valued at $850—had been pared down to only a farmhouse, a barn and 11 acres of land. In addition to this property, Ole Hurlbut held the notes of about ten friends, as well as money in savings accounts. In all, Ole Hurlbut's estate came to $5,528.90.[203]

Lydia Hurlbut

Lydia arranged a nice service in Huntington and Dennis Hurlbut took his place next to his first wife, Almira, in the couple's plot at the Old Coram Cemetery. (These burying grounds sat at the spot where the Coram Road almost meets River Road—at the Housatonic River—and then heads south for Stratford. Gideon Wakelee and Selah Blackman, were two of Ole Hurlbut's friends who turned the earth that day. The Hurlbuts' final resting place sat atop a fifty-foot-high mound, Coram Hill, on the western bank of the Housatonic River, and provided a secure bosom for many generations of Huntington residents. As we shall see though, it offered little rest for Dennis Hurlbut.[204]

A significant consideration surfaces here. When Lydia poisoned Dennis Hurlbut, it was the only time she resorted to arsenic when her back was not against the wall. Though this seems to contradict Lydia's standard methodology, it is by no means inconsistent with female murderers' efforts to improve their lives. Financial windfall isn't the only reason they kill; they also murder to improve their situations in life—a phrase that covers a lot of ground. When Lydia poisoned Ole Hurlbut, it was only a small variation on the theme of her murderous sociopathic pattern. Oddly enough, she may have thought her days ahead would be lavish, but except for the purchase of a few new dresses, Lydia really didn't know what to do with the money. She didn't shepherd money well and didn't get much joy out of it either.

Ole Hurlbut's farm was a magnet for a variety of friends who enjoyed his company. He had reached the age where he didn't take himself too seriously, and passed along a great many tips on shad fishing and other pastimes. Even after Ole Hurlbut expired, his friends maintained their habit of visiting his farm.[205]

Lydia continued to live there.

Because Huntington was such a small town, mail arrived through the post office in Derby, across the river. Since Lydia lived more than three miles from Derby, the fisherman William Thomas, used to pick up her mail when he fetched his own. One day, while bringing letters to Lydia, Thomas asked her if she would like to take in a baby.

William told Lydia of a widower in Derby who was saddled with a sick baby. Mr. Thomas said that Mr. Nelson Sherman had asked him if he knew anyone who would take the baby. Mr. Thomas continued, "When I got home, I was speaking to my wife about it, and she thought that Mrs. Hurlbut [Lydia] . . . would like it, as it would be company for her, and she wished you would take it."[206]

Lydia wasn't overjoyed at the prospect of caring for a sick child. She told Thomas, "I don't know where I could get milk from one cow, as it is necessary for the child to have it."[207]

Thomas countered, "Mr. Wakelee has plenty of cows, and as he was one of the neighbors, I could get him to furnish you with milk."

With that, Lydia said she would rather see Mr. Sherman herself, and only then would she consider bargaining with him. Thomas agreed to tell Nelson to stop down to see her.

Once again, Lydia's life seemed destined to intertwine with that of a needy man. However, even from the get-go, one is hard pressed to envision a way in which Lydia's life would be better for the entanglement. Was she lonely in the farmhouse in Coram? When it came to needy men, was she incapable of saying no? Despite the rumors about Nelson Sherman's dissipation, did she still see financial gain for herself at the end of the day? Unlike Lydia's previous killings, this next catastrophe winds up under a microscope and offers answers to at least some of these questions. The answers may not satisfy or be especially palatable, but we are about to come as close as we'll ever get to understanding the sociopathic personality of Lydia Danbury Struck Hurlbut Sherman.

CHAPTER 6

Horatio Nelson Sherman

Horatio Nelson Sherman was born in Machias, Maine on February 19, 1824. All his life, people referred to him as Nelson. Through his paternal grandmother, a longtime resident of Marshfield, Massachusetts, he was descended from Edward Doty, and John and Priscilla Mullens, of Mayflower fame. By way of his great grandfather, Ebenezer Sherman, he was descended from the most famous Mayflower passenger of all, Capt. Miles Standish.[208]

The forebears of his mother—Lydia Whitney O'Brien—determined the venue of Nelson's birth. Her people had a proud history of service in the American Revolution and were, at least to hear her tell it, the most prominent family in the First Congregational Church of Machias. (Though Lydia Whitney O'Brien was actually the illegitimate daughter of Col. Jeremiah O'Brien and his housekeeper, Thankful Whitney, in deference to the colonel—a bone fide Revolutionary War hero—the people of Machias kept the secret buried until recently. When—or if—Lydia Whitney Sherman ever learned of her true parentage is not known.)[209]

When Nelson's father, Aaron Simmons Sherman—a drummer boy in the Massachusetts militia during the Revolution—was nineteen, he hiked to Duxbury, a neighboring town of Marshfield, where he became a carpenter and joiner with a master whose specialty was church building. Aaron Sherman was an unusual carpenter because he also possessed a remarkable musical ear. He played the violin, but he also learned clarinet, drums, and cornet just to feed his native curiosity.[210]

In 1818, when only nineteen, Aaron Sherman traveled with his master to Columbia Falls, Maine to build the town's first Meeting House. After he completed his apprenticeship, at the age of twenty-one, he settled in Machias and started his own carpentry business. He built a few houses, but also helped in the construction of public buildings like the Machias county jail.[211]

Though raised a Baptist, there was no church of that persuasion in Machias so Aaron joined the Congregational Church where he met Lydia Whitney O'Brien. On March 10, 1823, when he was twenty-five and Lydia O'Brien nineteen, they wed. The Shermans eventually had thirteen children, the oldest of whom was Horatio Nelson Sherman.[212]

For a man who worked with his hands, winters in Washington County, Maine were particularly long and hard. Carpentry work dried up and Aaron and Lydia Whitney Sherman ultimately decided to move to Massachusetts. Despite the distress it must have caused Lydia Whitney Sherman's people in Machias, Aaron Sherman and his young family boarded a schooner and relocated to Bridgewater, Massachusetts, one of the earliest prominent mill seats of Plymouth County. Aaron Sherman drifted into pattern making. There was always work in Bridgewater for a skilled pattern maker, as America slowly geared up for its own industrial revolution. Aaron Sherman's pattern making skills made him an extremely well paid tradesman. He and his fellow workers concocted the wooden patterns that defined sand molds for the many thousands of parts that would ultimately combine to form machines to make household, commercial and military goods, and finally free America from the long-standing and despotic hold of English manufacturers.[213]

Aaron and Lydia Whitney Sherman got along well during the early years of their marriage, but they had a difficult time making ends meet, probably because of the thirteen children they birthed in the twenty-two years immediately following their nuptials. This strained the marriage to the point where Lydia Whitney and Aaron Sherman separated in 1855. By this time, all of the children—except the two youngest, Andrew, 12, and Charles, 8—were out of the house. In spite of their detached arrangement—and because of her pretentious disposition—Lydia Whitney Sherman refused to admit that she and her husband were separated to the point of staging a huge seventieth wedding anniversary celebration in 1893—twelve years after Aaron Sherman's death and thirty-eight years after their separation—at the home of her daughter, Mrs. Amelia Perkins, on the corner of Main and Oak Streets in Bridgewater.[214]

As a young man, their eldest son, Nelson Sherman, worked as a peddler out of Wareham, Massachusetts. Nelson attracted scores of friends and was described as a man who was generous to a fault. It was in Wareham that he met a local girl, Mary Snow Jones. They were married on July 1, 1849. Nelson was twenty-five and Mary was eighteen.[215] By the early spring of 1850, the couples' first child, Horatio Nelson Sherman, Jr. (Nellie) was born. That same year, Nelson accepted a job at Shelton Manufacturing Company in the Birmingham borough of Derby, Connecticut.

Derby's history as a manufacturing center is a textbook example of the 200 small water-powered manufacturing villages of Connecticut in the 1800s.

In 1830, the first factory for hoopskirts was built in the Birmingham borough. Eventually there would be twelve similar enterprises. Five years later, a brilliant physician, Dr. John Howe, gave up medicine and organized Howe Pin Company around his revolutionary pin-making machine. In 1836, a local industrialist Sheldon Smith bought land at the confluence of the Naugatuck and Housatonic Rivers, and created an industrial borough, Birmingham, in the Town of Derby. With Anson G. Phelps, the local selectmen drew streets through the property. The British engineer John Cloues laid out the roads, with the four principal

Horatio Nelson Sherman

thoroughfares named after his daughters and his wife—Elizabeth, Minerva, Caroline, and Olivia. Space for the Derby Green, or public common, was set aside, and Sheldon Smith donated land on the east of the public common for St. James Episcopal Church and balanced the gift with a similar piece on the north for the Methodist Church. Later, he donated still another plat on the west of the village common for the Second Congregational Church.

In 1837, entrepreneurs organized a firm that made paper from straw, followed by sheet-copper and copper-wire factories, an auger company, and a carriage axle and spring business. Textiles were not forgotten, as other enterprises sprang up to make flannels and satinets.[216]

Derby split into six sections, and the snorting little "factory village" of Birmingham—Section Number 6—was the economic heart. Men of industry built manufactories in Birmingham because of its great location at the nexus of the two rivers. They fashioned a dam on a canal that ran alongside the Naugatuck River—and later erected a twelve-foot masonry dam at the peak of navigation on the Housatonic River—both projects to harness cheap waterpower.[217]

The Naugatuck River and the canal coursed along the east side of Birmingham with riverbanks that were heavily wooded. Birmingham was a tidy little village with sidewalks of bluestone, and because workhorses' legs suffered on cobblestones, well-manicured dirt streets. Weekday mornings, shift bosses or superintendents called workers to task by clanging the bronze bells mounted in large belfries atop the manufactories. On the day of rest, clerics rang church bells instead as families made their way to Sunday services.

Mary and Nelson Sherman settled into a rented apartment next door to G. W. Shelton's palatial home on the east side of Caroline Street at the north end of the village.

Nelson Sherman showed all the same skill and natural aptitude with tools as his father Aaron. Nelson, who enjoyed a national reputation as one of the finest mechanics in the country, always got the best work at the Shelton tack and nail division, and could name his price wherever he chose to work. In fact, one newspaper noted, "So expert was he among machinery that the owners of the tack manufactory at Derby found it almost impossible to run their complicated machinery whenever he was absent for a day or two, and they therefore paid him the very highest wages for remaining with them."[218]

DERBY, CONNECTICUT

In the nineteenth century, Derby, Connecticut was divided into six districts, and the manufacturing village of Birmingham, at the center of everything, was designated District Number 6.

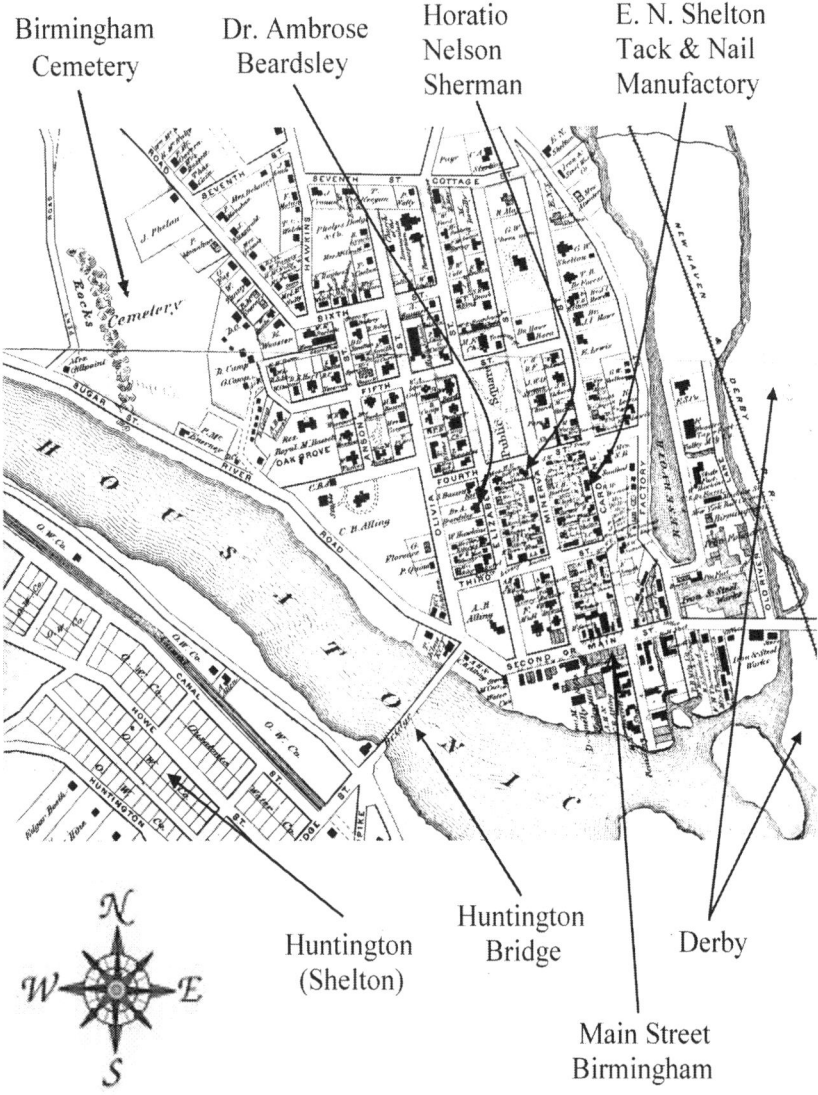

Birmingham Cemetery

Dr. Ambrose Beardsley

Horatio Nelson Sherman

E. N. Shelton Tack & Nail Manufactory

Huntington (Shelton)

Huntington Bridge

Derby

Main Street Birmingham

The industrious Nelson Sherman even held two patents. The first was a machine for making bed-screw bolts, once used in cord bedsteads. Nelson Sherman's machine—shaped like a five-foot cube—was sold outright to Shelton Manufacturing. The second patent was for a machine that cut and placed round leather heads on tacks—used in fastening down carpets. Nelson received a regular royalty for the use of this machine by Shelton Manufacturing.[219]

In 1851, Nelson's wife gave birth to another child, Mary Clarabel, who died three years later. Mary Sherman had more children. She delivered Ada (Addie) Snow in April 1856, followed by Ann Perkins in June 1860. Ann was a sickly child and died before her fifth birthday. The Sherman's last two children, Nathaniel Nye (Nattie) and Frank Henry (Frankie) came in November 1866 and December 1869, respectively.[220]

Nelson's mother, Lydia Whitney Sherman, visited her thirteen children and many grandchildren regularly and sometimes stayed for long periods of time. During the Civil War, for example, she stayed with Nelson's family for the greater part of the conflict.[221]

By 1855, at age thirty-one, Nelson became the superintendent of the tack and nail division of Shelton Manufacturing. His future looked bright indeed, as his annual salary soared to $3000 before the Civil War and twice that while the fighting was underway.[222] (This sounds extraordinary, but the same year that Nelson became superintendent at E. N. Shelton's Tack and Nail subsidiary, in Hartford, Samuel Colt paid Elisha King Root $5000 a year to run Colt Patent Fire-Arms—although ten times the size of Shelton Tack and Nail Division. The average yearly salary for a run-of-the-mill shop mechanic in 1855 was about $400.)[223]

The Nelson Shermans were doing so well that when Aaron and Lydia Whitney Sherman separated in 1855, Nelson invited his twelve-year-old brother, Andrew, to live with him. The boy stayed in Derby long enough to finish high school, and then he studied at New England divinity schools. During the Civil War, he served in two Connecticut Regiments, and in 1869, he entered the ministry of the Methodist Episcopal Church, only to embrace Congregationalism a few years later.[224]

In later life, Andrew Sherman remembered that his brother and sister-in-law, Mary, attended St. James Episcopal Church.[225] As a boy, Andrew Sherman watched as carpenters built the 500-foot-long wooden covered bridge across the Housatonic River to Huntington in 1857, replacing the storm damaged one built in 1839. The cleric looked back dreamily on the day when Nelson bought the "old Hinman place," on Minerva Street (southwest corner of Minerva and Fourth Streets, at the public square) in 1856. The house cost $2,050 and was slightly bigger than those around it. Nelson managed the purchase with $550 down, a $500 loan from Nelson Hinman, and a $1000 mortgage from Derby Savings Bank.[226]

The years rolled by. As the children grew, so did manufacturing in the Birmingham borough of Derby. The borough was insular; everything the Shermans needed was contained therein. Nelson was a man who worked hard and drank hard. At home, Nelson Sherman was domineering, but the Shermans were a fairly typical family living in an industrial village in Connecticut.

Nelson Sherman's happy life in Derby came to a shattering end on December 2, 1869 when his wife died from complications related to the birth of baby Frankie. Not only would Nelson miss her terribly, but he was saddled with all of the responsibilities of raising four children alone. His mother-in-law, Mary Jones, came to live with the Sherman family and was able to maintain stability in the household while she nursed the sickly infant. At first, Nelson's mother-in-law helped immensely, but in time this neurotic woman turned the Sherman household into a lunatic asylum. Nelson's mother-in-law was particularly tough on Sherman's favorite child, Addie. Nelson described the old lady as "being queer and finding a great deal of fault with Addie."[227]

In such a close-knit manufacturing village, news traveled faster in the barrooms and social clubs than by any other means, and Nelson quickly found a solution to his problem. Dennis Hurlbut and Mary Sherman died about seven weeks apart, and Nelson soon enough heard about the widow Lydia Hurlbut from the fisherman William Thomas. The grieving widower made contact as fast as he could, considering the emphasis on appropriate mourning periods and other social strictures common during the Victorian age.

On a sunny Sunday morning in early spring, Nelson Sherman accompanied some other fisherman to Lydia's farmhouse in Coram, Huntington. When he saw the chance, Nelson inquired whether Mrs. Hurlbut was the woman that his friend Thomas had mentioned. Lydia answered affirmatively, and Sherman said, "I am Mr. Sherman."

Lydia replied, "I suppose you are the man Mr. Thomas spoke to me about?" Lydia invited him into her kitchen.

Lydia began, "Mr. Thomas told me you wanted someone to take your baby to board."

Sherman replied, "Yes. I've got someone who I expected to do with, but I have another object in view. I want to get a housekeeper, as my mother-in-law is at my house and my daughter Addie cannot get along with her."[228] He then asked Lydia if she would consider keeping house for him. Lydia said she didn't know, as she had her own home to care for and didn't want to break up housekeeping. However, she would think about it.

Nelson Sherman wasn't about to give up so easily. He told Lydia that if she wanted to get her things stored, he would find her a place and it wouldn't cost her anything. But Lydia was still noncommittal.

Sherman returned to Lydia's place two weeks later and asked if she had made up her mind. She said that she had not, and the conversation took a strange, even desperate, turn. Nelson Sherman put forth a hasty proposition: If she would be willing to become his housekeeper and take care of his son Frankie, he would marry her. Naturally Lydia was stunned and flattered at the same time. Still, she told Nelson, before she moved in with him, they ought to become better acquainted. Sherman felt pressed to hire someone. He couldn't have the old woman in the house much longer. She was constantly making disturbances. Nelson's desperation escalated.

Nelson Sherman drove away that day and did not return for three weeks. Then he stopped by and flatly asked Lydia to be his wife. Again Lydia stood her ground. Sherman elaborated. If she wanted to sell her farm in Coram, he knew a man who would buy it.

In about two weeks, Sherman returned with two brothers, George and Henry Taylor. They looked at the place, liked it very much, and told Lydia they wanted to buy it. In turn, Lydia offered to rent. Once it appeared that Lydia had softened to the idea, Sherman stopped by frequently.

Finally on July 1, 1870, Henry Taylor leased the farm and moved his family into the main house. For the moment, Lydia stayed on as a boarder. A week later, Sherman returned and took Lydia for a long walk. He told Lydia that he had an interest (stock) of about $600 in the business where he worked, and could earn from $175-$200 a month. Hidden from Lydia was the fact that Nelson Sherman was no longer the wunderkind he had been before and during the Civil War when his salary was astonishing. In the space of only fifteen years, Nelson's hard drinking had taken him from a $250-a-month factory superintendent before the war, to a $500-a-month manufacturing boss during the conflict, to a $175-a-month dissipated machanic of late. Adding insult to injury, in 1859,

Hiram Kilburne, a local businessman, assumed ownership of the Nelsons' Minerva Street home—an effort to get some cash into the Sherman household. All in all, Nelson's finances were a mess.[229]

During this walk with Lydia, Nelson also mentioned that he was in debt $400 and he had a great deal of sickness in his family; he had lost one of his brothers a short time before, and he paid $100 a year to help his mother, who lived alone. Meanwhile, his daughter Addie was taking piano lessons. Obviously, expenses were running high. Sherman said that if he could get money to pay his debts, he thought he could get along fine.

Uncharacteristically, Lydia told him that she felt sorry for him and she thought of him as a perfect gentleman and would let him have money to pay his debts. He thanked Lydia, and declared "he could be a gentleman if he could get squared up once more."[230]

Lydia explained that she would go the next day to Bridgeport to draw the money from her savings account. She invited Nelson to come back to Coram that evening for the purse. Up to this time, Nelson Sherman had never been to see Lydia after supper. The following evening, he arrived at the Hurlbut farm with his daughter Addie and his son Nattie. Nelson was close to young Nattie, but fourteen-year-old Addie could do no wrong. She was "a lovely girl . . . one who was greatly admired in the village for her surpassing beauty and brilliancy of mind."[231]

Lydia gave Nelson $400 and told him to make good use of it. Sherman said he would.

Thereafter, whenever he traveled down to Lydia's farm in Coram, he brought one of his children—and sometimes two—with him. On one visit he left Addie with Lydia for a week. During that time, Addie decided she wouldn't go home again until Lydia went too. Addie also said that Frankie was very sick and she feared the baby would die. Lydia wouldn't leave Coram, but she finally persuaded the teenager to return home.

A few days later, Addie ran away. When Nelson got home from work, he couldn't find Addie but suspected she was at Lydia's place. He drove to Coram and found her there. Together Lydia and Nelson persuaded Addie to return home. It was obvious, Addie quickly built a strong attachment to Lydia, and the feeling seemed mutual.

The next time Nelson Sherman drove down to Lydia's farmhouse, she told him she was going to New Brunswick, New Jersey, to visit family. Nelson and Addie offered to accompany Lydia, and she graciously agreed. A few days later, they all traveled by train to spend some time at John Danbury's farm.

John was now a grocer in New Brunswick, and with his wife Elizabeth and family, lived and worked a farm in Piscataway Township (just north of New Brunswick). Nelson returned to Derby alone, leaving Lydia and Addie with the Danburys for a few extra days before they took the train back to Connecticut. Nelson met them at the train station, hired a hack, and they all returned to the house on Minerva Street. Lydia stayed overnight and then Nelson took her back to Coram the following morning. Nelson's mother-in-law, Mary Jones, did not understand that Lydia was part of a plan to get her out of the house and as a result was especially kind to Lydia.

Toward the end of that week, Nelson showed up at Lydia's place and asked Lydia again to move in with him—either as a housekeeper or as a wife. He stressed that young Frankie was very sick and that the family really needed her help.

As a temporary solution to their impasse, Lydia agreed to stay at the Minerva Street house for a little while. She settled in about the middle of July 1870. The next day, Nelson drove Lydia to a bank in Bridgeport, where she again withdrew money ($300) to help Nelson settle his debts and buy new clothes.

After two weeks, the live-in situation seemed to agree with both Lydia and Nelson, so Nelson suggested he and Lydia should marry at the Main Street home of his sister Amelia in Bridgewater, Massachusetts. That is, as soon as Frankie got a little better. They waited two more weeks.

Finally, on September 15, 1870, Lydia and Nelson traveled to Bridgewater and were wed. When the newlyweds left for home, intriguingly, Addie—who had gone to Bridgewater with them—stayed behind to "attend school." This brush with education lasted ten weeks. Lydia sent money to help out. When Addie eventually returned to Connecticut, Lydia met her at Union Station in New Haven and brought her back to Derby.[232]

Addie had only been home about a week when Nelson and his mother-in-law got into a fight. The whole matter concerned $75 that Nelson's mother-in-law was owed on a new piano. These verbal jousts between Nelson and his fractious mother-in-law escalated as "the old lady" finally understood that Lydia was there to stay, and she was expected to bow out.

In a moment of weakness, Nelson Sherman confessed to Lydia that he wished Frankie would die. In that event, the old lady wouldn't have to stay in the house another day.

Lydia was beginning to feel that same sense of claustrophobia she felt when her first husband was useless and she was burdened with six children. Day after day, she was "full of trouble, and not knowing what to do; she was tempted to give Frankie something."[233] She thought Frankie would be better off, and her husband would be happier.

Without realizing his mistake, Nelson mentioned the arsenic he kept in the house to deal with rats. He told Lydia that his mother-in-law used the arsenic to kill the pests while she was running the household.

Lydia didn't hesitate any longer. She put some arsenic in Frankie's milk and gave it to him just once. Little Frankie, quite feeble, was affected by the caustic effects of the arsenic almost immediately and began vomiting.

Nineteen-year-old Nellie ran over to Dr. Beardsley's house on Elizabeth Street, and asked him to come quickly. Beardsley arrived a short time later and examined young Frankie. The prognosis was mixed. Although Beardsley never thought the child was out of danger, he felt the young tyke was better for the moment. Beardsley gave Frankie something to settle his stomach, and returned later that evening only to find the infant sinking fast. He cautioned everyone that Frankie would not last much longer, and at 11 o'clock in the evening, November 16, 1870, little Frankie passed into eternity.

Dr. Ambrose Beardsley was a fifty-eight-year-old bear of a man who had practiced medicine in Burlington, Newtown, Redding and finally Derby. He was a practitioner who lived quite a bit differently than the average physician. The doctor, his wife and their children made their home on Elizabeth Street (close to the public square) right in the midst of his patients and the different manufactory buildings in the village. Dr. Beardsley was a jocose man who got a huge laugh out of life's small mishaps and ironies. He was the Derby town treasurer for twenty-five years, a warden of the Birmingham borough and the registrar of vital statistics. Beyond that, he was involved in charitable and religious activities and was active in community affairs, often giving orations at important events. In later life, Beardsley partnered with Samuel Orcutt to write *The History of the Old Town of Derby Connecticut 1642-1880*.[234]

Since patients had to send messengers to get the doctor when he was needed, living in the middle of the village made sense, but other doctors in Derby, like Dr. Charles Pinney, lived east of the Naugatuck River in a less-populated part of town. Lastly, Dr. Beardsley thought nothing of stopping in Healey's or Fay's saloons when he was in the neighborhood, always ready to hoist a glass of beer and gather the news of the day from regulars. Of the four or five physicians in the Derby-Huntington area, Dr. Beardsley had his ear closer to the ground (or bar) than any of them. If something was afoot—medical or otherwise—he knew about it.

Dr. Ambrose Beardsley

Dr. Ambrose Beardsley graduated from Berkshire Medical Institute in 1834. The school began operations in 1822 with 100 future physicians in its classrooms and the highest expectations. It opened in a remodeled stable in Pittsfield, Massachusetts, next to the Town House (Town Hall) and only a few steps from the graveyard behind the second meetinghouse. Since there was no legal method of providing medical schools with cadavers during most of the 1800s, Berkshire Medical students became infamous for their "resurrecting propensities."[235]

Unbridled competition among the growing number of medical schools forced Berkshire Medical Institute to carry a crushing debt load, yet it was still unable to pay its professors decent salaries. By 1867 though, enrollment had dropped to 35 and the yearly salaries of professors at

Berkshire Medical were an embarrassing $130. Unable to chart a viable future, in 1869 the school petitioned the Massachusetts General Assembly to cease operations. The school issued a total of 1,138 M.D. degrees.[236]

Little Frankie Sherman's passing should have piqued Beardsley's curiosity; or at least it should have hastened Mary Jones's departure from the Minerva Street home, but it accomplished neither. Nelson's mother-in-law used the tragedy to make still more trouble. She refused to leave before she was repaid $75 on the piano in the sitting room. Nelson didn't have the money, but promised to get it.

Within days, Lydia heard a terrible commotion coming from the sitting room. The old lady and Nelson were jawing so loudly that the neighbors could hear every word. Nelson stormed upstairs and Lydia scurried after him to discuss the matter. Nelson huffed that the old lady was "mussy" about the piano. Lydia insisted that Nelson pay Mary Jones for the piano because the ill feelings had begun to take on a life of their own.[237]

Help came from an odd quarter. At about this time, Henry Taylor bought Lydia's farm for $1100, with $300 down. Lydia gave Nelson $100 and told him to pay the woman, and shortly thereafter Nelson's mother-in-law was out of their lives.

The loss of his brother, wife and baby in such a short period of time, coupled with the stressful mother-in-law vs. daughter situation gave Nelson Sherman the excuse to drink even harder than usual, and to slack off work. Lydia supported the family for about six months. Not only was she paying the new bills, but she took care of a raft of old tabs that Nelson had ignored.

Christmas 1870 arrived amid snapping cold weather. In the days that followed, a huge snowstorm gathered in western New York, and worked its way across the state towards New England. By nightfall on December

30, four-foot drifts covered the railroad tracks near Rome, New York. Little Derby braced for a ravaging blizzard.[238]

Addie devoted a great deal of time to trimming St. James in preparation for Christmas Day. Quoting a reporter, "This young lady was in the very bloom of health, always vivacious and remarkably intelligent. She was the idol of her father and the favorite of many friends."[239]

Lydia remembered, "I furnished her with all her clothes and paid her dressmaking bills."

Lydia made Addie a Christmas present. Nelson received presents from Lydia too. On Christmas Eve, one of Addie's friends, Katy Hill, came to stay with her. In the late afternoon, the two girls braved the cold and walked to Main Street for some confectionery. They came back without delay, and soon thereafter Addie took sick with an upset stomach and vomiting.

Lydia went into Addie's room and found her doubled up with pain. Lydia asked her what she had been eating and Addie said nothing but candy. Fortunately, just as fast as the sour stomach came on, it relented. Addie appeared better.

The Shermans walked over to St. James Church to see the Christmas tree. When they returned, Addie lamented that she had a cold and went to bed. With the excitement of the holidays, no one gave it much thought.

Christmas morning, and Addie had a crushing headache. Still, Addie and Katy planned a sleepover at Katy's house. Nelson went out, and Lydia prepared a hearty meal for the children. Addie felt better and the girls started out to Katy's. On the way, they visited the Sherman's neighbor, Mary Hubbard, who lived in the northern half of the house with her husband Lewis. Addie got sick all over again. The friends returned to Addie's house and Katy went home alone.

Addie was sick the rest of the day. Lydia made up the sofa for the young girl so she wouldn't be alone on Christmas. When Nelson came home, he was shocked to see Addie so sick and rushed out to get Dr. Beardsley. When the physician arrived, he examined Addie and announced she had a fever, prescribed something for her, and offered to visit the next morning. A night's sleep accomplished nothing, for Addie was no better when Beardsley returned. In the afternoon he stopped in again, but did not become alarmed until he saw her on Thursday. At that point, Beardsley was so concerned he told Nelson and Lydia that Addie was a very sick young girl and he wasn't sure she would recover.

Of course with the recent deaths in his family, Nelson Sherman was beside himself. He consumed even more drink. However, as Dr. Beardsley commented, "Nelson was always a man of fine physique—a strong muscular man of enduring constitution—and was little impaired by his bad habits."[240] Despite his alcohol level, he functioned for the moment.

Dr. Beardsley ordered a brandy sling—brandy, water, sugar and lemon—for Addie. Lydia walked down to the store and bought a pint that afternoon, but in all the confusion, Nelson drank it.[241] Lydia got another pint in the evening and young Nellie hid it from his father. Nelson badgered Lydia to tell him where it was. She honestly didn't know, since Nellie concealed it. But Nelson was not to be denied. He stomped upstairs and loudly ordered his older son to tell him where he'd hidden the booze. At length, Nelson recovered the bottle, fixed a brandy sling for Addie and drank the rest himself.

Dr. Beardsley checked Addie again the next morning, but she refused to get better. Full of anxiety and guilt now, Lydia and Nelson sent someone to Milford for Dr. Dutton. In light of future events, it is very possible that Lydia was now trying to circumvent Dr. Beardsley, the Sherman's family physician, who lived practically in the Sherman's back yard.

The options can be debated, but Lydia seemed to harbor great intuition when it came to doctors—and others who might cause her trouble. In the end, she convinced Nelson to bring in the much older practitioner, Dr. Thomas A. Dutton, from out of town.

Though characterized as a man of noble bearing who showed more patience in any manner of circumstances than the average physician, the sixty-five-year-old Dr. Thomas Dutton's education was lackluster. He studied with his father, Dr. Hosea Dutton of Oxford and attended some lectures at Yale. Unfortunately, Dr. Hosea Dutton had spent himself into the poorhouse sending Thomas' older brother—and future Connecticut governor—Henry Dutton to Yale Law School. Truth told, Yale has no records of Thomas A. Dutton ever attending classes there, but local sources maintain that he did indeed attend.[242]

During his medical career, Dr. Dutton practiced medicine in Oxford, Newtown, Derby, and Milford before retiring to West Haven. Lastly, Dr. Dutton and his wife Lucinda suffered the most disastrous run of bad luck with their children. Lucinda Dutton birthed seven children between 1829 and 1844, but only one lived long enough to wed. The Dutton's youngest daughter, Isabella Catherine, married a Yale Medical School student, Byron Munson, in December 1867. She died of pneumonia a month later at twenty-two.[243]

At first, the messenger reported that he couldn't find Dr. Dutton, but Nelson would not be dissuaded. Hopping in a farm wagon, he headed the team for Milford. Much later in the evening, Nelson and the doctor arrived. The former was so drunk he couldn't walk straight. After all that trouble, Dr. Dutton didn't prescribe a thing for Addie. When Nelson asked Lydia for ten dollars to pay the physician, Lydia protested, and demanded to pay the doctor herself. Nelson stomped out.

The pressure mounted. Lydia claimed later that she felt so badly she decided to speed up the inevitable. "I had some arsenic in the house, and I mixed some in her tea and gave it to her twice."

Addie died in the morning hours of New Year's Eve—December 31, 1870—as a two-foot blizzard blanketed the Shermans' little corner of the world. A crowd of friends, relatives, and parishioners attended Addie's funeral service at St. James Episcopal Church and pallbearers placed her casket next to young Frankie's in the crypt of the local cemetery. The two would be buried when the snow melted and the ground thawed in the spring. The day after Addie's passing, Mary Jones returned to Derby for the funeral and stayed in the Minerva Street house for a couple of weeks.[244]

After Addie's passing, Nelson, now inconsolable, drank wildly. He spent every paycheck on liquor, forcing Lydia to use her own money for food and everything else. Nelson would order wood and coal, and Lydia paid for them out of her inheritance from Dennis Hurlbut.

At one point, Nelson's younger brother, Rev. Andrew Sherman, and his wife Arabella, came to spend a few days. Nelson remained in very bad humor the whole time. Rev. Andrew said to Lydia, "I understand that you have let Nelson have a good deal of money."

Lydia explained that she didn't want to give him the money, but he pestered her until she did. Lydia felt that "if Nelson would try to do right, [she] should not care anything about it."

Rev. Sherman ventured that he had heard about Nelson riding around with other women, announcing his shame of keeping such a wife. Lydia claimed ignorance of those notions, but conceded that Nelson was frequently away from home and squandered all his money.

No sooner had Andrew and his wife left Derby, than Nelson's other brother George arrived. George stayed about four weeks, went to Brooklyn, New York and then returned later for another three weeks.

George knew that Lydia was supporting the family, and he talked to Lydia quite a bit about this. Offhand, she commiserated that it was hard for her to support them and still give Nelson so much money. By this time, Nelson was working again, but he continued to drink all his earnings, while Lydia sat up nights waiting for him to come home.

Lydia confided in George that she was tempted to leave Nelson. George encouraged the separation before Nelson spent all her money. Moreover, it was George's view that once her money was spent, Nelson could get even worse. And if she refused to give him any money? Well, opined George, she might as well take her things and leave.

But Lydia didn't want to give up so fast. She brought up the temperance society idea.[245] She told George she wished he would prod Nelson to join the sobriety group. Lydia even got her neighbors, Lewis and Mary Hubbard, to convince members of the temperance "Division" to talk to Nelson. At first, he wasn't interested, but they kept after him and eventually he gave his consent—albeit without ending his drinking.

As a last effort, Lydia joined the Division, and then George brought Nelson and the two brothers joined together. Nelson pledged for a few weeks, brought home his pay, and told Lydia to use it as best she could. Nelson's sobriety was short-lived, and when he resumed drinking, it was with a vengeance. Finally he sold the piano for $325 and banked the money in Lydia's name. Despite apparent good intentions, Nelson only left the money there a few weeks.

Lost in all the mayhem of the Minerva Street household was the fact that Nelson's drinking was now symptomatic of something much more troublesome. Nelson was undoubtedly overwhelmed by the deaths in his family; but he had something bigger on his mind. Nelson had heard rumors about his new wife—ugly rumors—rumors that showed a level of perfidy and depravity beyond his comprehension. What was he to make of her? Was Lydia really a killer? How could he admit to himself—much less his friends and neighbors—that he had welcomed a murderess into his home? How could he have confided to her that he wished his own baby son would die? Moreover, how was he supposed to protect himself and his two remaining children, Nellie and Nattie? Should they keep eating the food that Lydia prepared for them, when common sense dictated otherwise? Nelson Sherman was a mess.

On Wednesday, April 26th, Nelson and a number of his friends hired a team and carriage and went to New Haven. Nelson told Lydia he would be back in the evening about 9 o'clock, but she didn't see him for days. During that time, she inquired of everyone if they knew his whereabouts. She heard all kinds of stories: He was in New Haven. He was down at Milford Point. He had $200 with him—though she was certain he had no money when she saw him last.

Tired of waiting and wondering what had happened to Nelson, Lydia went down to the Shelton tack factory to talk with the paymaster. He told her that Nelson had not taken his wages to buy liquor. However, by the way, he wanted Nelson to secure his tool bag, so it wouldn't be stolen or impounded by a creditor. Lydia explained to the paymaster that she was afraid Nelson had taken $300 out of her account at the bank and gone off on a drinking spree. The paymaster agreed to look into the matter.

When he saw Lydia later in the afternoon, he confirmed Nelson had indeed withdrawn the money from the bank. According to the bank cashier, Mr. Birdsey, Nelson put the money into the bank in Lydia's name simply to keep it from being factorized (taken by creditors).

When Lydia went back to Minerva Street, she told Nellie what had happened. The young man sympathized, and confided that Nelson wouldn't return until all the money was gone.

On Thursday evening—after Nelson had been gone for eight days—Nellie volunteered to go look for his father. Early Friday morning, Nellie accepted money from Lydia and he headed for New Haven looking for

Nelson. At first, Nellie couldn't find his father, but Nelson eventually showed up near the train depot. Nellie brought Nelson back to Derby with the team and carriage, but the older man still wasn't ready to face Lydia. Father and son reached Derby around 7 o'clock that evening, and left the team at the livery stable on Derby Avenue. Then Nellie walked over the causeway into Birmingham and up Minerva Street while Nelson slipped into the Union Hotel (also across from the railroad depot) to shoot the breeze with some friends.

When Nellie returned to the Minerva Street house, he told Lydia that he found his father, but left him down the street for a bit.

About 8 o'clock, Nelson returned home. Lydia met him at the door with the cheery salutation, "I'm glad you are alive."

He responded, "I supposed you did not know where I was?"

Lydia huffed, "How should I know?"

Nelson asked for young Nattie, who was already in bed. Lydia offered Nelson some supper but he didn't want any. Instead, Nelson went upstairs to Nattie's bedroom to retire.

A peculiar aberration comes to light at this time. Though the Sherman's were only married for four months, their marriage was troubled enough that the two did not sleep together. Lydia complained about this to Nelson and taunted him with divorce, but without resolution. Instead of sharing the same bed with Lydia, Nelson took to sleeping with his son Nattie upstairs while Lydia slept in a bedroom downstairs.[246]

By Saturday, Nelson was hung over and spent a languid day at home. Sunday, Lydia and Nelson talked about his propensity to take off for New Haven for days without notice, his drawing money from the bank, and spending his money as well as hers on liquor. Nelson admitted he was wrong. Sensing she was on a roll, Lydia asked Nelson point blank, "Don't you think we don't do right in not sleeping together?"

Nelson replied, "I don't know whether I do or not; I know too much."

Nelson went out at 4 o'clock in the afternoon and said he would not be gone long. Lydia didn't see him until 1:30 in the morning when he returned dead drunk.

On Monday, May 8, Nelson went to work as usual. His son Nellie, now working at Shelton's also, returned home and told Lydia that his father was not coming home to dinner and wanted Lydia to send something down to the shop for him, which she did. Nelson put in a full day and came home at 6 o'clock, after the rest of the family had already eaten. Lydia gave him some cocoa and he drank it with supper. He got up from the table, smoked a cigar out in the yard, and later went down the street to get some greens for the next day's dinner.

Lydia remembered, "I was in so much trouble on account of his drinking, and because he acted so about getting money and spending it, that I had given into the temptation of doing it again."[247]

While Nelson was gone, his stomach turned sour and he began vomiting violently. He returned home immediately, explained that he was sick and went to bed. Since liquor never made Nelson so sick, he had obviously ingested something else. For whatever reason, Lydia chose this moment to strike again. There was a pint of brandy in the house, and Lydia put some arsenic in it. Nelson drank some of the brandy and the next morning he was much worse. (Lydia later claimed that she didn't mean to kill Nelson—only to make him sick of liquor.)[248]

In a strange jumble of events, P.T. Barnum teamed up with William Cameron Coup and Dan Castillo in the traveling circus business in 1871, with a troop of 75 wagons, 200 horses, and 175 circus workers. The traveling band was called P. T. Barnum's Museum, Menagerie and Circus. By giving only a one-ring show at 7 o'clock each night—for 50 cents—Barnum was able to visit a new town each day. After performing in Bridgeport, Barnum's mesmerizing circus played Derby on Tuesday, May 9, 1871. Barnum's show was America's leading circus and it was enthusiastically welcomed all over New York, New England and the Middle Atlantic States.

In the late morning, Nelson curled on the couch and clutched his abdomen while Barnum's brightly-colored wagons, horses and elephants slowly made their way across the Huntington Bridge into Birmingham. They then paraded north on Olivia Street, east on Fourth Street—past the village green—and right by the Shermans' home. After plodding south down Caroline Street and east on Main, the troop set up the big top in the sprawling meadows on the north side of "the causeway" between Birmingham and Derby proper. While this exciting mélange marched by the couple's home, Lydia tried to get her husband up to a sitting position so he could watch the show through the front window, but it was no use. The arsenic had made Nelson so feeble, he remained supine while Barnum's extravaganza passed by.[249]

Launching quickly into her concerned spouse mode, Lydia sent for Dr. Beardsley, who came in the afternoon. When he arrived, Lydia met him at the door and fretted, "Sherman is very sick."

Beardsley went into the room and asked Nelson what was the matter, but got nothing but equivocations. "It may be one of my old spells," stated Nelson. The doctor told him he guessed that it was, and before he went away he cautioned that if Sherman did not give up his drinking and spreeing, he would die soon enough. He planned to revisit the matter when Nelson felt better. The doctor wrote out a prescription and left. At Lydia's request, Dr. Beardsley agreed to come back in the evening.

Nelson was sick all day. When Dr. Beardsley returned that night, he found Nelson no better. Beardsley gave him some medicine, and prescribed some brandy slings. The neighbor, Mrs. Hubbard, went down to Main Street and purchased the liquor for her friends. Lydia fixed a sling for Nelson and left the flask in a washstand next to the bed, allowing Nelson to nip at the bottle until it was gone. Feigning surprise,

Lydia pulled the empty flask from the stand, "What have you done with the brandy?" Nelson admitted he drank it, even as his health continued to deteriorate. On Thursday night, Lydia sent again for Dr. Beardsley, but he was not at home. Nelson continued downhill, so Lydia sent Nellie to fetch one of Derby's other physicians, Dr. Charles Pinney.

Amidst the stress of her marital woes—and her chosen course of salvation—Lydia wasn't thinking clearly. Pinney was another doctor that Lydia should have avoided with an iron will. He was born in South Windsor in 1831 and studied for Harvard at the Rogers Academy in East Hartford. After matriculating at Harvard in 1849-50, he enrolled at the Columbia's College of Physicians and Surgeons in New York.

Dr. Charles Pinney

In addition to his training at the medical school, Pinney blossomed under the private tutelage of Dr. Willard Parker. (While Parker was one of Pinney's professors, he also maintained a private practice and enjoyed a national reputation as a surgeon.)[250]

Pinney was a gifted physician and surgeon who wore a full beard and projected a professorial image, a man of science in a Parthenon of lesser practitioners. He and his wife Maria had one son who thought enough of his father's profession to become Dr. Royal Watson Pinney, also of Derby.[251]

Charles Pinney's new patient refused to improve. When Dr. Pinney arrived, he asked Lydia what Dr. Beardsley had done. As best she could, Lydia explained the details of the treatment, and Dr. Pinney penciled a quick note for Dr. Beardsley. The older physician finally arrived and Mary Hubbard gave him the paper. After reading the note, Dr. Beardsley changed the medicine.

Nelson Sherman grew worse through the night. Lydia, Lewis and Mary Hubbard, and Nelson's mother—who arrived at noon on Thursday—were up all night. Friday morning, Nelson asked for Dr. Beardsley. He came quickly and found Nelson in an exceedingly low state. Nelson died around 8 o'clock that morning. It was a beautiful, clear spring day—May 12, 1871.

Nelson Sherman was a favorite with the townspeople of Derby. They loved him for his generosity and ebullient personality. He had been elected to office a number of times, but always resigned because Shelton's came first. At uncertain times, his work demanded his complete attention. Sherman was also in the Masonic fraternity, the members of whom "resolved to ferret out the true cause of his death." The public mood, combined with their own medical suspicions, convinced the doctors to seek a post mortem examination of Nelson Sherman's remains.[252]

Dr. Beardsley, as the attending physician, conducted the Sherman matter in a most unusual way. Rather than ask for a post mortem examination in his own right—tantamount to calling Lydia a murderess—Beardsley had the foresight to include Drs. Gould Shelton and Charles Pinney as consultants on the case. Only after all three men studied Nelson Sherman's remains and agreed on the most likely cause of death—arsenical poisoning—was permission for a post mortem requested. Lydia would have a hard time demurring in the face of three respected physicians.[253]

Dr. Pinney was actually the one who asked Lydia if she had any objections to a post mortem examination. She did not. Leaving no stone unturned, they next asked Nelson's mother, Lydia Whitney Sherman, if she would consent to the examination. She readily agreed.[254]

Dr. Gould Abijah Shelton was another top-notch medical talent of nineteenth century Connecticut. The Town of Shelton is named for his forebears, and Gould Shelton added in grand style to a medical dynasty that dated to 1790. Born in 1841, Dr. Shelton prepared for college at Easton Academy and entered Yale with the class of 1866. After graduating from Yale College, he completed the requirements for a medical degree at Yale Medical College. (Running boldly against the grain in medical education—usually offering brief programs and handsome profits for its professors—Yale and Harvard were among the first two schools to switch to two- and then three-year courses of study, as was the proposal of the still fledgling American Medical Association. By 1880, there were ten medical schools with expanded programs.)[255]

A handsome man, Dr. Shelton was considerably younger than his colleagues, having practiced medicine for only a brief period of time. However, his superior schooling made him a welcome addition to the consulting team. Indeed, in the early 1870s, Dr. Gould Shelton's medical education placed him in the very highest echelon of practicing physicians.

After securing permission all around, Dr. Pinney obtained the necessary legal papers, and the examination commenced Saturday morning, May 13. Drs. Pinney, Shelton and Beardsley were the only persons present.[256]

Nelson Sherman's mother-in-law, who had stayed at the Minerva Street house since the day after Nelson died—kept a close eye on Lydia. By June 6—about three weeks down the road—she had seen enough. Mary Jones was so frightened that she arranged a trip to her home in Boonton, New Jersey for Nellie and Nattie. They would be safe there.

Dr. Pinney, assisted by Dr. Beardsley, adroitly removed the stomach and half of the liver from Nelson Sherman's remains, wrapped them carefully in cloth and sealed them in glass bottles that were placed in a small wooden box. Without delay, Dr. Pinney drove the remains to New Haven and deposited the bottled missives of criminality into the hands of the noted Yale physician and chemist Dr. George Frederick Barker. Nelson's soul was given the traditional Episcopalian Funeral Mass at St. James Church, and his remains were buried in the old village cemetery next to his wife and children.

Lydia had no clue at the time, but Dr. Barker was about to exchange her love of arsenic escapes for a one-way ticket to the Connecticut State Prison at Wethersfield. Lydia hoodwinked a number of doctors in Manhattan and the Huntington-Derby area of Connecticut, but as we shall see, most physicians couldn't even stand in the shadow of Dr. George F. Barker. The day that Lydia's husband died, May 12, 1871, was the day her luck ran out.

Not only was Dr. George Barker an 1863 graduate of Albany Medical College, but at the request of the legendary Yale chemistry professor, Benjamin Silliman, Dr. Barker accepted a post as Demonstrator of Chemistry at Yale Medical College. During the Yale commencement exercises of 1867, Barker was appointed Professor of Physiological Chemistry and Toxicology at the Medical Institution of Yale College. Lastly, in 1870 Barker's *A Text Book of Elementary Chemistry, Theoretical and Organic*—intended as a new edition of Professor Silliman's *Chemistry*—appeared in print. Barker's classic text introduced modern nomenclature and notation for the first time in this country.[257]

It gets better. As a sideline, Dr. Barker, brilliant medical doctor, professor, chemist and toxicologist, helped the State of Connecticut by giving compelling testimony on poisons in difficult murder trails. Barker was a good looking man with a mustache that swept down a good twelve inches on both sides of his face, mixing with great shocks of hair from his sideburns—a look only a man possessing extreme self-confidence could pull off. The pince-nez glasses that sat on the bridge of his nose—dramatized by a thin black cord traveling vertically from his eyeglasses to his lapel and then draped loosely around the collar of his white shirt—added a curious mix of intelligence and heart. He made quite an impression on a jury.

It took nearly three weeks for Dr. George Barker to conduct his analysis of Nelson Sherman's stomach and liver. He insisted on thoroughness. After spending nearly twenty-four hours creating a workable mixture of pure yellow precipitate of arsenious sulphide, Barker produced a number of arsenic compounds with only the addition of a single component. This represented a series of simple tests for arsenic trioxide, the typical white powder purchased at the druggist's shop for killing rats. Then Dr. Barker ran three different tests on the organs: first, a portion of the matter was tested using the 1845 screening methodology of

Drs. Carl Fresenius and August von Babo; second, some of the solution was tested using the Reinsch test, discussed early. This evaluation, named

Dr. George Frederick Barker

after the German chemist Hugo Reinsch, was a crude test that narrowed the suspect chemical to arsenic, antimony or mercury. Still more of the mixture was subjected to the 1840 Marsh test, the most sensitive analytical test for arsenic at the time. In the end, all of Dr. Barker's tests were positive. Nelson Sherman's liver was fairly saturated with arsenic.[258]

Dr. Barker's turned over the report to Dr. Pinney at the beginning of the week of June 5, 1871. The contents of the report were privileged, but

Derby was far too small a village to keep such a huge secret. In no time, Barker's findings hit the streets of Derby like horse manure from a team of draft horses. Nelson Sherman's poisoned liver was titillating enough, but had Lydia poisoned anyone else besides her third husband? If the wildest suspicions proved correct, Lydia would be the biggest female killer America had ever produced. Could a housewife in tiny Derby, Connecticut be such a monster?

CHAPTER 7
Arrest and Preliminary Hearing

After Dr. Charles Pinney received Dr. Barker's written evaluation of Nelson Sherman's stomach and liver, he launched a formal complaint with Deputy Sheriff Henry Blakeman. Following procedure, Blakeman went to see Derby's town attorney, Col. William Wooster, who advised the sheriff to proceed slowly. Col. Wooster commanded an enormous amount of respect and people generally accepted his advice. Deputy Sheriff Blakeman took Wooster's admonition seriously and waited until Friday, June 9 to make a move, even though he knew that news of the investigation was wafting through the village like a marsh fog.

Meanwhile, grand juror Abijah Gilbert made a formal complaint to Derby's justice of the peace Seabury Platt who acted more reassuringly and issued an arrest warrant. At length, the warrant was handed over to Deputy Sheriff Blakeman, now fairly winding the stem off his pocket watch as he waited to get Lydia behind bars. However, keeping Col. Wooster's cautionary words firmly in mind, Blakeman still held back on the handcuffing.[259]

Blakeman heard rumors about Lydia leaving town, so he went to talk with her neighbors. They did nothing to quell his concerns. Blakeman was so anxious to know what Lydia's plans were that he called at her Minerva Street house on Friday to ask if she had a piano for sale. Overcome with uncertainty, but loathe to act irresponsibly, Sheriff Blakeman stationed a surveillance team outside Lydia's house beginning that night.[260]

The caution of Col. Wooster stemmed from a problem most lawyers would have understood intimately, but the townspeople of Derby probably couldn't fathom at all. True, Professor Barker had conducted a magnificent forensic examination, and yes, he would vanquish the doubters in court, but proving Lydia Sherman administered the arsenic to her drunken husband wasn't possible. In a circumstantial case like this, Lydia might have been able to win an acquittal. How could the State of Connecticut ensure that Lydia wouldn't walk right out of the courtroom and begin again her depraved love affair with arsenic?

Col. Wooster aimed to buttress the existing case by connecting Lydia with other crimes, if possible. By exhuming the bodies of the two Sherman children and Ole Hurlbut, Lydia's involvement in their deaths—if indeed Dr. Barker found more arsenic—would build a case that Lydia could not possibly sidestep. Even if Lydia escaped justice in the Nelson Sherman case, she could not evade responsibility in Ole Hurlbut's death because Wooster was confident he could show that Lydia and Dennis Hurlbut were the only two people in their Coram farmhouse when Dennis took sick and died. It would be worth the wait if some solid evidence could be lifted from the three corpses in Birmingham and Coram Cemeteries.

Although it remains a mystery who originally broached the subject of exhuming the bodies of the two Sherman children, the idea surfaced all the same. To advance this ghoulish scheme, Dr. Beardsley and grand juror Gilbert made clandestine plans to proceed. Their arrangements may have been surreptitious at the outset, but word got out. The Masonic friends of Ole Hurlbut—who hung out at Nathan's Hall on Main Street—quickly moved to have his body exhumed too. Beardsley and Gilbert acquiesced, and befitting a case laced with intrigue, the three bodies were scheduled for exhumation on Saturday night June 10, under the cover of darkness.[261] This sounds a bit theatrical, but in a village of only 2,000 souls, the possibility that Lydia would get wind of these machinations was likely and no one's idea of an ideal outcome.

The night after Deputy Sheriff Blakeman posted a team of watchmen outside Lydia's home, Dr. Beardsley's band of midnight raiders gathered in the gloom of the old Birmingham Cemetery for a task grizzly enough to chill Lucifer. A heavy fog blanketed the village that night—with only a shrouded half moon for light. Dr. Pinney, gravedigger Scott Baker, and Sheriff Blakeman—who carried a deep-green globe lantern with a clear glass bull's eye at the center—filled out the exhuming party of four. They found the graves. The first shovel broke ground and soon the two coffins holding the Sherman children were jostled to the surface. The men removed the covers, and Blakeman turned the concentrated rays from the lantern's eye upon the children's faces. The gravedigger, uncharacteristically, let out a gasp, which unleashed the emotions of the others. They all knew the children and remembered seeing their happy faces. Now, the men saw visages as appalling and cold as the case they hoped to solve. Dr. Pinney unwrapped the necessary surgical implements and went to work. Soon he completed his solemn task. He removed the tainted stomachs and livers from the bodies of Addie and Frankie, placed them in jars, and then boxed them carefully. Drs. Beardsley and Pinney commented on how well the organs were preserved. (Remember that from the Civil War until 1910, arsenic was the main ingredient in embalming.) Soon enough, Baker lowered the child-sized coffins back to their resting places, refilled the earth and went home.[262]

Dr. Gould Shelton replaced Dr. Beardsley as the small party crept across the Huntington Bridge and then trundled the three miles down to the Coram Cemetery, where Ole Hurlbut reposed. Gideon Wakelee and Selah Blackman joined them at the cemetery. (Positive identification would be important.) The group started the procedure again.

However, while carrying out their spine-chilling work, the five men were startled by interlopers. Wakelee and Blackman had just raised the crusty coffin of Ole Hurlbut to the surface, when some laboring men juddered by with a wagon and team of horses. They saw a bright light and distinguished the outlines of live humans up on the heavily wooded hilltop. They reined in their horses. After a breathless silence, one shouted in a tentative tone, "For God's sake, what devilish work is going on up there?"

Nothing followed. Sheriff Blakeman doused the light, and Dr. Shelton, Dr. Pinney, Gideon Wakelee and Selah Blackman stood motionless. The outsiders jumped off their wagon and jogged more than half way up the the rutted road that flanked the southern approach to the poorly kept cemetery. There they stopped and again shouted in the same hollow voice, "Who's there? . . . What's the matter there?" Still receiving no answer, they retreated—and their enigmatic shadows rapidly disappeared into the darkness, not to return.[263]

The exhuming continued until accomplishment, and early the next morning (Sunday), Dr. Pinney brought the boxed specimens to Dr. Barker's home in New Haven.[264]

As if Lydia had gotten word of the nocturnal pursuits of Drs. Bearsley and Pinney and their band of grave robbers, on Monday she shocked her lookouts by buying a train ticket to New Brunswick, New Jersey. Ghastly rumors were swirling around Derby, an unsettling change for a such a quiet little village. Just as Deputy Sheriff Blakeman expected, on Tuesday morning, Lydia closed up the Minerva Street house and took the New Haven train south. She settled into a comfortable seat in one of the parlor cars and by noon was in New Brunswick for a nice visit with her sister Ann. But Blakeman was prepared. He telegraphed Charles Oliver, the chief of police at New Brunswick, explained the situation, and requested that Lydia be watched closely. Chief Oliver cheerfuly obliged.[265]

Undercover police followed Lydia and Ann around New Jersey, as the two women enjoyed their reunion, shopped, and even spent a week in

Burlington visiting the aunt who raised Ann. All the while, U.S. Deputy Marshall (Detective) John Mitchell and a few other operatives, including a woman, tracked Lydia and her sister like bloodhounds. As directed, Detective Mitchell reported back on a regular basis to New Brunswick and Derby. It wasn't particularly interesting work, but Chief Oliver had no intention of losing Lydia on his watch.[266]

On Wednesday, June 28, 1871, Dr. Barker arranged for his report on the three bodies exhumed the night of June 10 to be hand-delivered to grand juror Abijah Gilbert in Derby. The report was brief and to the point—"To: A. H. Gilbert, Derby, Connecticut . . . Analysis of stomachs of Hurlbut and the Sherman children is complete. Quantities of arsenic found in all three. (signed) George F. Barker."[267]

In addition to Dr. Barker's analysis, the police questioned George Peck, the druggist doing business on Main Street in Derby. Peck had been in business for eight years and remembered that Lydia had come to his shop to buy arsenic in the warm spring days of 1871, perhaps a few weeks before her husband's last illness. Peck couldn't remember the date exactly, but it was after the good weather had arrived and his doors were propped open. Lydia asked for help in selecting rat poison and George Peck suggested arsenic, as it was as good as any of the alternatives—and cheaper. As with other druggists, Peck didn't like putting arsenic on his scales. Instead he poured out approximately one ounce, tied it up in paper and gave it to Lydia. Peck vaguely remembered that Nattie, the little boy, was with Lydia and also that she had made some remark about her house being overrun with rats.[268]

When Sheriff Blakeman got Dr. Barker's report, he bolted into action. He telegraphed Chief Oliver at New Brunswick and told him to arrest Lydia without delay. It was finally time to bring in the "Queen Poisoner."[269]

That very afternoon, Blakeman took the train to Hartford and got a requisition order from Governor Marshall Jewell—intended for Governor Theodore Randolph of the Garden State—for the extradition of Lydia Sherman. The following morning, Blakeman was on the early morning train to New Brunswick. Upon arrival, he hustled to meet with Chief of Police Charles Oliver. When all the facts were on the table, the two constructed a trap.

Learning by telegraph from the detectives shadowing Lydia that she and Ann were on a morning train coming through from Philadelphia, Sheriff Blakeman managed to jump a train to Trenton. After successfully hopping on the New Brunswick-bound train, he searched each car for the two women. However, the train was so long and so crowded that Blakeman couldn't find them. Eventually, all three of them got off the train in New Brunswick. It was close to 10:50 a.m.[270]

Besides Blakeman, other lawmen were waiting at the New Brunswick depot. A patrolman asked Lydia and Ann to step into the ladies' room at the station. The two women did as requested and Sheriff Blakeman finally made his appearance, "Excuse me, Mrs. Sherman, but I have a warrant for your arrest."

Lydia's piercing black eyes shot glances at Blakeman, but not a muscle moved or nerve quivered. "Arrest?" she echoed with perfect nonchalance. "What for, sir?"

Blakeman replied, "For murder, ma'am!"[271]

Lydia's face didn't drain or flush. She merely replied, "Oh, is that all?" Then looking at Blakeman, she smiled slightly and asked tauntingly, "Well, what are you going to do to me?"[272]

The officers took the two women to Ann Nafey's home where Lydia packed her belongings. Thereafter, she appeared at the office of New Brunswick District Attorney Charles B. Herbert where she remained until 4 o'clock in the afternoon. After Herbert rechecked all the paperwork,

Sheriff Blakeman and Detective Mitchell escorted Lydia back to Derby by train. It was Friday night, June 30. Lydia took up residence again in the house on Minerva Street, with two officers watching her around the clock.[273]

Lydia stayed under house arrest from July 1 until July 11 when she was bound over for trial—an odd and eerie interlude to say the least. Lydia couldn't go to church on Sunday, but was allowed to give interviews to reporters in her front sitting room. Besides these intensely curious reporters, Lydia had no visitors at all.

On July 2, the village was particularly quiet because the horse cars didn't run on Sundays. A reporter for *The Sun* captured the mood perfectly, "The dark, smooth waters of the old Naugatuck course along here at the bottom of what looks like the deep ravine. . . . At the summit of the west bank, where lies the chief part of the old village of Derby, there is a broad, dusty street, with white cottages on either side; the church bells are ringing mournfully, and scores of children are on their way to Sunday school. There is one house, perhaps a little larger than the rest, at which all the children stop for a moment and take a peep through the white pickets."[274]

While the neighborhood kids allowed their imaginations to run wild, Lydia stayed in the southern part of the house, accompanied by the two officers of the law. Day and night, they watched.

On Monday, July 3, Lydia was taken before Derby justice of the peace Seabury Platt to establish a date for her preliminary hearing—a two-day examination of the facts to determine Lydia's eligibility for trial on the charge of murder.

Connecticut's grand jury system began in colonial times, when it became customary for courts to assemble grand juries in capital cases. The earliest law was passed in 1643, and the superior courts specified in

1784 a grand jury of eighteen be chosen "to enquire after and present such criminal offenses . . . where there should be occasion."[275]

In the late nineteenth century, a movement arose to abolish the grand jury system with criticism centering on the grand jury's perceived role as a "rubber stamp" for prosecutors. In its place, many critics advocated a preliminary hearing (examination), conducted before a single judge in a public adversarial setting. In theory, this method would be simpler, cheaper, and more effective as a screening mechanism.[276] This was the forum prescribed in the murder case against Lydia Sherman.

After the usual formalities, the state scheduled the preliminary examination for Thursday July 6. Lydia still had some inheritance money from Dennis Hurlbut, so she was able to secure the services of an excellent lawyer, Samuel Gardner of Derby. Gardner in turn hired the best associate he could find in New Haven—Attorney George Watrous. Lydia's case was front-page news all over the country, and lawyers undoubtedly ached to take second chair to Sam Gardner. Money wasn't necessarily an issue.[277]

On Wednesday, the same reporter from *The Sun* marveled, "This quaint little town has been shaken to its very center by the revelations in the allegedly wholesale poisoning cases in which Mrs. Lydia Sherman is the central and only suspect. . . . Mrs. Sherman heard the stray rumors flying about, but she treated them in a completely unnerved manner, and never even to the casual observer displayed the slightest annoyance at what the neighbors said."[278]

Sheriff Blakeman's officers permitted reporters, including the one from *The Sun*, to interview Lydia for an hour the day before her preliminary hearing. One journalist noted that her house was "on a beautiful street in old Birmingham" and that there was "a set of croquet implements, [all ready] for the players" on the south lawn.[279]

A reporter, from the *New York World*, interviewed Lydia the same day. His observations were keen, "The room was small, but having an air of coziness, the furniture being simple and comfortable, and carpet clean and neat. A little clock ticked sharply on the mantel, and on its right and left were some simple mantel ornaments. The largest picture in the room was a portrait of young Nellie Sherman [the son]. There was also a picture of Addie taken when quite small. A large looking glass, with a few more pictures, French fantasy pieces, and a very well executed water scene, sketched by Nelson, completed the ornaments. Mrs. Sherman was seated on one side of a large sofa, with a pillow for a rest when she wished to recline. . . . She sat with a pin in her hand, with which she kept picking at the flower patterns on her clothing, probably more from the force of the habit. . . .Her manner was quite cool and collected. When she spoke, she talked off-hand and free. I should say that she was a woman of little intellect, but a great deal of firmness—and not a little cunning."[280]

"[Lydia] rose, smiled, and extended her hand. Her bright black eyes, almost wicked in their expression, rested for a moment on those of the reporter, and then with a lightning-like sweep took in his entire figure, hat, cane, and all. She motioned him to his seat, and with the most perfect ease opened a conversation. She chatted away about the heat, her friends in New Jersey, her keepers who sat by, and other subjects of passing interest. She was in a fine humor, and laughed heartily whenever anything amusing was said."[281]

"She [has] a very dark complexion, black hair and jet black eyes, and has very much the look of an Italian. . . .She is forty-seven years of age. . . .Her mind is good, but lacks culture, although she uses fair language in conversation, and is not wholly illiterate."[282]

When the reporter mentioned her arrest, Lydia bragged, "I laughed at Mr. Blakeman. My sister was frightened out of her wits . . . but I stood firm. I never allow anything to throw me off my balance. (Here Mrs. Sherman looked at the reporter with the coldest, most callus smile he'd ever seen on a human face.)"[283]

Elaborate preparations were made for the preliminary examination. Nelson Sherman's mother-in-law, Mary Jones, and Cornelius Struck (the stepson by her first marriage who suspected foul play years earlier) arrived for the hearing. The prosecution summoned a large number of witnesses, and court administrators engaged a public concert room [Nathan's Hall] to accommodate the crowds.[284]

Birmingham's Main Street, a fairly short street packed with shops and offices, ran east and west at the lower, southern end of Caroline, Minerva, Elizabeth and Olivia Streets—close to the Housatonic River. Nathan's Hall, a brick business block built in 1851, sat on the south side of Main Street—almost across from the foot of Minerva Street—and on one of the strangest pieces of land in all of Derby. Nathan's Hall had three shops at the street level and the building rose only three stories, even as the street pitched fifteen degrees to the east. The back of Nathan's Hall—which faced the Housatonic River and accommodated a forty-five degree drop off from Main Street—stood six stories tall with the lower three stories a rabbit warren of tenements for workers in local factories.[285]

From Main Street, the second floor housed professional offices—including that of the people's attorney, Col. Wooster. It also served as the center of government for the Birmingham borough, and sheltered the town offices, a jail and the chief of police's quarters. The top floor offered a big concert and dance hall that the people also used for more than half a century as the venue for court proceedings, elections, and social events. This concert hall staged performances of Uncle Tom's Cabin, the lectures of Henry Ward Beecher, and Wendell Phillips, the abolitionist. Presidential candidate James Garfield spoke at Nathan's Hall in the autumn of 1880.[286]

Nathan's Hall, Derby, Connecticut

From first light on July 6, the summer heat began to bake Derby. Residents who weren't nailed down to a permanent job turned out well before 9 o'clock to get good seats for Lydia Sherman's preliminary examination. The ladies of Derby formed the largest part of the almost 500 in attendance. Also present were Mary Jones, Cornelius Struck, Lt. George Sherman and Rev. Andrew Sherman (brothers of the deceased), and lastly, Nelson Sherman's son, Nellie.[287]

A sizable platform on one end of the hall afforded space for the justice, lawyers, officers, witnesses and the accused. When everyone was seated and the paperwork arranged just so, Justice Platt declared the proceedings open. Col. William Wooster and the Yale-educated State Prosecuting Attorney Eleazer Foster appeared for the people. Wooster's law partner, the universally loved Scottish immigrant, Attorney David Torrance, sat in from time to time, mostly during the trial phase of the proceedings.

During the Civil War, Torrance served as a captain under Lt. Col. William Wooster of the Twenty-ninth Regiment Connecticut Volunteers (Colored). He was imprisoned at Libby and Belle Isle before an exchange enabled him to return to the fighting. Ultimately Torrance rose to the rank of colonel himself. After the war, Torrance studied law in Wooster's New Haven office until the two partnered in Wooster & Torrance in 1868. They worked together until Torrance became a superior court judge in 1885. He went on to serve as Connecticut's chief justice from 1901-1906.

Lydia's defense team was first-rate. Princeton-educated Samuel M. Gardner's trial partner, George Watrous, graduated in the famous Yale class of 1853, which included Hartford Attorney Henry Robinson and the Norwich newspaperman Isaac Bromley. Colleagues and criminals considered Watrous one of the finest lawyers in Connecticut, inasmuch as "his intellect was acute, his industry was indefatigable, and his ambition was directed exclusively to success in his profession."[288] Grand juror Abijah Gilbert, who was later credited with developing most of the strong, circumstantial evidence against Lydia, was also in the courtroom.[289]

Seabury Platt practiced as an attorney, but also functioned as justice of the peace for Derby; therefore he was referred to as "Justice Platt" throughout the preliminary examination of Lydia Sherman. After presentation of the evidence, it would be up to Justice Platt to determine if probable cause existed for Lydia Sherman to be bound over for trail. An interesting difference between "justice" in the 1870s and that of contemporary times centers on the standard salutation of an accused felon after the service of an arrest warrant. Lydia would now be referred to as "the prisoner" (rather than today's "accused") by the judges, jurors, bailiffs, jailors and witnesses, going forward.

The preliminary examination varied considerably from any forthcoming trial because the purpose of the former is simply to determine the answer to two simple questions. Firstly, did the alleged crime occur in the jurisdiction of the court? And secondly, is there probable cause to believe that the accused committed the crime? Therefore, in a preliminary hearing, the rules of evidence are relaxed considerably. Hearsay evidence is allowed and evidence that would clearly be disallowed at trial may also be let in during the preliminary.

At the end of the preliminary hearing, the judge—in this case Seabury Platt—had to decide if sufficient evidence was presented to believe that the prisoner committed the crime. If so, the prisoner was "held to answer." At that point, the court scheduled an arraignment, and demanded a plea from the prisoner: guilty or not guilty. If the response was not guilty, the court set a date for the trial.[290]

In short, the prosecution at Lydia's—the prisoner's—preliminary hearing offered only the most damning evidence. Rather than waste a lot of time trying to discredit the prosecution's witnesses, her lawyers wisely acted as moderators, making sure the prosecutor stayed within reasonable bounds. Since the decision of Justice Platt was the final and only word in this preliminary hearing, there was no need for theatrics.[291]

At half past nine, Lydia made her appearance. She entered the big room with a nonchalant air and walked firmly to the platform. As she strode, she gazed around upon the audience indifferently, and seemed not the least bit concerned. She was dressed in a fashionable suit of thin gray summer material, handsomely trimmed with a brighter collar and under sleeves, silk gloves, and a beautiful straw hat with white flowers and wheat heads. A thin blue veil covered her face. She took a seat and looked her accusers square in the face. Her dark eyes flashed sharply through her veil at the silent, mesmerized crowd. Two deputy sheriffs sat by her side throughout the proceedings.

Col. Wooster opened the proceedings by reading the complaint made by grand juror Gilbert. It charged that Horatio Nelson Sherman died of a poison called arsenic. Moreover, this lethal substance, prosecutors believed, was administered to Sherman by his wife Lydia. The facts of the case were set forth and Lydia was formally accused of murder.[292]

During the reading of the facts, newspapers of every stripe were fond of recalling that Lydia "sat as still as a statue—not a muscle moving and not the slightest change overspreading her face."[293]

The parade of witnesses began with Nelson's son, Nellie Sherman, sworn and seated on the platform. He said simply that he was the son of Nelson Sherman and that he had lived in Derby up to the middle of June—about a month after his father's death—but then move to Boonton, New Jersey.

Nellie remembered that his father took sick on Monday night, May 8. Before that, Nelson commenced a drinking spree in New Haven that lasted more than a week. Nellie explained how he had gone to New Haven to get his father on Friday, May 5.

Back in the Minerva Street house, Nellie saw little of Nelson over the next few days, but described him as sober.

When Nellie got home from work on Tuesday night, his father was sick in bed, vomiting almost continuously. Nelson remained in bed all day. Though he clearly had stomach trouble, he also suffered from labored breathing. This continued for two more days until he died at 8 o'clock Friday morning.

Nellie explained that when Lydia first moved into the Sherman home as a nursemaid and housekeeper, the family consisted of Nelson, Sr., Nellie, Addie, Nattie, the infant Frankie, and Nellie's grandmother, Mary Jones. Nelson and Lydia seemed to get along fine for a while, but then two months before Nelson died, some sort of a marital problem surfaced. Apparently, Lydia and Nelson did not share a bed at night, but Nellie had no idea what the problem was.

He explained to those present that Addie and Frankie were dead. When it came to Nelson Sherman's illness, Nellie claimed that he never saw Lydia give him any medicine and that Dr. Beardsley was first summoned on Tuesday morning.

Col. Wooster stepped in and attempted to have Nellie explain what he knew about Addie's death, but George Watrous objected on the basis that Lydia was accused of killing her husband and any other cases should be off limits. However, Justice Platt decided to admit the testimony, subject to objections by counsel as the information came to light.

Nellie continued. Addie fell ill on Christmas Eve. When Nellie returned from church, she was lying on the sofa in the front sitting room and told him she'd been vomiting. Addie just kept getting worse and finally died on New Years Eve, 1870. Near the end, she was very hoarse, making it difficult for her to speak. Nellie recalled that Addie felt Lydia treated her very kindly and was very fond of her.

Upon cross-examination, Nellie explained that he'd always lived in the family. Frankie, the baby, had health problems from the time he was born. Then the prosecution encouraged Nellie to offer more details of his search for Nelson Sherman when he was missing in New Haven. Since Nellie only ran into his father in the last few minutes of the drinking spree, he had little to offer.

On the Monday night on which his father was taken sick, the family had hot chocolate with supper, although Nellie did not know who made it. When Nelson Sherman fell ill, Lydia sent Nellie to get Dr. Beardsley. To Nellie, his father seemed worn out. Toward the end of his illness, Dr. Pinney checked his father. During Nelson Sherman's last sickness, medicines were accessible to everyone in the house.

After his father's death, Nellie remained in the Minerva Street house and remembered Lydia saying she intended to remain there and take in boarders. Lydia had mentioned these plans to Lewis and Mary Hubbard next door, so this was common knowledge.

Upon prompting, Nellie told the court that he had a steel trap for rats, but his father talked him out of using it. Nelson preferred to give the rats arsenic instead. But when Nellie went down into the cellar for the arsenic, it was gone. When Nelson questioned Lydia about the missing poison, she joked, "I guess the rats have carried it off, paper and all." The matter was dropped, and young Nellie's testimony ended.

While Nellie delivered his testimony, Lydia sat perfectly still. She watched closely and didn't seem the slightest bit concerned even when the testimony was most damning. When Nellie spoke of his father's search for the arsenic, "a half smile fluoridated around her mouth, and the fan which she held in her hand went up to her face with a quick spasmodic jerk."[294]

After a recess for dinner, the court reconvened with the first appearance of Dr. Ambrose Beardsley. The doctor testified that he knew Nelson Sherman for twenty years and attended him in his last illness, until he died at 8 o'clock on the morning of May 12.

Dr. Beardsley remembered when he first stopped at the Sherman house on Tuesday of that week; Lydia met him at the door and exclaimed, "Oh Doctor, I'm so glad you've come. Nelson is very sick."

Then when Beardsley went into the bedroom, Nelson said softly, "I'm dreadfully sick, but I guess it's just one of my turns." Nelson's symptoms were grave pains in the pit of his stomach, hot skin, parched throat and mouth, considerable thirst, and excessive nervousness.

When Dr. Beardsley went down into the dining room, Lydia followed. Beardsley asked her if she could think of anything amiss lately. Lydia mentioned the drinking spree in New Haven and that he'd been sick since he got home. Dr. Beardsley prescribed an eighth of a grain of morphine along with a "blue pill." (Blue pill was "blue mass" whose ingredients varied widely, but always contained a significant amount of mercury.) Beardsley also put a mustard plaster on Sherman's stomach.[295]

Beardsley visited again at 11:00 o'clock that evening only to find more thirst, soreness in the bowels, rapid pulse, and general diffused heat all over the body. The next morning Sherman's stomach seemed better, but he was feebler. His thirst continued, and he had a hoarseness of the throat and bony dry skin.

By Thursday morning, Beardsley was alarmed. Nelson Sherman had an unquenchable thirst, could keep nothing on his stomach but a little bread, and presented a feeble pulse and cold extremities. Beardsley turned to Lydia, "These symptoms cannot be the effects of a debauch. They are not the symptoms of any ordinary disease. I don't understand his vomiting. What has he taken?"

She replied, "Nothing Doctor, except what you ordered. I have been particular to taste everything I've given him."[296]

Among the other medicines, Dr. Beardsley told the court he had ordered some brandy slings. In spite of all the intense care and medicine, Sherman got worse all day long and finally Dr. Pinney was called. He examined Nelson Sherman and then left a prescription for substrate of bismuth (similar to Pepto Bismol) subject to Dr. Beardsley's approval. By dawn on Friday, Sherman was moribund. All of his symptoms persisted. If anything, they were stronger. He died at 8 o'clock that morning.[297]

Beardsley suspected poisoning, but couldn't make up his mind. Nelson Sherman sometimes drank freely, and often got sick from the effects of the alcohol. However, those spells did not affect him this way. In Beardsley's opinion, Sherman's symptoms mimicked those of arsenical poisoning, but he was hesitant because there were three important symptoms missing: purging, delirium, and convulsions. The symptoms did not comport exactly. Just before Sherman died, Dr. Beardsley confessed to him, "Mr. Sherman. I don't understand this excess vomiting. You must have taken something." Nelson shook his head in disagreement.

Lydia's damning dilemma was that she had sole care of Nelson Sherman during his last illness. She claimed not to have given him anything of nourishment because he couldn't hold it down, but how was that to be proven? The day after Nelson took sick, the contents of his stomach were showing up yellow and looked like healthy bile, but this changed quickly. By the following day, the aspirated elements were colored dark brown and were highly offensive to the smell.

Although Lydia's counsel objected, Dr. Beardsley also explained in detail all the particulars of Addie's death. Nelson Sherman had called him between 11:00 and 12:00 o'clock in the evening, when Addie began vomiting. Beardsley found her with pain in the head and bowels, quick pulse, excessive thirst, and vomiting. Beardsley gave her a laxative, and did not see her again until morning, when she was much the same. She continued the same way until Thursday when her symptoms expanded. She had "soreness and tenderness of the bowels, swelling, confused redness about the hips, constant gnawing pains in the stomach and bowels, a leaden appearance about the eyes, coldness of the extremities, and general symptoms looking towards collapse."[298]

Beardsley was undecided in his diagnosis, and conferred with Dr. Dutton of Milford. Dutton wasn't able to get there until Friday evening, when he examined Addie and left a prescription for chloric ether (a narcotic agent). She passed a very distressed night, and died at 11 o'clock on Saturday morning, New Years Eve.

Beardsley suggested a post mortem examination to Nelson Sherman, but he wouldn't hear of it. Beardsley did not think Addie died of disease and he recorded his suspicions of arsenical poisoning in his notes.

Dr. Beardsley was also called to attend to the infant Frankie November 15 of that year. Beardsley found him to be a feeble child, who was completely taken over by vomiting and purging. During the summer, Frankie had been quite ill with cholera infantum, but had no attack so severe as the one in November. When Dr. Beardsley stopped back the following morning, he told Mary Jones that it was no use. The child couldn't live out the day—and the doctor was right. While New England endured the overcast days of late autumn, Frankie died.

Dr. Beardsley tried to be fair though. He noted that Lydia was always there, "[Lydia] was assiduous in her attention to both Addie and her father during their last illness, and took, as I thought, every possible care of them. Mr. Sherman was in the habit of drinking to excess, and at times he would get low-spirited. I think during the last 24 hours particularly . . . his symptoms were decidedly those of arsenical poisoning. It is not necessary that the three symptoms—purging, delirium, and convulsions—should have been present. I have known cases of arsenical poison where the symptoms were not so marked as in this case."[299]

Lydia managed to maintain her composure while Dr. Beardsley was on the stand, probably because she understood general practitioners and knew the right things to do and say. Her acting skills were unsurpassed, and remember, she'd fooled more than a dozen physicians before she even met Dr. Beardsley. A good guess is that Lydia considered the whole process quite easy by this time. Clearly, she was unconcerned by family practitioners, and felt she would ultimately be acquitted of the charges.

So said, Lydia had never met anyone like the next witness—Dr. George Barker of Yale. Not to put to fine a point on it, but Lydia probably didn't even know that men like Barker existed. Lydia's baptism by fire was at hand.

Dr. George Frederick Barker brought two very rare items to the preliminary hearing—a profound knowledge of chemistry and a welcome scientific clarity of speech. The crowd liked him.

In a nutshell, Dr. Barker laid out in the most intimate detail all tests he had run on the stomach and liver of Nelson Sherman. Dr. Barker had received Nelson Sherman's stomach and liver from Dr. Pinney May 13, the day that Drs. Beardsley, Pinney and Shelton performed the post mortem in the sitting room of Nelson Sherman's home. Nelson Sherman's stomach and liver were submitted to the usual processes for discovering metallic poisons. In the stomach, both bismuth and arsenic were found, but judging by the amount of arsenic, Barker knew that Nelson Sherman had died of arsenical poisoning.

On June 11—the day after the midnight exhumations in the cemeteries—Dr. Pinney delivered to Dr. Barker's home the stomachs and livers of Addie and Frankie Sherman, as well as that of Dennis Hurlbut. Addie's liver showed arsenic distinctly and Dr. Barker had no doubt that she died of arsenical poisoning. Little Frankie's liver also contained arsenic and he died from it.

Dr. Barker then told the court about his examination of the disinterred organs of Dennis Hurlbut. Barker found the level of arsenic in Hurlbut's liver was "enormous, certainly the maximum amount a human system is capable of absorbing."[300] In truth, Dr. Barker didn't even bother examining Hurlbut's stomach after he finished with the liver. Without question, Hurlbut died of arsenical poisoning.

While Dr. Barker delivered his testimony, Lydia exhibited signs of nervousness. "She twitched about in her chair and agitated her face violently. Her great black eyes watched every movement of the professor's lips with an intensity that was painful. When the professor spoke of the enormous quantities of arsenic found in Mr. Hurlbut's liver, a "Mmmm" went through the audience, and for the first time, the black eyes of the prisoner sought the floor."[301]

When Dr. Barker finished his testimony, the court adjourned for the day and Lydia regained her composure long enough to walk out with the same look of indifference she had displayed walking in. In the peaceful village of Derby, one of the most remarkable records of crime the nation had ever countenanced came to light slowly. Although the few remaining witnesses would seem unnecessary after Dr. Barker's testimony, Justice Platt wanted to be sure that he had conducted a thorough hearing.

The second day of the preliminary was to begin at 9 a.m. the following day, but the hours before the proceeding featured an unusual meeting. Very few people knew it at the time, but Lydia sent for George Peck, the druggist. Peck, unaware and curious, went to the house on Minerva Street. Lydia mentioned buying the arsenic at his shop in the early spring and the circumstances surrounding the purchase. Peck remembered the purchase, but that morning Lydia refreshed his memory anyway.[302]

An hour before the hearing resumed, a similar sized crowd to that of the day before assembled. Public interest continued unabated as the ladies of Derby flocked to Nathan's Hall in droves. Though many of them couldn't hear a word in the big hall, they were satisfied just seeing Lydia's rigid figure.

Lydia entered at 9 o'clock, and, "tapped lightly up the aisle, turning neither to the right nor left as she advanced. Reaching the steps that led to the platform, she sprang up them with the agility of a cat, and seated herself with a magnificent sweep in the chair, which had been provided."[303]

The newspapers reported that she dressed even nicer than the day before and appeared as unconcerned as ever. Once or twice she turned her face toward the audience, but appeared oblivious to the large crowd.

Lydia watched her counsel, Sam Gardner, very closely all day, but that was the only evidence of anxiety she exhibited. Connecticut's Prosecuting Attorney Eleazer Foster occupied a seat near Col. Wooster.[304]

Though the townspeople weren't disappointed, the testimony of the remaining witnesses was not earth shaking. The first witness called was Captain Scott Baker, the sexton of the Birmingham Cemetery who hoisted up the young victims' remains in June. Baker simply said that he knew exactly where the Shermans were buried and the coffins were marked with engraved plates. (No chance of an error.)

Gideon Wakelee, a good friend of the late Dennis Hurlbut, was called next. He mentioned that he attended the funeral of Ole Hurlbut and the two men's farms were close to one another. Wakelee was one of the men who exhumed Ole Hurlbut's remains on the creepy night of June 10. Wakelee watched as Sheriff Blakeman removed the lid of the coffin and he (Wakelee) saw the remains of Ole Hurlbut. He recognized him immediately. Wakelee also knew Lydia. He told the audience that he was going by Hurlbut's house one day in his farm wagon when [Lydia] came out and urgently conveyed that Hurlbut was sick and wanted to see him. Wakelee found his friend in bed, and visited him twice after that. Damningly, he testified, "His wife [Lydia] had sole care of him. Hurlbut had no server. His family consisted of himself and his wife. No one had ever lived in the house with him [after Lydia arrived]."[305]

Selah Blackman's testimony followed and he swore that he was present when Ole Hurlbut was first interred. He was also present when his friend was disinterred on June 10, and "The remains were those of Mr. Hurlbut."

The next witness was Nelson Sherman's mother-in-law, Mary Jones. Lydia and Nelson sometimes referred to her as "the old lady," and there was great tension between Lydia and Mary Jones. However, Mrs. Jones's testimony was unfocused and she was unable to do any damage.

She mentioned that Lydia had resided in Mr. Sherman's house about four weeks before their marriage. Regarding young Frankie, Mary Jones said that Lydia had little to do with the care of Frankie. It was Mary Jones who took the responsibility for Frankie's care. Once when Mary Jones had Frankie dressed up and sitting on the floor, Lydia came into the room and blurted out, "Grandmother, what are you going to do with little Frank?" Mary answered, "I'm going to have him home again as I had him before he was ever sick." While Frankie was playing about, he suddenly began vomiting. Dr. Beardsley was called to the house, but didn't get there until the evening hours. After the vomiting, Frankie failed rapidly and lived only until the following night.

She continued, "Mr. Sherman and [Lydia] did not live very happily. They occupied the same room while I lived in the house. I frequently heard "angry words" being used between them."[306] There were also angry words between Mary Jones and Lydia.

Then Mary offered, "Nelson said he was afraid Nattie would be taken sick as Addie had been." Mary Jones tried to comfort him by saying she thought it was not a danger.

Mrs. Jones had come to Derby for Addie's funeral, arriving the day after her death. Although she didn't feel welcome, she remained until January 9, 1871.

Mary Jones also traveled to Derby for Nelson Sherman's funeral, which was held two days after his passing, on May 14, 1871. She stayed until June 9, when she took Nattie and Nellie with her to Boonton, New Jersey to protect them.

At this point in the hearing, Mary Jones tried to paint Lydia as a wayward woman. Speaking of the days after Nelson's death, she said, "A week from the next Wednesday, she was at a picnic of the Sons of Temperance, and on the next evening she was at a Temperance Festival, and again on Friday night. She remained out until one o'clock the last night."[307]

On one occasion when Mr. And Mrs. Sherman quarreled, Mary Jones heard him tell her to take her things and leave. Apparently, she never heard her upbraid him about his habits, and she also held that "Lydia was very kind to Addie and the boy. She loved that little boy." When it was hinted to her that Lydia had something to do with Frankie's death, she thought for a moment and countered, "[I do] not believe [Lydia] could do such a thing. Besides . . . if she did wish to do anything of the kind she had no opportunity [because] I took care of the child."

The Shermans hired a housekeeper, Ellen Harrington, a young woman from Derby, who gave some short testimony next. She began work for the Shermans during Addie's illness and remained until two weeks after Nelson Sherman's funeral. During that time, she had not prepared any of the food or medicine for Sherman. "I didn't assist in preparing anything," was the extent of her testimony.

The audience was attentive to the testimony of these witnesses, but was moved to another loud "Mmmm" with Deputy Sheriff Blakeman's words. Sheriff Blakeman took the stand, and although he was unable to connect Lydia with any poisonings, he was able to bring her together with the purchase of arsenic. He said, "On my way homeward after the arrest of Mrs. Sherman . . . on the cars from New Brunswick to New York . . . I had conversation with her. I introduced the conversation myself, but not with a view to obtaining information to be used against her at some subsequent time. I offered no inducement to make her talk. I simply told her that whatever she said, she had better tell the truth. I did not represent anything to get her to talk. I did not tell her that I knew she had purchased arsenic. . . I told her that some druggist had said that she purchased arsenic [from] him, and I told her that she had better tell if that was so. I had not heard so. It was a misrepresentation on my part."[308]

At this point the crowd let out the loud gasp.

Blakeman continued, "I asked Mrs. Sherman if she had ever had any arsenic in the house. She replied, 'Yes, Mr. Sherman had some last winter.'

I asked, 'What did he use it for?'

She answered, 'To kill rats with.'

I then asked, 'Did you kill any rats with it?'

She answered, 'We did. We found one dead in the cellar.'

I said, 'What did you do with the rest of it? Did you use it all to kill rats?'

She replied, 'I think. . . No, we put the rest of it on a shelf, and when I asked Mr. Sherman for it, he said that he had thrown it into the stove. . . .'

When asked about where the arsenic had originally come from, Lydia replied, 'I bought it myself from Peck the druggist.'"

At that point, all the witnesses had given their testimony and Justice Platt adjourned court until the following Monday at 1 o'clock in the afternoon.

At this juncture, newspapermen were up in the air. They felt Lydia would be bound over for trial, but they also thought she could get an acquittal in superior court. They pondered, "It has been proven beyond question that the four victims, whose stomachs were examined, died of poison, but there is not the slightest proof that Mrs. Sherman administered it. There is no doubt in their minds that she did, but there was no legal proof of it. In the case of Hurlbut, the evidence seemed stronger because she was the only one in the house with him. Beyond that, in his case, there was a strong motive in the form of money and property, a motive that did not exist in the other cases."[309]

The State of Connecticut's strategy was simple. It would rely on the Nelson Sherman case to secure a conviction, even though conviction on circumstantial evidence wasn't a certainty. If they couldn't make a murder charge stick in New Haven County, then they could always hand Lydia Sherman to authorities across the Housatonic River in Fairfield County and let her stand trial for the murder of Ole Hurlbut. One way or another, they would get her behind bars.

At 1 o'clock in the afternoon on Monday, July 10, a large crowd gathered at Nathan's Hall to hear Justice Platt's decision in the Lydia Sherman matter.

Lydia entered the building, escorted by Sheriff Blakeman, and at once all eyes were turned on the prisoner. She appeared a little worn, but as unconcerned as ever. She was dressed well, as on the preceding days of the examination. The heat of the room was oppressive, and at one time before the proceedings commenced, the prisoner seemed faint.[310] Luckily, "...this was noticed by a beautiful young lady among the spectators, who tendered her a fan. The bright black eyes turned with a grateful look toward the fair donor, and the fan was accepted with a smile. It is hardly necessary to add the young lady at once became a target for feminine eyes, and for her polite and thoughtful action, [she] received a good share of unworthy comment."[311]

Col. Wooster at last arose and announced that counsel had agreed to submit the case to his honor without argument, whereupon Justice Platt rendered the following decision—

> The first question to be decided relates to the admissibility of evidence touching the alleged death by poison of two members of the family of Horatio N. Sherman, deceased. It is an undoubted

rule of law . . . the public prosecution will not ordinarily be permitted to prove the commission of other indistinct crimes—charged in the indictment in order to establish the guilt of the prisoner. In this case, testimony has been presented to show that within the period of six months prior to the demise of Mr. Sherman, two of his children died under circumstances similar to those surrounding his death, and exhibited similar indications of arsenical poisoning, all of the parties named being members of the same family with the same prisoner. These events are closely allied to that of Sherman's death in the circumstances of time, place, and party as well as in the symptoms at death . . . so close indeed as to give character to the principal facts under consideration, to wit, the manner of said Mr. Sherman's death. They tend to show in the first place that Sherman's death was not result of accidental poisoning. Secondly the arsenic had been for some time kept in Sherman's house, and was presumptively in possession of the prisoner or accessible to her. The evidence therefore is regarded as admissible.

The evidence in relation to the death of Dennis Hurlbut stands upon a different footing. That event is not closely allied to the principal one either as to time, place, or parties. Dennis Hurlbut died about a year and a half ago in an adjoining town, and was in no way connected with the family of Mr. Sherman, save that the prisoner was at that time Mr. Hurlbut's wife. The chief ground for the admission of this evidence seems to be that because the prisoner is strongly suspected of having been the cause of Mr. Hurlbut's death, therefore she is presumptively guilty of the crime now laid to her charge. Such evidence is easily obtained as liable to great abuse. The evidence relating to Hurlbut is therefore excluded.

Without reviewing at length the evidence that has been presented as affecting the guilt or innocence of the prisoner, I do find and am of the opinion that probable ground exists for supporting the complaint, and I'm compelled to order that the prisoner be committed to the custody of the keeper of the jail in and for the county of New Haven, there to remain until she shall be discharged by due course of law." [312]

During the delivery of Justice Platt's decision, Lydia gave no sign to indicate shock or shame. She listened carefully, waved her fan briskly, but did not betray her emotions in any way. Mr. Watrous asked that sufficient time be allowed for the prisoner to put her affairs in order before being taken to jail. Lydia wanted her siblings in New Jersey to take care of her household effects, but Justice Platt deferred to Sheriff Blakeman, who was in no mood for indulgences. The sheriff wanted Lydia in the county jail as soon as possible—and that was that.

Justice Platt ordered Lydia to the New Haven County jail on Tuesday, July 11, 1871 to await trial for murder. She would be in the custody of Captain Charles Webster, a decent man who, while not breaking any rules, allowed Lydia considerable latitude while she was at the Whalley Avenue fortress. Since a male jailer is at a disadvantage when taking care of female prisoners, Captain Webster's wife, Jennette, facilitated matters greatly.

Lydia Sherman was forty-five, and as she came closer to the tedium of unhurried time, she also began to realize that her days as a free woman might well be over.

CHAPTER 8
Trial in New Haven

The formal indictment for murder came down on September 21, 1871, and Lydia's trial was scheduled for November 12, 1871, only three weeks hence. At the request of the attorneys for "the prisoner," the matter was postponed until Tuesday, December 19, 1871. This was the first in a series of near-monthly postponements that eventually pushed the courtroom drama all the way to Tuesday, April 16, 1872.[313]

Unfortunately for Lydia's legal battle, she inadvertently became the victim of some prejudicial events in far off Indiana. In January 1872, an Indianapolis jury found Elizabeth Wharton not guilty of poisoning two men—one died; one lived. Wharton's guilt seemed comfortably beyond a reasonable doubt, but she walked. The verdict in the Elizabeth Wharton case attenuated the focus of prosecutors like the state's Prosecuting Attorney Eleazer Foster and physicians like Dr. George Barker in a way that nothing else could. Though tartar emetic (antimony) was the presumptive poison of choice in the Elizabeth Wharton case—for the legal authorities of the State of Connecticut, this was clearly a distinction without a difference. Connecticut had to make sure that Lydia Sherman did not escape justice the way Elizabeth Wharton did.[314]

To confuse matters even further, Lydia's sanity had been an issue from the start. Wrote one paper, "The deaths are established facts, the presence of poison is testified to by physicians [at the preliminary hearing], and all that remains is to prove that she administered it and that she is of sound mind. Her conduct since her imprisonment is not such as to confirm this theory. She has talked most incoherently of herself and her family and exhibited many signs of insanity."[315]

The McNaughton rule, which focuses on whether or not the accused knows the difference between right and wrong, first made its appearance in 1843, so Lydia's state of mind was a legitimate concern. However, her chances of hiding behind the McNaughton rule were slim. Members of the justice system were wary of Lydia, but they were also well aware of her duplicity. In the end, they refused to accept her impressions of insanity and proceeded to trial. [316]

Municipal improvements were underway in New Haven and its impressive City Hall stood completed in 1862. However, the new Court House, on the north side of City Hall, wasn't completed until 1873. As a result, the Superior Court utilized space inside City Hall in April 1872 when Lydia Sherman went on trial for murder. [317]

In Lydia's Connecticut, the presence of a state Supreme Court justice was mandatory in capital cases. For this hearing, Chief Justice John D. Park filled that role. He served as chief justice of the state from 1874 to 1889 when he was forced to retire on his seventieth birthday. For Lydia Sherman's murder trial in New Haven Superior Court, Chief Justice John Park ably assisted Judge David C. Sanford of New Haven. [318]

Lydia Sherman's trial for first-degree murder only lasted eight days, including the deliberations of the jury and the delivery of the verdict. During the Gilded Age, major trials only ran from Tuesday to Friday, so this case was heard from April 16 to April 19 and then from April 23 to April 26 of the second week.

The prisoner entered the courtroom on schedule. She appeared unusually cheerful, wearing a neat black alpaca dress, trimmed with silk velvet, and a woolen shawl of mixed black-and-white. A white straw hat, trimmed with black velvet and brown plume sat neatly on her head. Over her face drooped a thin lace veil, through which her features were

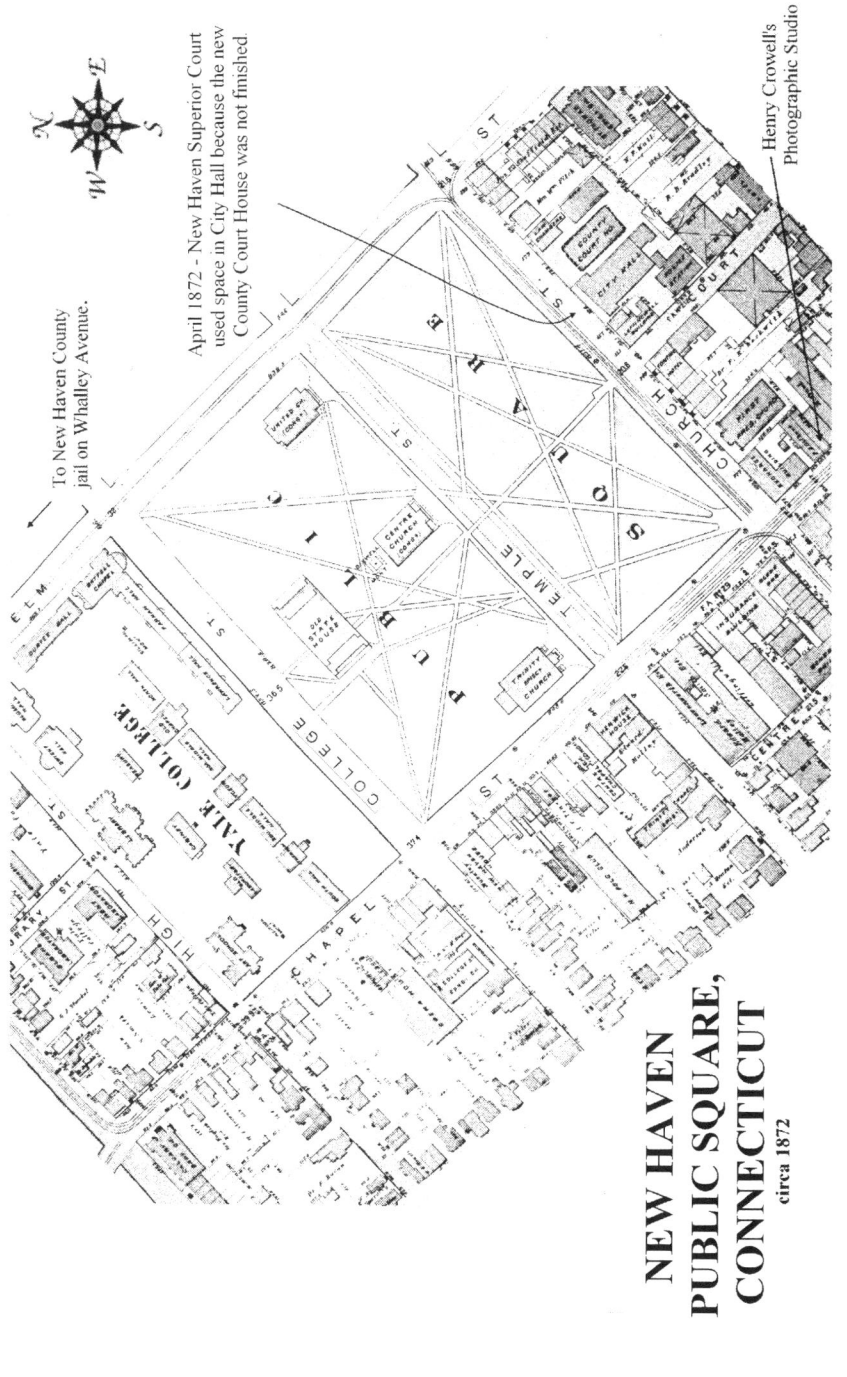

unmistakable. She wore black kid gloves. After the jury was empanelled, she left the prisoner's box and took a seat next to her legal team.[319]

A little before 11 o'clock, Judge David Sanford took his seat on the bench accompanied by Justice John Park. Atty. Eleazer Foster, Col. William Wooster, and Col. David Torrance appeared as counsel for the state. Attorneys George Watrous and Samuel Gardner stood for Mrs. Sherman.

At 11 o'clock, State's Attorney Foster arose and read from his notes, "The grand jury has indicted Lydia Sherman for the murder of Horatio Nelson Sherman and I move for the court that she be put on trial."

After establishing that Lydia had not yet entered a plea, the wheels of justice continued. Lydia arose and the clerk began to read the indictment. Attorney Watrous interrupted. "Is it necessary that she should stand? The indictment is that long?"

Judge Sanford said that it was not necessary for Lydia to stand and George Watrous walked over to Lydia and informed her that she might sit down. She smiled and declined. The reading of the indictment proceeded with Lydia listening carefully, all the while maintaining a perfect calmness. The indictment listed four counts:

(1) That Mrs. Sherman did knowingly put arsenic in [hot] chocolate on May 8, 1871 and give it to her husband, Nelson Sherman; (2) that at diverse times, between May 8-12, 1871, Mrs. Sherman mixed arsenic in her husband's gruel; (3) that Mrs. Sherman mixed arsenic in certain "slings" given to her husband between May 8-12, 1871; and (4) the final charge was a repetition of the first, but with a legal thoroughness and accuracy that surpassed the understanding of the average citizen.[320]

At last, the clerk asked, "To this indictment what is your plea, guilty or not guilty?"

Lydia replied with rapidity, "Not guilty, sir."

Judge Sanford then commanded, "Call the jury, Mr. Sheriff."

The jury was composed of twelve men from the nearby towns of East Haven, North Haven, Hamden, Essex, Cheshire, and Madison. Most of the men were middle aged and more than half were farmers. The remaining jurors were merchants, church sextons and ships' carpenters. In an orderly fashion they filed into the courtroom and took their seats in the jury box.

At this juncture, three people entered the courtroom. Lydia's sister, Ann Nafey, of New Brunswick, New Jersey, walked up to the dock. Lydia rose with a bright smile, grasped her sister's hand and kissed her heartily, while tears ran down her cheeks. Lydia suppressed the tears quickly, and immediately afterwards shook hands and kissed her brother-in-law John Nafey. Lastly, Lydia's brothers Joseph and John Danbury, both of New Brunswick, kissed her.[321]

Ann Nafey was two years older than Lydia and was also a petite woman—short and weighing about 100 pounds. However, while Lydia was olive-skinned with deep-brown eyes, Ann had a fair complexion and blue eyes. Their personalities were different too. Ann was nervous and easily rattled while Lydia was calm and unconcerned. Other siblings, like Ellsworth Danbury of New Brunswick—who had passed away in the 1860s—were small and nervous too. Lydia was different; somehow she seemed constitutionally more unruffled than her siblings.

The proceedings began with the sheriff calling out Dr. Ambrose Beardsley's name. The doctor was quickly sworn in and took the stand.

Dr. Beardsley started off slowly, explaining that he was the family physician of the Shermans, and was called to see his patient on Tuesday morning, May 9, 1871. Lydia met him at the door and expressed how relieved she was to see him. When Beardsley examined Nelson Sherman, his symptoms included nausea, vomiting, parched mouth and throat, unquenchable thirst, sharp pain in the pit of the stomach, racking pain in the bowels, hot dry skin, quick pulse, and some faintness. The patient also informed Dr. Beardsley that he had been off on a spree for the last week.

Beardsley was well aware of Sherman's sprees, though he testified later that Nelson could go weeks without drinking at all. Besides, Nelson Sherman had been a big drinker all his adult life and in a factory village like the Birmingham borough of Derby, most men drank more than they should. After examining Sherman, Dr. Beardsley asked Lydia why she gave him money. Lydia said that she had tried to control Nelson because he had spent $1,200 to $1,500 of her money on his binges, but he proved impossible to restrain. Dr. Beardsley gave Sherman one-eighth grain of morphine and a one-grain blue pill, to be taken every two hours, after which Beardsley left. Beardsley went on to describe his visits and subsequent autopsy.

Beardsley continued his testimony by adding that Sherman had "turns" after his sprees, for example on December 9 and at other times. According to Nelson Sherman, this sickness and vomiting were not unlike "the old turns." However Dr. Beardsley felt differently. Unlike previous cases, the insatiable thirst, burning throat, intense pain in the pit of the stomach, gripping pain in the bowels, and hurried respiration were symptomatic of something else. In Dr. Beardsley's opinion, Nelson Sharma did not die of natural disease.

Beardsley had no doubt that Nelson Sherman's death was caused by poison—white arsenic (arsenic trioxide) to be precise. During Sherman's last illness, Lydia had full charge of him, and claimed she could get along fine without help. She was always in the room, and apparently did what she could for him. In a particularly damning way, Dr. Beardsley explained that at one point, around Wednesday, Sherman had begun to mend, only to worsen again on Thursday. In Beardsley's opinion, the recurrence of symptoms after abatement was caused by the administration of another dose of poison.

At the conclusion of Dr. Beardsley's testimony, which continued until almost 4 o'clock, the lawyers for both sides gathered in consultation. Fairly quickly, State's Attorney Foster announced they would go no further with the testimony for the day. The prosecution then asked that the jury be allowed to retire. They wanted to bring evidence of the prisoner's guilt in three other deaths before the court.

Judge Sanford granted this request for a private meeting and excused the jury until Wednesday morning at 9:30. The witnesses were also excused.

The prosecution offered that on November 15, 1870, Nelson Sherman's baby, Frankie, fell sick and died a day later; that on December 25, 1870, his child, Addie, became sick and died six days later; that the prisoner's previous husband Dennis Hurlbut died on January 20, 1870; and that they all died with the same symptoms and their symptoms were all those of arsenical poison. The prosecution wished to show by this history that the defendant knew the use of arsenic and had used it with felonious intent. Prosecutors for the state wanted desperately to include the damning evidence of poison collected from the Birmingham and Coram Cemeteries on the night of June 10, 1871.

Naturally Lydia's lawyers fought fiercely to keep this evidence out. For the better part of an hour, Mr. Watrous claimed that evidence had not been found factual, but was being made by prosecution to prejudice judges and jury by proving Mrs. Sherman was a dangerous woman, and hence capable of the crime for which she was charged.

The arguments lasted until 6:45 in the evening, at which time the court adjourned. Judge Sanford reserved judgment until the following day.

By 9:30 the following day, the courtroom was packed and included a large number of women, many from Birmingham. Each day, Derby's entrepreneurs conveyed carriages full of people back and forth from the scene of the crime to the scene of the trial. Even old-timers couldn't remember a time when Church Street in New Haven had been so crowded.

Sheriff Scott of the New Haven County jail brought Lydia in and seated her between the two lawyers at the defendant's table. She wore the same clothes as the previous day. Her brothers Joseph and John, her sister Ann, and her brother-in-law John sat close by. Lydia's son, John Struck, arrived from Boston and swiftly took a seat close behind his mother.

The first order of business was for Judge Sanford to rule on the admissibility of the evidence collected from the two Sherman children and Ole Hurlbut. His decision was simplicity itself. Since the indictment accused Lydia of murdering only Nelson Sherman, evidence of other criminal acts could not be allowed. This was an important win for the defense. Had this evidence been admitted, there would have been little doubt of a guilty verdict. The opinion of Judges Sanford and Park met with general approval and fair-minded people saw the ruling as just. Though this represented a substantial triumph for Lydia, as we shall see, the victory was Pyrrhic.[322]

The prosecution was left with a single count of murder and now had to give serious thought as to whether or not Lydia Sherman could be convicted. After the forensic testimony, there would be no doubt about the presence of arsenic in Nelson Sherman's body. The difficulty would be in making a connection between the poison and Lydia (as the delivery agent).[323]

Dr. Beardsley was asked to return to the stand for still more questioning. In an effort to be concise, Beardsley pointed out that the previous day he spoke of constrictions in Nelson Sherman's throat and a resultant hoarseness. He wanted to amend his testimony to show that Sherman could only speak in a whisper.

In the usual question and answer format, Beardsley noted that Nelson Sherman only took tea, bread, water, and thin gruel in his last few days. Also, the doctor said that an ordinarily poisonous dose of arsenic might not be detected by taste. Beardsley also pointed out that Sherman was a strong man who somewhat tolerated his excessive drinking habits. Surprisingly, during his last illness, the forty-five-year-old Sherman maintained a remarkably clear and collected mind. In response to questions regarding Sherman spirits, Beardsley maintained that the mechanic was rather jovial. In fact, Beardsley never saw him despondent, except when under the influence of liquor.

On cross-examination by Attorney Watrous, Dr. Beardsley had to admit that during Sherman's illness, Lydia was attentive and devoted to his welfare—as far as he could see.

When questioned about other medicines Dr. Beardsley gave Sherman, the physician answered, "a weak solution of ipecac with an aromatic to allay purging; the purgative pill was mostly aloes and rhubarb and one grain of the extract of mandrake; the blue pill is mostly of mercury; it is a mild form of mercury." (The doctor did not know the exact ingredients.)

At this point, Watrous shifted to the most important matter by asking Dr. Beardsley, "What quantity of arsenic is sufficient to produce death?" Beardsley answered, "From three to five grains; there are instances where two and a half grains caused death."[324]

Watrous wanted to introduce other cases of arsenical poisoning, and since Victorian wallpapers contained Paris Green—an arsenic compound—he asked Dr. Beardsley if there were other cases of poisoning caused by persons sleeping in rooms with green wallpaper? The doctor parried, "There are cases where they have been affected, but not killed."[325]

Next Watrous tried to find some mistake in procedure by asking where Sherman's body was from the time he died until the post mortem examination on Saturday morning. Beardsley answered, "It was in the front room where he died." After that, "I don't know where it was or in whose charge; I took no part in making the incisions, but I assisted in packing the specimens." Stubbornly Watrous tried to get Beardsley to admit that the storage jars and the transport box were unclean, but failed.

The prosecution then called Nelson Sherman's son, Nellie. The young man explained again his journey to New Haven to collect Nelson after his father's last drunk fest. Nellie asked Lydia for the money to go to New Haven, but she held out for the longest time. Finally she gave him some money and he took the 9:15 evening train from the Derby Station. Nellie checked the Park House in New Haven, and while waiting out a rainstorm at the train station, his father showed up. The two walked around for a while and then finally got into Nelson's carriage and headed back to Derby. They arrived at the Union House in Derby at about 7:00 in the evening. At that point, Nelson went into the hotel while young Nellie walked home. Nelson at long last returned to the house on Minerva Street at 8 o'clock Friday night.[326]

Nelson stayed home Saturday and Sunday, and returned to work at 6:30 Monday morning. Nellie remembers his father hanging a grindstone at the shop for the purpose of grinding his tools. Before lunchtime, Nelson asked his son to have Lydia send him down some dinner so he could keep working. Nellie saw his father off and on for the next few hours, but when young Nellie returned to the house on Minerva Street at 9 o'clock that night, Lydia said Nelson was vomiting and had gone to bed.[327]

By morning, Nelson wanted his son to get Dr. Beardsley. Nelson's condition went downhill all week despite visits from Drs. Beardsley and Pinney. Young Nellie, in response to a question from the state's attorney, explained that Lydia had sole care of his father until Thursday noon when

Nelson's mother, Mrs. Lydia Whitney Sherman, arrived. After that, both women took care of Nelson.[328]

Judge Sanford called for recess until two o'clock.

On cross-examination in the early afternoon, Nellie mentioned two items that the audience in the courtroom found titillating yet confusing. Nellie said that his father did not sleep with his mother because of some marital trouble. He also said that he didn't know when they were married.[329]

Next on the stand was Dr. Charles Pinney. He attended Nelson Sherman on Thursday night before he died and found him suffering with all the symptoms of arsenical poisoning. He gave Sherman a prescription for subnitrate of bismuth to allay the pain. Dr. Pinney also explained that although Lydia consented to the post mortem examination, she did not know that organs were removed from her husband's remains and taken to Yale. Pinney told her simply that the examination showed inflammation of the stomach.[330]

Dr. Pinney then told the court of his visit to Dr. Beardsley, the visit where they both agreed that a post mortem was in order. For whatever reason, Dr. Pinney then went over to Huntington to find Dr. Shelton. Come Saturday morning, the three doctors went to the Sherman House on Minerva Street and saw Nelson Sherman's sheet-draped body laid out in the front parlor. While Dr. Beardsley exposed the body, Dr. Pinney repeated the request for the post mortem exam and Lydia offered no objection. She even went so far as to say her "husband's death was peculiar and she would like to have an autopsy done."[331]

After the stomach and liver were packaged (the box measured 16" long x 12" wide x 8" high), Dr. Pinney drove directly to New Haven and gave it to Dr. Barker, who removed the glass jars from the box in Dr. Pinney presence.[332]

Attorney Watrous for the defense tried to poke holes in the methodology of the three doctors, but did not help the defense's case at all because he came across as petty and grasping at straws. Drs. Beardsley and Pinney agreed on virtually everything, despite the efforts of George Watrous to show them at odds. In fact, the whole cross-examination hurt far more than helped the defense.[333]

Still, Watrous did score on one small point. He got Dr. Pinney to admit that in nineteen years of medical practice, he never treated a case of arsenical poisoning.[334] Nevertheless, Pinney was well schooled on the symptoms of arsenical poisoning and knew Nelson Sherman's symptoms to the very last one.

With that, Judge Sanford adjourned the proceedings until 9:30 the following day. Professor Barker's testimony was postponed until then.

On the third day of the trial, a cloudy Thursday morning with rain expected any moment, Dr. Gould Shelton gave testimony on the poisonous qualities of bismuth—or better stated, the lack thereof. Naturally George Watrous and Sam Gardner wanted the jury to believe that the bismuth given to Nelson Sherman by Dr. Pinney was the cause of his death, but it was ridiculous argument. Subnitrate of bismuth was widely used to soothe stomach distress.[335]

Mrs. Lydia Whitney Sherman, mother of Nelson Sherman, followed Dr. Shelton to the stand. She was "a bright looking old lady, ready to tell her story faster than the lawyers and judges could take it down."[336] She was also a no-nonsense woman who at times gave very sharp replies. Mrs. Sherman averred that she was only at the Minerva Street house when the funeral of her granddaughter Addie was held in January 1871, and again when her son fell desperately ill. At Addie's funeral, and without any provocation from the older woman, Lydia told her that if things did not go on differently, she would leave Nelson. After all, she had money and friends. Naturally, the mourning grandmother was shocked.[337]

Nelson Sherman's mother stayed with him in his last twenty hours of life, and she thought he behaved strangely in matters pertaining to his wife. For example, when he heard Lydia go down into the cellar, he asked his mother to get his wallet, and he handed her a wad of money, saying, "Mother, take this money, and give it to Nellie, and tell him to . . . make good use of it."

But the day after Nelson did that, Lydia was in the sitting room and asked, "Mother, you have that money of Nelson's?"

The older woman said, "No, I have not."

When Lydia pressed the issue, Nelson's mother finally confessed to giving it to the young man.

Lydia said it was "all very strange" because Nelson had told her that she should have it. From that point forward, Lydia was rather surly toward her mother-in-law.[338]

Lydia also told the older woman, "I had about made up my mind to leave Nelson, but as things have turned out, I'm very glad I did not."[339]

Then Mr. Watrous bore in on a particularly delicate matter. He elicited from Mrs. Lydia Whitney Sherman that her son Nelson had committed the care of the boy Nattie to his wife Lydia. With his mother in the bedroom, Sherman had said to Lydia, "I want you to promise before God and man that you will protect this dear boy of mine," and she swore, "I will." He repeated it twice over, at his mother's request, the second time with Mr. Hubbard present. (Nelson's mother told the court that she thought he would make a good witness.)[340]

The servant girl Ellen Harrington was called next, and testified that she lived at the Shermans' house at the time Nelson Sherman died. She had lived there a number of months and stayed until three weeks after

Sherman's death. She was in Ansonia on the Monday night that Nelson Sherman was taken sick and didn't return until after supper.³⁴¹

George Peck followed. For eight years he had been a druggist on Main Street in Birmingham. He couldn't remember exactly when Lydia stopped at his shop to buy arsenic, perhaps a few weeks before Nelson Sherman's last illness. Peck testified, "It was after the warm days had come, and the store doors were wide open. I think Nattie, the little boy, a bright child, was with Lydia when she purchased it."³⁴² Lydia remarked that they were overrun with rats and she inquired what was best to kill them. Peck mentioned other exterminators, and suggested that arsenic was as good as the others, and cheaper. Peck also added, "I think she may have said that she did not like to have it around."³⁴³

Then Peck dropped a bombshell. He mentioned that Lydia sent for him the last day of the preliminary examination. Peck went to her house, not having any idea what she wished to say to him. Up to that point, no one knew that Lydia had coached Peck before he gave testimony at the preliminary hearing"³⁴⁴

Dr. George Barker was the last witness of the day. Barker testified to the examination of the liver and stomach—as given at the head of his report—finding 0.485 grains of white arsenic in six and two-thirds ounces of liver—equal to 5 grains for the whole liver, a perfect lethal dose.³⁴⁵

Again Lydia's counsel George Watrous did what he could to rattle Dr. Barker. Watrous was trying to make it appear that bismuth and arsenic were alike in appearance, and that the former often contains traces of the latter. In short, Watrous evidently wanted to show that Nelson Sherman was killed, either by a drug mix-up or by the impurity of the bismuth.³⁴⁶

It was late in the day, and Dr. Barker settled the matter handily. He said that he had examined the bismuth sold by the Derby druggist and found no trace of arsenic in it.³⁴⁷

The fourth day, Friday, April 19, the day after the rains had come and gone, the weather got brighter and more cheerful for everyone—except Lydia. Dr. Barker was expected to be on the stand all day and Lydia was about to be eviscerated.

Professor Barker resumed his testimony with the results of a chemical analysis of the deceased's stomach and liver. As the case proceeded, the public interest appeared to increase, and the trial became the leading theme of conversation.[348]

Dr. Barker's testimony was threefold—how poisons act on the human body, what constitutes a lethal dose of arsenic, and whether or not impurities or contamination rendered his examination invalid.[349]

Since Dr. Barker found very little arsenic in Nelson Sherman stomach, the logical question was: How long does it take for arsenic to find its way to the liver?

Barker started slowly but warmed to his subject as he proceeded, "White arsenic taken into the stomach is removed therefrom by absorption, and as it has not been detected in either the lymph or the chyle (a milky lymphatic fluid and emulsified fat), it had to have taken place in the blood. It has been detected in the urine within one hour after it had been taken. The liver acquires its maximum quantity—in the opinion of several authorities—from fifteen to eighteen hours after administration."[350]

Prosecutor Foster then asked, "Does it pass off from the liver?"

Barker replied, "It is eliminated from the liver, and may entirely disappear in . . .eight to fifteen days . . . depending on the quantity and other circumstances."[351]

As an example of Barker's ability to relate to a jury, he answered one of Fosters questions this way, "When arsenic is taken more rapidly than it is absorbed or eliminated, then it may be considered accumulation in the same sense as apple pie if taken faster than it is secreted."[352]

As Lydia fidgeted in her seat, Barker next described the three stages of symptoms associated with arsenical poisoning. "The first (local) symptoms—agonizing pains in the stomach, accompanied by vomiting, and unquenchable thirst—appear within an hour of taking the arsenic. The second stage of symptoms (remote)—great prostration of strength, anxiety and depression of the mind, and a peculiar lividity of the face including the blue line under the eye—usually present themselves in from one to eight days. Many people die in the throes of stage two symptoms. Should the patient survive, the (tertiary) symptoms of arsenical poisoning affect the nervous system: coma, delirium, and convulsions manifest themselves now. All of these symptoms may not be present." Barker brought the courtroom to a deathly silence when he said finally, "The patient may recover from all the symptoms that may be called primary, and may die from the secondary effects of the poison years afterwards."[353]

The prosecution finished the questioning of Dr. Barker with a simple query: "What in your opinion was the cause of the death of Nelson Sherman?" Dr. Barker's answer was no less trenchant, "Assuming the stomach and liver I analyzed to be those of Sherman, my opinion, in view of the symptoms stated, is that he died from the effects of a dose of arsenic."[354]

The defense attorney could not possibly repair the damage of Dr. Barker's testimony, but he made one good point. He enticed Dr. Barker to admit that he had never seen a person die by arsenical poisoning . . . . Moreover, Barker had no experience of it as a medical practitioner. Everything Barker knew, he learned from books and testimony.[355]

Watrous then spent considerable time asking every question he could think of to discredit Barker, even reading from a book purporting that someone once died of bismuth. Dr Barker, confident and dashing as ever, said coolly, "Let me see the book."

He examined the copyright date and the passage in question. Then, he simply dismissed it: "I do not believe it. It has been contradicted."

Professor Barker quoted from Wormsley and Otto, both leading authorities on poisons, who notably never mentioned bismuth as a poison. At every turn, Professor Barker left Watrous short of the mark.[356]

George Watrous grew decidedly nervous.

Lydia Sherman's demeanor changed notably too. She had so far preserved an imperturbable calmness, but during Professor Barker's testimony she became antsy. She clearly appreciated the damaging nature of the testimony and the inability of her counsel to vitiate its damage or to rattle the brilliant Dr. Barker.[357]

The final witness on Friday was William Ford, a peace officer in Derby—as was Nelson Sherman. Apparently Ford met Sherman at the Derby Depot Sunday afternoon, two days after the latter got back from his binge in New Haven. The two men walked around town as Ford checked doors, investigated a break-in at Fay's saloon, and then wiled away an hour at Peck's druggist shop. Ford left Sherman at 10:15 in the evening at his Minerva Street home. According to Ford, Nelson Sherman was sober and looked fine.[358]

Since the court would now recess for the weekend, Judge Sanford admonished the jurors not to read accounts of the trial in the newspapers, nor talk about it. With a light tap of the gavel, Judge Sanford adjourned the court until Tuesday, April 23 at 9:30 in the morning.

When court reconvened on Tuesday, a noticeably smaller crowd gathered in the morning, but by afternoon the courtroom was full. As with other days, there was a fair sprinkling of ministers and doctors in the crowd. Of interest, though, were two unusual spectators: Former U.S. Congressman Richard Hubbard and Hartford Mayor Henry Robinson sat in for a little while on Tuesday morning. Richard Hubbard was one of

Hartford's preeminent lawyers, having studied under the indomitable William Hungerford. Owing to the enormous amount of newspaper coverage of the Lydia Sherman murder case, Richard Hubbard probably knew he had something in common with Lydia. Hubbard was also orphaned at an early age. The Roberts family of East Hartford raised him, and despite an appalling lack of funds, Hubbard managed to graduate from Yale in 1839 and was admitted to the Hartford bar in 1842.[359]

The ubiquitous Henry Robinson had become Mayor of Hartford just a few days earlier, but was also a highly respected lawyer, having graduated from Yale in 1853 with George Watrous and then studied law in his brother Lucius' firm. Hubbard and Robinson were not in court to gawk. Good lawyers love to watch their peers work and that was the point of this visit to New Haven.[360]

Lydia's face betrayed a heightened level of anxiety. Now that the most important forensic witnesses had completed their testimony, the state sought some kind of a motive for Lydia's actions. That said, most of the testimony was invasive, even prurient. The audience of course had come for this part of the show, but Lydia didn't like it. With the exception of Dr. Barker's testimony, the first week was a breeze for Lydia compared to the second, and her behavior bore this out.

The state began with William Downes, a man who had worked under Nelson Sherman for the last fifteen years at Shelton's Tack and Nail Division. Downes had helped Sherman hang the grindstone in the factory on the Monday before he got sick. Downes and Sherman worked until 5 o'clock in the afternoon and then helped three other workers empty a pitcher of beer outside the shop.[361] Downes finished his testimony by saying, "There was nothing unusual in the beer, and nothing poisonous."[362]

Nelson Sherman's brother George Sherman from Brooklyn followed Downes. In the fifteen weeks before Nelson Sherman's passed away,

George spent about seven weeks—in two separate stays—with the Shermans. He noticed in the first four-week stay that Lydia and Nelson did not live happily together. They talked angrily to one another, using "very hard words." George heard Nelson tell Lydia "She could take what things she brought and leave."

Her reply? "Very well."[363]

During George's last three-week stay, Lydia called his attention to the fact that she and Nelson did not share the same bed. Lydia complained to George a lot even saying that she preferred when Nelson came home with a couple of drinks in him because he treated her better than when he was sober.[364]

George's recollection was that Lydia was full of complaints. She complained that when she was sick, Nelson never even asked how she was doing. Lydia felt that Nelson was ashamed to be seen on the street with her and refused to take her out in society. Lydia, George relayed, was convinced that Nelson did not love or respect her. She was also convinced that when he went on his sprees, he kept company with other women. (Remember, Nelson's other brother, Andrew, helped Lydia solidify these notions.) Lydia talked twice to George about divorce, even going so far as to talk about different lawyers.[365]

Curiously enough, Lydia's reputation—as a result of her marriage to Ole Hurlbut—was that of a gold digger. However, before she married Nelson Sherman, she lent him $700. Since their marriage, she had contributed $1,800 toward keeping the family afloat. Lydia told George that Nelson wouldn't have stayed with her at all if she hadn't given him so much money. These comments were made just before George went back to Brooklyn on April 22. By that time, George noticed that Nelson didn't even speak to Lydia unless there was no choice, and sometimes he refused to pass food to her at the table, handing it to others instead.[366] Three weeks later, Nelson was dead.

George traveled from Brooklyn to Derby the day after his brother died. He remembered that Lydia talked incessantly about what Nelson ate. Lydia explained that he came home from work on Monday and ate the fish that she had warmed up for him in the oven. Apparently at supper, he drank a cup of chocolate, though he didn't finish it. After supper, he went out into the yard and smoked a while. At some point he came to the door and asked Lydia if he should walk to the market to get spinach. (Lydia thought he was in remarkably high spirits.) Apparently, Nelson usually went down to the market to order the food he wanted and had the groceries sent up to the house. When the packages arrived, Lydia found out what she was expected to prepare for dinner and supper.[367]

At one point during Mr. Watrous's cross-examination, he asked George Sherman, "Did you not say that Mrs. Sherman was a jewel of a woman?" To this, George shouted, "Never!" But Watrous wasn't about to give up. He followed with, "And that there was not one woman in a thousand that would come there and do as she did?" Again George Sherman shouted, "Never!" But the witness weakened, and finally said simply he objected to the word "thousand." Watrous bore in, "If [you] did not say a "thousand," how many women did you have in mind?" At that point, the courtroom exploded into laughter.[368]

Toward the end of his testimony, George said unhappily that he had heard a rumor after his brother's death that portions of his body had been taken away. He spoke to Dr. Beardsley about it, but received no satisfactory explanation. George was indignant that such rumors should be on the street when the family knew nothing of the matter.[369]

The next witness, Orrin Lathrop, saw Nelson Sherman on Monday night when Sherman went out to buy spinach. Lathrop ran into him on Main Street in front of Henry Florence's grocery store between 6 and 7 o'clock. (Florence's grocery store was about 100 feet from Peck's druggist shop.) Sherman was standing on the sidewalk with his back against a tree, looking pale. He wasn't feeling well and wanted to go home. For whatever reason, Lathrop left Sherman there and went around to the post office.[370]

Nelson Sherman's mother-in-law, Mary Jones, was sworn in next. She said she was a visitor at Sherman's home from June 28, 1863 to December 22, 1870. Mary Jones said she received a telegram from Nelson Sherman on December 30, saying his daughter Addie was very sick. She quickly traveled back to Derby and arrived the following day. However, Addie was already dead. Five months later on May 12, 1871 she received a telegram saying that her son-in-law was dead. She got to Derby on May 13 and remained until June 6, 1871.[371]

In a conversation with Mary Jones, shortly after Addie died, Sherman expressed worry that his little Nattie would become sick too. At that point, Lydia came in and accused Nelson of always finding fault with her. If he admitted dissatisfaction with her care of the children, she would leave the house that night. Mary Jones begged Lydia to be quiet, for Nelson had never said a word against her. Lydia claimed she knew better. According to Mary Jones, up to that time she and Nelson had never been alone together long enough for him to complain of Lydia, for she always came in right after he did. As if to punctuate her comments, Mrs. Jones said Lydia was angrier than she'd ever seen a person before.

After Nelson's death, Lydia said she wished to keep the rental of the Minerva Street house. She thought she would keep borders, as she knew plenty of gentlemen who would board with her. Lastly, Mary Jones admitted that before Lydia arrived she (Mrs. Jones) had used arsenic on the rats.[372]

Dr. Beardsley was asked to take the stand again to explain in detail the different medications that Sherman was given. The prescription left by Dr. Pinney was composed of hydrocyanic acid dilute, subnitrate of bismuth, pulverized gum Arabic, water and simple syrup all rubbed together. The dosage was left to Dr. Beardsley, who instructed Lydia to give her husband one teaspoon full every two hours, if he could hold it down.[373]

Although Dr. Beardsley's testimony bordered on the repetitious, Attorney Foster crossed a few "t"s and dotted a few "i"s before allowing Mr. Watrous to cross-examine the witness.

Though he tried desperately to make some points, Watrous was snake bitten. Inadvertently, he kept strengthening the case for the prosecution! For example, he asked Dr. Beardsley, "If in place of the five grains of bismuth, there were five grains of arsenic, it would have caused death, would it not? Beardsley answered, "I think it would, but Sherman had the symptoms of death before he took that prescription." Beardsley smiled at the defense attorney.[374]

The defense's problem with Dr. Beardsley was that he was a man known for his jocose nature. If humor could be found, Beardsley would find it. Since he was the catalyst behind the movement to convict Lydia—and with Dr. Barker's expert testimony that little difficulty appeared surmounted—Dr. Beardsley was particularly prone to toying with the defense. In sum, Beardsley felt that the proceedings had already achieved their goal, so he could have some fun.

When the defense asked him whether or not bismuth was poisonous, Beardsley joked that "bismuth wasn't any more poisonous than a jackknife. If a person took enough of either, he would die from the effects. In thus being capable of producing death, they might be called poisonous."[375]

When Mr. Watrous finished with Dr. Beardsley, attorneys for the state—Foster, Wooster and Torrance—felt they had constructed a fairly respectable gallows, so they rested their case.

True, they had failed to establish a believable motive, or to demonstrate to a reasonable certainty that the accused administered the arsenic, but they had done the best they could. Attempting to make the decisions of a sociopath reasonable to the average person is not always possible.

On this fifth day of the trial, a Tuesday, Lydia did an astounding thing. For a number of days, a sketch artist from New York tried to draw a picture of her in court. It was Lydia's son John Struck who noticed the

There are only two known photographs of Lydia Sherman, both taken by Henry Cowell on April 23, 1872. The harsher picture on the left—turned into newspaper engravings—seems to have been reproduced from the picture that Lydia gave to reporters. The photo on the right—heavily lighted from above and mildly overexposed—makes Lydia look younger than her years.

artist's hand moving and alerted his mother. As a result, throughout the afternoon Lydia kept moving her head and covering her face with her gloved hands to foil the artist's efforts. John Struck felt that his mother should never appear in an illustrated paper, but Lydia knew that she would wind up in the police gazettes whether she liked it or not, so she came up with an idea.[376]

Learning from Sheriff Scott in the late afternoon that the artist had rendered a particularly bad image of her, Lydia grew excited and held a short consultation with her siblings. Afterward, she approached Warden Webster—who often extended himself for Lydia beyond what was customary—and asked if they could stop at a photography studio on the way back to the jail. She wanted to have a picture taken for the press. Webster acquiesced.[377]

Late that afternoon, instead of traveling north from the courthouse to Elm Street, and then west to the New Haven County jail on Whalley Avenue, the posse turned south to Chapel Street. There were a number of photography galleries along this boulevard, and Lydia quickly ducked into Henry Cowell's Photographic Studio at 303 Chapel Street and had her portrait done. (The picture is the photo on the cover of this book.) Finally Lydia was at ease, knowing that she wouldn't be "caricatured in the pictorial press."[378]

On April 24, the sixth day of the trial, Lydia's defense team finally got their chance to stem the tide. Public opinion was decidedly against their client, but Watrous and Gardner mounted the best defense they could. The courtroom was densely crowded. The morning session opened at 9:40.

Mr. Watrous arose and said that perhaps a word of explanation was necessary for the jury. Watrous then proceeded to tell the whole story of Sherman's spree in New Haven and the events of the subsequent three days leading up to his illness. In particular, Watrous focused on the fact that Lydia was a good wife, took excellent care of her husband when he was sick, and Nelson Sherman thought enough of Lydia that he made her swear to take care of his little son. Lydia did not try to hide the fact that she bought arsenic from George Peck, the druggist, and she even refreshed his memory on the details of the purchase at the time of the preliminary hearing. Watrous sought to punctuate the problem by saying, "The arsenic was bought because there was evident need for it. The house was overrun with rats, which got into the well, and carried off potatoes by the bushel."[379]

The first witness for the defense was Lewis Hubbard. Since Lewis and Mary Hubbard lived in the north side of the Minerva Street house for the past twelve years, they had more to offer than most. Lewis Hubbard knew Nelson Sherman for eighteen years because they both worked at Shelton's. Though Hubbard knew that Nelson Sherman was sick, he didn't see Nelson until he asked for Hubbard on Wednesday night of his final week. Hubbard went to Sherman's room and shook hands with him. The former said, "Mr. Hubbard, I feel as though I am going to die. Are my dues paid in the lodge?" (Nelson Sherman's concern with his dues at the Knights of Pythias had to do with funeral expenses to which Lydia would be entitled.) Hubbard told him that his dues were paid until July 1 and even offered a receipt if Sherman didn't have one. He next visited Sherman Thursday night at 6 o'clock. He stayed with Nelson through the night, as did Hubbard's wife, Mary, Lydia, and Nelson's mother. Lewis Hubbard was there on Friday morning when Sherman died.[380]

Watrous was able to elicit from Hubbard a fairly good report of Lydia's care of Sherman. Hubbard said "I saw nothing different from what is seen between any man and wife under the same circumstances. She manifested a great deal of feeling for him all the time during his sickness. Hubbard was also forced to admit that during the past few years Sherman binged sometimes once a month, then maybe once in three months, and then back to once a month.[381]

Then Watrous got Lewis Hubbard to verify an important piece of evidence. Hubbard confirmed everyone knew Lydia bought arsenic to kill the rats that sometimes got out of hand around the Minerva Street house. He could remember Lydia showing him a slop-pail with a dead rat in it.

He even said that "a rat . . . got into the well, and all the water had to be pumped out that time."³⁸²

Lastly, Hubbard mentioned that Mr. Shelton—Nelson Sherman's employer, who by this time virtually owned the Minerva Street house—wanted him to get the rent off Lydia's hands, so that he could rent the rooms to other parties.³⁸³

On cross-examination by Mr. Foster, Hubbard said that by Thursday night he was asked to mix the brandy slings about every fifteen minutes. Nelson needed them often.³⁸⁴

After Lewis Hubbard gave his testimony, the court adjourned until 2 o'clock in the afternoon, when the witness continued. Hubbard admitted he assured the men at the shop on Monday and talked with his wife Mary about the case a few times.

Rev. Leonidas Baldwin of St. James Episcopal Church took the stand next and testified that he made three calls on Sherman during his illness. The first and second were on Thursday evening, and the third was at 7 o'clock the morning Sherman died. Rev. Baldwin said, "As far as [he] observed, Lydia's behavior was such as became a wife under the circumstances."³⁸⁵

Ichabod Allen, whom Nelson Sherman knew for about fifteen years, took the stand and said that he saw Sherman the Sunday night before he died, between 10 and 11 o'clock. Part of that time, the two were in Captain Healy's saloon. When the time came to leave, they walked up Minerva Street. In the opinion of Allen, Sherman was neither intoxicated nor sober. Mr. Allen stated that Sherman felt "people had tried to kill him and injure him, and that he would show them that he would come out on top of the heap and beat them all."³⁸⁶

Ichabod Allen admitted repeating Sherman's remarks in a conversation with Dr. Beardsley and some other friends over beers in the barroom of the Bassett House. Apparently Mr. Allen and his friends at the bar felt, "No one was trying to injure Sherman anymore than he was himself and if [he] could keep to work and be steady, he would get along well enough."[387]

It was the most peculiar set of circumstances. Since the passing of Ole Hurlbut, many in the village suspected that Lydia was a poisoner. Nelson Sherman himself didn't trust Lydia. He claimed that he "knew too much," and insisted that young Nattie sleep with him. Yet he still ate and drank what Lydia prepared, lived in the same house with her, bought arsenic as needed to control the rats at the Minerva Street house—and told her about it. When he made Lydia swear "before God and man" to take care of Nattie, was he saying he trusted her? Or, perhaps he meant just the opposite—a threat—if she harmed Nattie after making such a promise, she'd be breaking a covenant.

Nelson Sherman was living a nightmare, but others thought his paranoia was unfounded. There were only a few people in Derby who had assimilated the evidence correctly.

Following Ichabod Allen was Lewis Hubbard's wife, Mary. She had been to visit Nelson Sherman on Wednesday and right through Thursday night while he was sick. She was also there on Friday morning, but had gone back to her own place just before he died. Mary Hubbard also testified to Lydia's kindly manner toward her husband. She felt that Lydia's conduct during her marriage to Nelson was as well as husband-and-wife in general, and that Nelson preferred to have Lydia take care of him.

Strangely enough, after Nelson Sherman's passing, it was Mary Hubbard who asked Lydia if she knew that her husband's stomach had been sent to New Haven for examination. Mary Hubbard couldn't remember how she found out about the extracted body part going to New Haven. She did not think it was a secret since she was not cautioned when told. Lydia showed a complete lack of concern regarding the removal of her husband's stomach. Neither was she displeased; she just didn't seem to care.[388]

Lastly, a minor character in the drama, Philip Meyers of Derby was sworn in. He had seen Nelson Sherman in John Miller's saloon for a few minutes the Sunday before he passed. Meyers didn't notice Sherman's condition except to know that he didn't think Sherman had been drinking.[389] Although the defense aimed to show that Nelson was sober that night, each witness put him in a different saloon, where he drank . . . coffee?

With that George Watrous announced, "We rest, if the court pleases." But again State's Attorney Eleazer Foster proposed to offer evidence in regard to other cases that had been ruled out in the beginning of the hearing. Foster argued that the defense claimed Sherman's death was an accident or suicide, and it was up to the state to remove these presumptions.

At this point, Connecticut's Chief Justice John Park weighed in, saying that nothing had happened during the course of the trial to change his decision. The evidence of other cases of arsenical poisoning remained excluded.

Trial Day Seven—Thursday, April 25—was of more interest to the public than any day in the trial to date. The courtroom opened at 9:30 and was full to overflowing all day long. Four attorneys—two for the prosecution and two for the defense—gave final arguments. Col. Wooster opened for the prosecution, followed by Mr. Gardner for the defense. Attorney Foster then closed for the state and Mr. Watrous for Lydia Sherman. In a startling reversal of form, Lydia wept a little before court opened.

Col. Wooster began by reviewing and criticizing the evidence for the defense. Wooster claimed that the defense had failed to show anything except that the accused had lived on moderately good terms with the deceased, and had entirely failed to break down the testimony for the state.

At the close of Col. Wooster's two-hour argument, Lydia Sherman suddenly burst into tears. One newspaper report noted, "She seemed more, than at any time we have observed her, deeply impressed with the gravity of her situation. She also wept at nearly all the touching references made by counsel in their remarks . . . . After this, she seemed unable to regain her calmness and wept freely through the day."[390]

Mr. Gardner followed for the defense. He stuck almost exclusively to the amicable relations between Nelson and Lydia Sherman, and the complete absence of motive. He also mentioned the prisoner's efforts to reform her husband, to lift him up to a higher plane of manhood than that to which he had fallen by the use of the "fiery liquid." Attorney Gardner's argument dragged along wearily with the exception of one good point: the prisoner purchased the arsenic so openly in Derby. She could have gone to New Haven and purchased it without any fear of detection, but she didn't. Lastly, Gardner insisted that Nelson Sherman, in the act of dying, had asked Lydia to take care of his son Nattie, in the presence of God and man; this showed that no matter what others may have observed or felt to be their angry disagreements, Sherman passed from this life with a loving confidence in his wife.[391]

State's Attorney Foster, at 2:15, began the closing remarks for the prosecution. He said there was no reasonable doubt as to presence of arsenic in the liver of Nelson Sherman. The defense had completely failed to shake the testimony of Dr. Barker. He then opined that there was an unbroken chain of circumstantial evidence to show that Lydia put it there, and with a sufficient motive. Ahhh, motive. Foster had to show motive and that he did next. He averred, "The case presents domestic relations of an unhappy character—distrust, coldness and jealousy, so much so that when Mr. Sherman's corpse lay there, the prisoner said to his mother, 'I had resolved to leave Nelson, but now I'm glad I did not.'"

Later in his remarks, Foster said, "Lydia felt she was scorned and her affection for him on his deathbed was the affection of Delilah, when she caressed Samson that she might shear his locks."[392]

Mr. Watrous finished the defense's plea. His argument was strongly negative and consisted of an attempt to show that there was no reasonable proof of the charge of murder made against Lydia. Mr. Watrous made a wanton attack on Dr. Barker, remarks that made no friends in the gallery or jury box for Lydia.

The court then adjourned to 9:30 in the morning on Friday, April 26.

On Friday morning, as the different players in this Greek tragedy readied themselves for the last act—the denouement of this murder and madness—a massive cloud rack socked in New Haven, as if a Divine Magistrate in a terrifying theophany was setting the stage for justice borne of vengeance.[393]

Chief Justice John Park began the proceedings by charging the jury. In the process, he found strongly against Lydia. At the same time, he instructed the jury that it was in their purview to find Lydia guilty of murder in the second degree, if they so chose.

While awaiting the verdict, the courtroom came alive with activity bordering on the festive. Throughout the room, men and women animatedly discussed the case. It was reminiscent of a teacher-less grade school class.

Lydia laughed heartily at the wild scene in the courtroom. She chatted amiably with her relatives.

While all this noisy socializing was going on, the door of the jury room suddenly swung open. The courtroom fell deadly silent. The crowd waited for a signal of some sort. False alarm: The jury simply wanted the statute books on the degrees of murder.[394]

Of course, such a request was quite a signal for those with courtroom experience. If the jury were leaning toward convicting Lydia of first-degree murder, they wouldn't need the statute books. Conversely, if they wanted to spare her the gallows, but make sure that she never walked free again, then they would need to study the penalties for the lesser degrees of murder in Connecticut.

The audience didn't need to wait much longer. In less than an hour, the jury had a verdict and informed Judges Park and Sanford. The twelve-man jury found Lydia Sherman guilty of second-degree murder in the arsenical poisoning of her husband, Horatio Nelson Sherman.

Lydia looked like an effigy. She stood a moment or two without so much as a muscle twitching. Then she sank back into her chair and hid her ashen face in her fan. A murmur of relief and satisfaction swept over the courtroom. Ann Nafey and John Struck cried. Joseph and John Danbury and their brother-in-law John Nafey tried to comfort them, but were also moved. Lydia's attorneys of course were stunned.[395]

The original balloting looked like this: For conviction in the second degree, 9; for acquittal, 3. A second ballot sealed Lydia fate: the verdict as rendered was unanimous.

With Chief Justice of the State John Park assisting Judge Sanford, the possibility of winning an appeal based on a point of law or procedure was nil. Lydia's counsel, most people speculated, would not even bother with an appeal, but attorneys Watrous and Gardner had ten days in which to take exception to the ruling.[396]

At the close of the proceedings, an open carriage whisked Lydia back to the New Haven County jail, where for nine long months, she awaited an appeal. In early May 1872, George Watrous filed a motion for appeal to the Connecticut Supreme Court of Errors on the grounds of the admissibility of certain evidence. The court's calendar was so crowded that the appeal couldn't be heard until the end of September 1872. However, the appeal was pointless. As stated, the chances of a reversal were miniscule, and there was an outstanding bench warrant for Lydia on the Hurlbut matter. The three extra arsenic-saturated bodies obviated any chance of Lydia ever walking free due to court order. George Watrous and Sam Gardner—and everyone else—knew that the "Queen Poisoner," the "Poison Fiend," this twisted sociopath in sensible shoes, would spend the rest of her natural life behind bars.[397]

Though everyone knew that the penalty for second-degree murder was life in prison, the formality of sentencing was postponed until after the appeals process played itself out. Thus, the result, when announced, would satisfy most because Connecticut residents were squeamish about executing women. In his *History of Hartford County*, J. Hammond Trumbull mentions hanging "witches" in 1648. Two other "witches," Rebecca Greensmith and Mary Barnes, were hung from an elm tree on Hartford's Albany turnpike in 1663. But these executions haunted the people of the Nutmeg State. Second-degree murder would confine Lydia to prison for life and, speaking broadly, the judge, jury, and public were satisfied.[398]

Once Lydia was back at New Haven County jail, her composure completely disappeared. She stretched out on her bed and wept openly.[399]

CHAPTER 9
Wethersfield Prison & Lydia's Passing

Toward the end of her eighteen-month stay at the New Haven County jail, on December 28, 1872, Lydia confessed killing her children and husbands to Warden Charles Webster and his wife Jennette.[400] Contemporary accounts say that the confession was not used against Lydia in court, though there is language in Judge David Sanford's sentencing remarks that make it obvious he was aware of the confession and its deplorable contents. The contents of the document leaked two weeks before Judge Sanford's sentence came down on January 11, 1873. Nevertheless, Connecticut state law did not give him leeway in the sentencing. The punishment for second-degree murder: life imprisonment.

For the first time, Lydia's crimes were laid bare for the world to see. On January 13, 1873, the *New York Herald* broke the story. By her count, Lydia had used arsenic to poison two husbands and six children. Lydia maintained that the death of Dennis Hurlbut was inexplicable and the passing of her oldest child, Lydia, was the result of natural causes. She suggested that Ole Hurlbut might have ingested the arsenic in a clumsy mix-up or even taken it on purpose. If there is uncertainty in these two deaths, Lydia of course does not get the benefit of the doubt. She is generally credited with killing ten people—three husbands and seven children.

Lydia's confession is extraordinary for another reason. From 1979 to 1983, members of the FBI's Behavioral Science Unit interviewed thirty-six convicted male sex killers—twenty-nine of whom were successive murderers. Males of this bent actually enjoy reliving and retelling the details of their crimes, especially the most chilling parts, and agents had no trouble getting these killers to cooperate. Conversely, female sequential killers have a natural aversion to discussing their misdeeds. Not surprisingly, there is no definitive study of female multiple murderesses to match the study done by the FBI on men.ABs. Deborah Shurman-Kauflin tried to replicate the FBI's study with female successive killers and approached twenty-six subjects. Only seven agreed to help. So said, Lydia's uninvited confession—where she recounts her murders in intimate detail—stands virtually unprecedented in the literature.[401]

On the day of Lydia's scheduled sentencing, Saturday, January 11, 1873, hundreds of people squeezed into New Haven's superior court. Lydia kept her veil close to her face and entered the courtroom a little after 9:30. Her confidant, Warden Charles Webster, walked with her. She took a seat in front of the judge, who asked her if she had anything to say. George Watrous, her counsel, answered for her in the negative. The usual formalities consumed a few minutes and then Judge David Sanford announced Lydia's sentence. The ghostly silence of the spectators caused the judge's firm voice to echo around the oversized room. His remarks were meant as a simple legal pronouncement, but they froze everyone—

> It is an unpleasant duty which this court has to discharge, but it is one from which it has no disposition to shrink. You, Mrs. Sherman, were . . . indicted for feloniously, willfully, and with malice aforethought, killing Horatio N. Sherman, your husband, by means of a deadly poison, by you administered. . . . If you had been found guilty of that, the verdict would have been murder in the first degree. You were tried by a jury of your own countrymen, which was largely of your own selection. You were ably defended by talented counsel. After a full, fair, and impartial trial, you were found guilty of murder in the second degree. It is the opinion of the court that the jury had been fully justified in

rendering a verdict of murder in the first degree, the penalty of which is death upon the gallows. Recent developments have fully vindicated the soundness of that opinion. The jury was not satisfied that the evidence warranted such a verdict, and therefore convicted you of murder in the second degree. So you have escaped the gallows, only to live surrounded by prison walls for life. The court has no discretion in fixing the punishment. The only sentence it can pronounce is that provided by the statutes, which is that you, Lydia Sherman, found guilty of murder in the second degree, be imprisoned in the Connecticut State Prison for the period of your natural life.[402]

Lydia showed no emotion. She would one day die in the Wethersfield Prison, but as she had done for the duration of the trial, she kept her emotions under control to the extent that she could. Soon thereafter, she left the courtroom with Captain Webster and—thanks to the usual New England January snows—was brought back to the New Haven County jail in a sleigh.[403] Reporters were led to believe that she would be transferred to the Wethersfield prison later that week or, at the very latest, the following week. However, Warden Webster decided to let the turmoil die down before he effected the transfer.

Lydia was undoubtedly happy to stay longer in New Haven thanks to Captain Webster and his wife, who treated her more kindly than she had any right to expect. Unlike the unforgiving accommodations that lay ahead at Wethersfield, the New Haven County jail was downright cushy. Lydia's cell was carpeted and a comfortable bed took up a large share of the narrow unit. What extra space remained was given over to articles for sewing, her toiletries, and personal items. There was also a large Bible, which Lydia claimed to read prodigiously of late. This isn't likely since there is nothing to indicate that Lydia read anything else at any time in her life.[404]

After returning from the courthouse, Captain Webster allowed a reporter from the *New Haven Palladium* to visit with Lydia.

Knowing all about the confession, this enterprising reporter asked Lydia if she would like to let the whole world know the truth. Lydia couldn't decide—

"I kept feeling so bad and I though I could give all up to Christ and confess to him and all would be right. . . . That is what I thought. I lay awake nights thinking about it. I could not sleep and I could not eat. Mrs. Webster will tell you that I did not eat anything. Finally one night, I made up my mind that I would give myself to Christ and confess everything, and I did. I knelt down, and said I was sorry, and asked him to forgive me. I felt better then. I felt that the burden was gone and that I was forgiven. Then I felt that I must confess it to the world. I felt that was my duty to do that, that others might be warned. I felt that I could not be forgiven unless that was done. In the morning, I called to Mrs. Webster. This was on Thursday the 26th of December. I called her in and I said, 'Mrs. Webster, I am a very wicked woman.' and she said she felt I was not very wicked now. I said, 'but I have been a very wicked woman, haven't I?'

She said, 'I know you have been, but I think [you have] become a good woman.'

I said, 'I felt that I wanted to let everybody know how bad I had been, and that I could not be forgiven unless I did.' She spoke to Mr. Webster, and he came in the next morning and asked me if I wanted to make a confession, and I said I did. Then of course I told him. After I made up my mind . . . and after I told him all, the oppression was gone from my heart, and ever since I have been perfectly contented and my mind is at ease.'"[405]

Lydia continued—

"I felt that I know God has forgiven me, and then after I am done here I shall have a home then with him. I made up my mind that I would give up everything in this world and not think nor care for anything here. I think it was on Christmas that Mrs. Crumb came here to talk to me, and that it was she and her talking to me and praying with me that helped me to do this, and a great deal was owing to [Rev.] Mr. Lutz. He was here on Christmas day. Mrs. Crumb was the means of my making up my mind finally to give myself up to Christ. I would like the world to know how I felt. I feel that I have given up all hold on the world, and that I have given Christ my heart and that my trust is in him. Years ago, I was a professor of religion, and always thought I had a religion, but I know now that I never was a Christian. I always used to think I was, but I know I was not, or I would not have done as I did."[406]

The *Palladium* reporter remarked that her quarters at the Wethersfield Prison would certainly not be as nice as her New Haven accommodations, and she claimed she didn't care. Lydia told him she placed herself entirely in God's hands, and she was ready to bear her fate. She also said she wanted Christian people to know how she felt and to have them point to her case as a warning to others.

Lydia was "perfectly willing to receive her sentence and die in prison, but hoped that even there she [could] find means of doing some good."[407]

As she finished her interview with the reporter from the *Palladium*, Lydia wanted to say something about Captain Webster and his wife Jennette. By way of thanks, she noted, "I have been here eighteen months today, and I have not had an unkind word spoken to me. I have been allowed a great many privileges and my time has passed pleasantly. I have been treated very kindly."[408] Later, the reporter described Lydia's appearance, "She was dressed plainly in a . . . black alpaca dress and white apron, and wore a collar and earrings. Her hair was combed down smoothly, and she looked like a neat and orderly person. She was quite calm, though but two hours before she had received the horrible sentence, and she conversed in a pleasant and affable manner. When speaking of her confession and her feeling she was very earnest, and seemed to be thoroughly imbued with what she gave expression to.[409]

While Lydia waited for transfer, Rev. Mr. Goodsell visited her. In recounting his talk with her, he stressed, "she appears to be a person born with no moral sense whatever, with not the slightest idea of right and wrong, and yet not. . . a person of loose habits or deep passions."[410]

Lydia was finally transferred to the Connecticut State Prison at Wethersfield on February 3, 1873. As Lydia settled into the Connecticut Prison—just one more place where time had no meaning and life no purpose—reporters continued to have their fun. At about this time, Gen. Frank Wheaton was battling the Modoc Indians in Northern California and Oregon—west of the Cascade Mountains. The small tribe of Modocs had settled on the Klamath reservation, but a splinter group commanded by a Brave, Captain Jack, rebelled. Thanks to liquor and supplies sold to them by unscrupulous white traders, Captain Jack and his followers became roving marauders, preying on the white settlers of the area. One newspaperman mused, "The government proposes to set up Mrs. Sherman of Connecticut in the boardinghouse business in Modoc country."[411]

Lydia offered reporters in the Hartford area a number of different versions of why she made the confession and why she committed the murders in the first place. As for the confession, she ventured, "A burden of years—one which had weighed upon her days, and which sleep could not ease—had been taken from her mind, and that she was now a happier woman than she had ever been. In her sleep, the torments of remorse had harrowed her in a manner she could not describe. For several days, she had been visited by several persons for the purpose of giving religious advice and consolation; and yesterday [December 25,1872] she spent the afternoon in conversation with three persons upon religious subjects.[412]

The three persons Lydia referred to included Rev. Mr. Lutz of New Haven, Mrs. Crumb, a spiritual advisor who prayed with Lydia on Christmas Day, and of course, Jennette Webster, the warden's wife.

When it came to a motive for the murders, Lydia, at times, offered some fairly prosaic explanations. At other times she relied on her old line, "I was downhearted and much discouraged." Searching wildly for something new for reporters, once she even said, "The devil was in [me]."[413] The truth, however, was something even Lydia might not have understood. For sociopaths like Lydia Sherman, "human life is as valuable as a used tissue. [Murder] actually is easier for them. The hedonistic comfort of material gain outweighs the price of human life."[414]

Wethersfield Prison

The Connecticut State Prison at Wethersfield was built in 1827 employing inmates to lay up the hard brownstone walls surrounding the main complex at the fore. The main building—containing all the cellblocks, offices, hospital, chapel and wardens' quarters—was brownstone on the outside, with concrete floors and cellblocks on the inside.

Just as the reporter for the *Palladium* had speculated, Lydia's accommodations were not anywhere near as snug in Wethersfield as they had been in New Haven. The concrete floors especially were cold on the feet and dreary on the spirit.

The Town of Wethersfield began as a shipbuilding village and import-export center. However, by the beginning of the 1800s, it was a typical Yankee farming enclave, built around the huge spire of the First Congregational Church, with a few ancient seed businesses, a couple of small markets and 3,800 residents. The new prison sat on one and a half acres of a seventeen-acre tract purchased by the state. The remainder of the land was used to grow crops. The prison's brownstone walls shot eighteen feet into the air and formed a 336-foot by 435-foot penitentiary.[415] Dark and foreboding, it rested on the north side of Wethersfield abutting a small cove that was once an oxbow in the Connecticut River.[416]

After forty-three years of service—and now housing almost 200 inmates—the old prison cried out for remodeling. In July 1869, the state legislature passed an act directing the water commissioners of Hartford "to supply the Connecticut State Prison with pure and wholesome water."[417] The 100-hogshead cistern under the exercise yard would still supply some water, but the inmates would now get their drinking water from the limpid streams of Trout Brook in West Hartford.[418] The Hartford Water Works wasted no time acceding to the wishes of the legislature and had good clean water flowing into the prison within a year, although plumbing fixtures inside the prison wouldn't come online until later. In addition to the new water supply, coal from the prison's stockpile was converted to gas for lighting.[419]

Though Indiana completed a women's prison by 1873, women felons in Connecticut occupied a separate wing in the Wethersfield prison until a separate facility in Niantic was completed in 1930. Just like the male convicts, the women prisoners tended to be in for murder or robbery. Male or female, they all lived in five-by-eight cells with only a primitive bed for company. A reporter characterized Lydia cell in this manner: "Her cell is a model of neatness, and is handsomely decorated with pictures and knick-knacks."[420]

One small difference between male and female inmates was that the former engaged in contract labor making mechanics tools, shoes, boots and cigars in the different shop buildings. The latter stayed in their cellblocks or in the laundry and busied themselves with sewing, picking wool, knitting, spooling, needlepoint and fancy work.

At the Wethersfield Prison, the female department made the clothing for all the inmates, and Lydia was correspondingly busy. She occupied the farthest corner of the room and always sat with her back to the door. When visitors entered, she never even turned around. For obvious reasons, Lydia had no part in the cooking at the prison.[421]

The women in the prison were not completely isolated from the men. A door in the masonry wall allowed workers (men) to access the women's quarters, and the women worked alongside male inmates in the laundry room and other places. However, women and men enjoyed separate exercise yards.

The intermingling of the sexes—beyond their work—was unauthorized and a real blunder. In an inquiry conducted in 1879, former guards gave testimony that Rev. Mr. William Green—a cleric from Litchfield County who killed his wife—and Lydia "had special dinners served [to] them. They ate together." In the same hearing, Matron Sarah Waterhouse and James McCabe (a burglar doing seven years) were rumored to have had an intimate relationship.[422]

Though the men were barred from even the simplest luxuries, the women prisoners fared better. For example, the women's cells only had bars on the doors. There were solid panels to the sides of the doors with a latticework of three-inch stellate holes drilled in the upper half for ventilation. The women were also allowed to hang frilly pink curtains inside their cell doors. Held back by sashes, the inmates closed them when they dressed and undressed or attended to their private business.

As the days turned into weeks, Lydia's crimes were soon enough history, but the press had done an incredible job of spreading her practices. A Philadelphia entrepreneur, Erastus Elmer Barclay published a small pamphlet *The Poison Fiend!* (printed in English and in German). As an author and publisher, Barclay covered his lurid pamphlets in bright colors, and added beautiful pen and ink drawings to thrill readers. There were others in the field, but none so successful as Barclay, who made a good living from 1841 to 1880 with these thrilling offerings. After the Civil War, he even tried four-color covers, but reverted back to single-color covers in purple, maroon or navy blue.

After searching for an explanation for the poisoning of a German family near Chicago, those investigating the case discovered an illustrated copy of *The Poison Fiend!*—Lydia's story—among the family's possessions. The Malinski family was poor, and the final conclusion was that the mother—gathering inspiration from Lydia Sherman—decided to put the whole clan out of its misery with a pitcher of poisoned coffee.[423]

Despite Lydia's heartfelt confession to Christ and her selfless yearning to do her time in prison quietly and perhaps "be of some use to others," it wasn't long before she concocted her yellow-faced escape plan and strode out the prison door.

Arriving in Springfield, Lydia went to the Pynchon House. Without registering her name, she secured a room and slept well.[424] The next morning, she bought prêt-à-porter traveling and morning dresses, toilet articles, towels, a fan, perfumery, and two satchels in which to put these items. Afterwards, Lydia went back to the hotel, ravenously ate dinner, and caught the afternoon train for Worcester at 1 o'clock.

She couldn't decide—Boston or Providence? For a woman who was noted for her cunning, it tasks the imagination to discover how much of Lydia's decisions, behavior and plans were spur-of-the-moment affairs. Ultimately, she chose Providence, arriving there at 7 o'clock in the evening. She checked into the Central Hotel, masquerading as Mrs. Brown of Philadelphia. Lydia later claimed that the Philadelphia hometown wasn't a lie because she had lived there at one time. However, like so many things Lydia said, this wasn't true either. She had worked for the Maxon family in Saylorsburg, Pennsylvania (north of Allentown) for a few months, but never lived in Philadelphia.

This presents a fascinating oddity about Lydia's sense of values. She would go to great lengths to rationalize a lie—or not to tell one in the first place—while she was capable of killing ten people with no real remorse. Even the most casual observer might ask—Was this something that she learned in Hornerstown as a child? Was Lydia influenced by the raw elements of life on the Clayton's farm, where the care of a wagon or hay rake was infinitely more important than the life of a steer, pig, or chicken? Why exactly did Lydia put such a paltry value on human life? Once again, history hides the complete answers from us.

At the hotel, Lydia became fast friends with the proprietor's wife, Mrs. Ellery Sears, and her mother, Mrs. Annie Thornton. Lydia's plan, she explained, was to get work for a month and then go see her sister Ann in New Brunswick, New Jersey. The two Rhode Island women were quick to help Lydia, and mentioned a widower with three children in East

Providence who needed a housekeeper. This was perfect because the widower sounded a lot like the needy men that Lydia gravitated toward. Accordingly, she trudged to East Providence. The widower wasn't at home, and Lydia returned to the Central Hotel without landing a job. (Apparently, while in Providence, she missed out on a second job opportunity as well.)

After Lydia got back from East Providence, she was exhausted. Sitting down on the front steps of the hotel, she engaged in conversation with the elder woman, Annie Thornton, who at some point inquired again of Lydia's last name. The escaped prisoner froze. She had forgotten her alias. Rather than miss a beat, Lydia blurted out, "Mrs. Moore." She thought the error would go unnoticed. It did not. Quickly enough, the two Rhode Island women put their heads together and figured out the real identity of their guest. At the first opportunity, they sent a messenger to notify the police.[425]

The next morning, Lydia heard a knock at her bedchamber. When she opened the door, a stranger walked in. Lydia thought perhaps it was the "widower" or someone else who wanted to engage her. The stranger—Detective Frederic Waldron as it turned out—began talking about the Sherman case. Lydia claimed ignorance, but was asked to accompany the detective to the station house. There, the chief of police questioned her for a long time and then put her in a cell. While she waited, Detective Waldron handed her a napkin ring engraved "Lydia." The game was over.

Newspapermen always had their fun with Lydia, and her escape and recapture was no exception. One paper quipped as she fled, "If she will turn her attention to [poisoning] the potato bugs, the people will rise up and call her blessed."[426] The *Augusta Chronicle* [Ga.] wrote, "Mrs. Lydia Sherman, the poisoner, has been recaptured. We were in hopes that she would fascinate and marry [Gen.] Ben Butler."[427]

Warden Hewes of the Wethersfield prison was notified immediately and sent Deputy Warden Martin to collect Lydia. She slept a little in the Providence station house that night and was on a train that pulled into Hartford at 11 o'clock the following morning (June 6). A large crowd had gathered at the station, but guards whisked Lydia out the smoking car and into a hack waiting on the blind side of the train. She landed back at Wethersfield in a flash. Lydia had been gone one week.[428]

A number of reporters were allowed to interview Lydia, as she stood in her cell behind the grated door, her small hand gripping one of the bars. She talked freely and even corrected a few misconceptions about her escape. Lydia seemed remarkably cheerful, considering that it had been her habit to turn her face from visitors and few people had ever seen her. All the while Warden Hewes stood close by.

Allowing such an interview seems a bit irregular, but Warden Hewes had a hidden agenda. Rampant rumors charged that unfinished renovations at the prison—particularly missing locks on the inmates cells that were actually in place by the end of 1876—had somehow aided in Lydia's escape. By allowing the prisoner to regale the assembled reporters with all the finer points of her escape, it would set the record straight with the public and absolve Warden Hewes and his staff of any wrongdoing or negligence in the matter. The interview achieved its goal for Hewes and most of the prison officers. As we shall see though, nothing could save Sarah Waterhouse.

Lydia told reporters that while in Providence, she tried to get housekeeping employment in two different homes. If for any reason the East Providence widower didn't work out, there was also a clergyman a few miles outside the city with an invalid wife who needed help.

At one point, Warden Hewes remarked that it was lucky for the widower that he hadn't taken Lydia into his service. Lydia flashed a most peculiar smile and said that she didn't know.

During the conversation with reporters, Lydia had nice things to say about Sarah Waterhouse, injecting that the matron never knew at any time of Lydia's escape plans. Along the same lines, she told Warden Hewes that she was glad to get back and was sorry that she had tried to escape—even adding that before she got half way to Hartford, she wished herself back at the Wethersfield prison. (Everyone knew Lydia's comments were simply attempts to avoid punishment.)

Lydia's demeanor throughout the interviews was perfectly cool, and those present felt that she actually enjoyed giving descriptions of her travels.[429]

A reporter for the *New York Times,* who participated in this June 6 interview, finished his replay of the conversation by writing, "The woman is a strange character, full of deceit and cunning under the cover of a smooth tongue, and might deceive the very elect, by her plausibility and simulated good nature. There has hardly been one like her in criminal history of this country—one so utterly depraved, with no moral sense whatsoever—and her speedy capture is a matter as profoundly worthy of congratulations as it would have been deeply disgraceful had the State of Connecticut lost possession of her."[430]

To the general public, the ultimate responsibility for the escape fell to Warden Hewes—and he should have been completely beside himself with Lydia's embarrassing stunt—but the warden, like most men, was at least in some part amused by Lydia. Besides, even the harshest taskmaster realized that Warden Hewes could not possibly have kept perpetual tabs on 200 men and women. Matron Sarah Waterhouse would be the one to actually pay the price, and pay she did. By 1877, Waterhouse's hard work and attention to detail had vaulted her to the princessly salary of $268 a year. After Lydia's escape, Hewes cut the matron's pay 35 percent to $173. The goal of course was to humiliate her into retirement, a goal that inexorably came to fruition the following year.

In 1878, Sarah Waterhouse's seven-year career as an officer of the Connecticut State Prison at Wethersfield came to a close.[431]

When Lydia first disappeared, Warden Hewes offered a $500 reward to anyone who helped with the capture of his infamous prisoner. Within a week of Lydia's return to Wethersfield, Mrs. Ellery Sears of the Central Hotel in Providence was awarded $500 by the State of Connecticut for aiding in the capture of one of the worst killers in American history.[432]

After Lydia's brazen breakout, she was confined to her cell much of the time and watched far more closely. It was June 1877 and Lydia had been behind bars for four years and three months. She was fifty-two years old and finally had to come to the conclusion that she would never walk free again. Her health began to deteriorate. Unlike her prior charade, now her skin actually took on a jaundiced color. Although never diagnosed correctly, she was clearly suffering from organ failure—probably the liver. Covering her face and hands with pigmented wax for a year might have been a contributing factor. The truth will never be known, as no investigation ensued.

Lydia became seriously ill about May 8, 1878. In an ironic twist of fate, she suffered extreme abdominal pain, had spasmodic attacks of nausea and fainting spells—similar to the symptoms suffered by her victims.[433] A week before her death, the prison chaplain, Rev. Mr. George Wooding had a long talk with her. Among other things, Lydia requested that the chaplain write to her son, if she should die. Rev. Wooding felt that Lydia's health was on a downhill trajectory, and if she wanted to dictate anything, she should do it immediately. But Lydia felt too weak to talk. The chaplain returned on Sunday and Lydia still did not have the strength to dictate anything. Finally on Monday, when she was very feeble and failing rapidly, she whispered her few wishes.[434]

She wanted her son John—now living in New Jersey—notified of her death. She did not want her remains sent to him, as it would be an unnecessary expense and cause him needless problems.

However, she did not want her remains buried in the small potter's field behind the prison, but in the village cemetery instead. In an effort to complete this transaction, Lydia reached inside her undergarment and pulled out a "bosom pad." Tearing it open, she removed a small folded piece of paper, inside of which was a $50 bill. She handed it to the chaplain and explained that he should use the money to secure her a proper Methodist burial.[435]

From his talks with Lydia, Chaplain Wooding believed that "as far it was in her nature to be remorseful, she really did feel penitent; that she often expressed sorrow that she administered poison to her first husband."[436] She also claimed to have been a consistent member of the Methodist Church and repeated that she "was a poor, weak woman, who was unable to resist a great temptation, which came to her when she was burdened with the care of a sick and complaining husband, and with poverty."[437]

Twenty-four hours before she died, Lydia lost consciousness and never opened her eyes again. Her death was an agonizing one, but people in the prison thought she did not suffer in body or mind as much as others may have wished or imagined. One particularly poetic reporter wrote, "She was like a person dying from a sudden and fatal poisoning; it was an actual death, produced by deep-seated disease, which had been dragging her toward the grave for many years. Though dying from an extraneous cause . . . it seemed as if the scenes of the dying, who had been destroyed by her own hand, were being reenacted.[438]

She died at noon on Thursday, May 16, 1878. She was only fifty-three. Though everyone seemed quite confident that Lydia expired as a result of some type of liver disease, the prison medical officer, Dr.

Roswell Fox, decided that the cause of death more closely resembled "General Disability."[439]

A number of people asked Warden Hewes to deliver the body to a scientific institution for dissection, but he dismissed the idea.

Rev. Mr. Wooding forwarded Lydia's request that she be buried off the prison grounds to Warden Hewes, who gave his consent. He saw to it that Lydia Sherman was interred in the Ancient Burying Ground behind the First Congregational Church in Wethersfield. The chaplain made the arrangements. The sexton of the village cemetery supplied a plot at the southeast edge of the property. The funeral took place on May 17. There were no formal exercises except at the gravesite, where only Chaplain Wooding, a gravedigger and a few curious villagers assembled. The chaplain read the rites of the Methodist Episcopal Church and Lydia's remains were lowered "to mingle with the dust." [440]

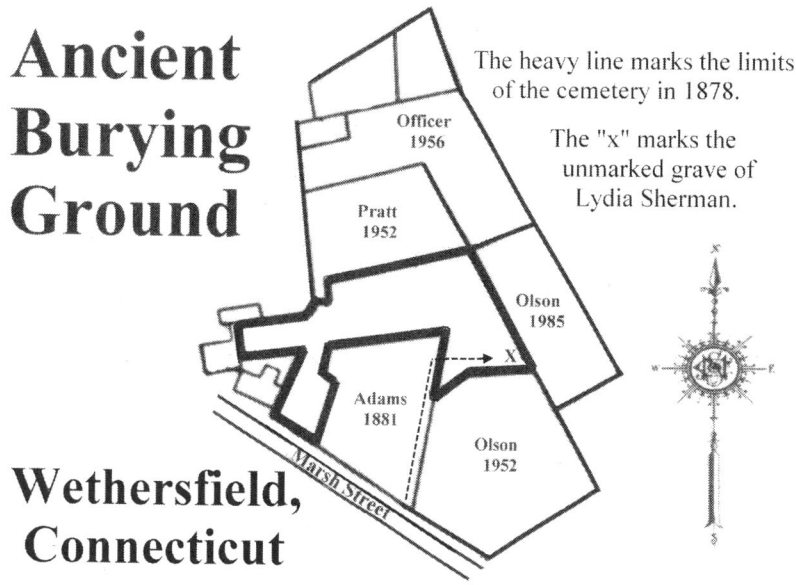

Lydia's gravesite: Use the easternmost entrance to the Ancient Burying Ground on Marsh Street. About 100 feet ahead—on the right side of the road—is the Veterans Memorial. Lydia's final resting place is due east of this monument, near the woods.

Postscript:

Considering that Lydia spent considerable time deceiving the physicians of the nineteenth century, it is curious that she is buried amidst at least a dozen doctors. These graves are all that remain of a small band of American medical practitioners representing different centuries. Included in this company is the final resting place of a highly respected diagnostician of the twentieth century— Dr. Robert D. Murphy—the author's father.

Sometimes Lydia's insentient life—as near as a full accounting of the existing evidence allows—appears to be nothing more than a random collection of ironies. As an infant, she was placed out to enable others to go on. Then time slipped away and she began to murder at a level never seen before—so that she could go on. She killed those closest to her, the people she should have protected unto death. Her tumultuous life ended and she came to rest in a verdant place without the despondency that dogged her days. And life goes on.

APPENDIX A

Lydia's Confession

Lydia Sherman's confession was completed on December 28, 1872, at the New Haven County jail, with the help of Warden Charles Webster and his wife Jennette. Lydia Sherman was barely literate, so Charles and Jennette Webster did the actual recording. Beyond her dismal education, Lydia had a terrible memory for names and dates. As such, even in this confession—where she made an effort to be honest—the document is full of errors. Below is a transcription of the original confession with corrections contained in brackets.

The Confession

I was born near the town of Burlington [in Trenton], New Jersey, December 24, 1824. My mother died when I was nine years [months] old, and I was sent to live with my uncle, Mr. John Claygay [Clayton—actually Lydia was first sent to live with John Clayton's mother, Widow J. Clayton.] I never attended school much, being able to go only about three months in the year. At sixteen [fifteen and a half] years of age, I went to New Brunswick with my two brothers, and afterward to live with the Rev. Mr. Van Amburgh in Jacksonville [Lebanon, N.J.], twenty-five miles from New Brunswick. I lived there for three years, then return to New Brunswick and learned to be a tailoress. I work for three months without pay and was then employed by Mr. Owen [Owens]. He was a class leader in the Methodist church of which I became a member. It was there that I met Mr. Edward Struck, who was a devoted Christian up to a few months before his death. I was his wife eighteen years; he has been dead about eight years [since May, 1864]. Our first child we called Lydia, and after her birth we went to New York and resided near

Elizabeth and Houston Streets [244 Elizabeth Street]. In New York, we had two boys. Afterward, we move to Carmansville [Carmensville] where we had four children born. At the end of that time, Mr. Struck obtained an appointment on the Metropolitan Police force. Six months later, we lost our daughter, age twenty-two months, by the measles. About this time, my husband was transferred to Manhattanville, and we move to 125th Street. Then occurred our first trouble, which came about in this way:

On May and came up to Stratton's Hotel [St. Nicholas Hotel] on the Bloomingdale road [Broadway], and made a disturbance in the barroom. He attacked the bartender with a knife and immediately the cry of murder was sounded. Just at this time, the Manhattanville stage came along, and on it was a detective [Dep. Sheriff James E. Merriam] who heard the cry. He rushed into the hotel, but finding he was powerless to accomplish anything, he asked for the assistance of a policeman. There was none near, and he endeavored to quiet the man by talking to him, but could not succeed. The man appeared deranged. The detective struck him with a cane, but the man would not desist. He struck the officer with a knife, when the latter drew a pistol, and [Merriam] shot the man dead.

The stage drove on and soon met Mr. Struck, and as he was a policeman, the driver told him the circumstances about the killing of the man at the hotel. Mr. Struck started immediately for the hotel, and when he reached there he found the man was dead. Word was sent to the Manhattanville police station, and doctors gave it as their opinion that the man was deranged. My husband reported at headquarters, and soon after a rumor prevailed that he would not arrest the man, because he [the longshoreman] had a pistol. This is incorrect, but the employees of the hotel testify that Mr. Struck was at the place and was afraid to go in. The result was that he was discharged from the police force. I sent for Capt. Hart [Hartt], but when he came my husband would neither look, speak, nor have anything to do with him. The captain said he was out of his mind, and advised me to have been sent to an asylum.

One night after this, he was acting very badly, and I called in police Sergeant Mc— [Officer Watson Wagner], who lived in the lower part of our house. The sergeant advised me to put him out of the way, as he would never be any good to me or himself again. I asked him what he meant, and he told me to get a certain quantity of arsenic and give him some of it. I paid ten cents for it, put it in some oatmeal gruel, and gave him some of it during the afternoon. That night he was very ill, and at 8 o'clock the next morning he died.

The following July [1864], I made up my mind my two little children, Mary Ann, six years old, and Edward, two years younger, would be better off if they were out of the way, so after thinking the matter over for several days, I made them some of the same kind of gruel their father had eaten. They only survived a short time.

The doctors said that the children died of gastric fever. They had not the least suspicion of the truth.

I continue to keep the house, and had four children with me at the time. My son, George Whitfield, who was then fourteen years of age, was living with me. In the latter part of August [1865], he was taken sick, and I sent for doctor Oviatt [Elliott]. He said the boy had painters' colic, and as he did not improve I became discouraged and mixed some arsenic in his tea. He died the next day, and the doctor said it was painters' colic.

Then my little daughter Ann Eliza took the chills and fever, and was continually sick. This made me down hearted and discouraged again. I had some arsenic in the house which I purchased in Harlem, and I put it in the medicine I bought for her to cure the chills. I gave it to her twice, and she was taken sick as the others were, and died about noon four days afterward. "She was the happiest child I ever saw."

I then kept house until the following May, going out as usual to do nursing. About that time, Lydia, my eldest daughter, went to New York with work, was taken sick, and after an illness of twenty-one days, she died a natural death. I never gave her anything the doctor did not order. Then I went to Sailorsville, Pa., with a family named Maxom [Maxon]. It was not a profitable venture, so I returned to New York and went to live with my stepdaughter, Mrs. Thompson. Then I took a situation with Mr. Cochran who kept a sewing machine establishment in Canal Street. There I became acquainted with Mr. James Curtiss [Curtis]. He asked me to go to Stratford, Connecticut, to take care of his aged mother and keep house for them. I consented to go for $8.00 per month. I lived there eight months. One day, Mr. John Fairchild, in whose store I bought our groceries, asked me if I would like to keep house for a man who had just lost his wife. In this way, I became acquainted with Mr. Hurlburt [Hurlbut] who lived in Coram, Huntington. After I had been a few days with him, he asked me to marry him, which I did November 22, 1868. The ceremony was performed by the Rev. Mr. Morton in his own house. We lived happily for fourteen months. About three months after we were married, Mr. Hurlburt [Hurlbut] made his will. He was subject to fits of dizziness.

One day he was unwell, and he ate clams and drank cider with saleratus in it. Then he became worse. On one occasion he made me drink cider and saleratus, after which I became very sick and dizzy, and I took to vomiting. Finally, Mr. Hurlburt [Hurlbut] became worse, and about 5 o'clock one morning the old man died. Now I wish to say that I never gave Mr. Hurlburt [Hurlbut] anything that would cause sickness, though there may have been arsenic mixed with the saleratus, which he put into the cider.

About two months after Hurlburt [Hurlbut] died, I heard that Horatio N. Sherman of Birmingham wanted me to take a little baby to board. I met Mr. Sherman one Sunday morning. He introduced himself to me, and said that he had another object in calling besides getting me to take care of his baby. He wanted me as his housekeeper, because his mother-in-law and his daughter could not get along well together. I said I would think about. Two weeks later he came again and offer to marry me. I told him we ought to be better acquainted. He said that he was compelled to get someone, as he could not have the old woman in the house, as she was creating a constant disturbance. He then went away, and I didn't see him for three or four weeks; but at the end of that time he found me a tenant for my farm, which ended in my lending him $300.

In July 1870, I lend him $300 more, and on the 3rd [15th] of September 1870, we went to Mr. Sherman's sister's house in Bridgewater, Massachusetts and were married.

After we had been married about two months, Mr. Sherman said one day that he wished his babe (Frankie) would die, as then the old woman should not stay another day in the house. I was full of trouble, and never knowing what to do, I was tempted to get him (Frankie) something to get him out of the way, because I thought he would be better off. They had arsenic in the house. The old lady had used it before the poison rats. I put some of it in some milk, and only gave to him once. Being quite feeble, he began to be sick and vomit. I sent for a doctor, but he said the child was not out of danger, though he was better. This was in the forenoon. That night, the child died at 11 o'clock. This was November 15 [16], 1870.

Mr. Sherman then took to drink, and I supported the family for about six months. During this time, I found that he had dissipated the money I gave him, instead of paying his bills with it, so I had to pay out about $300 more for him. Then came Christmas, and Ada devoted a great deal of time in decorating the church. I furnished her with all her clothes and paid her dressmaking bills. On Christmas Eve, Ada was taken sick and

Dr. Beardsley was again sent for. He prescribed a brandy-sling for her, but Mr. Sherman drank all the liquor I bought. I couldn't keep a drop for Ada. The next morning she was no better, and we sent for Dr. Dutton of Milford. When the doctor came, Mr. Sherman was so drunk that he could not walk straight. Mr. Sherman asked me for $10 to pay the doctor. I refused to give it to him, saying that I would pay the doctor myself. Then he got mad and went out.

That made me feel so bad that I was tempted to do as I had done before. I had some arsenic in the house, which I mixed in her [Addie's] tea and gave to her twice. She died the next morning.

Mr. Sherman began drinking more than ever. Sunday he went out and returned very drunk. Monday he went out again and returned in the evening. He drank a cup of chocolate and then went out to get some greens for dinner.

While he was gone, he was taken sick, and he came home immediately. I had about a pint of brandy in the house, and I put some arsenic in it. That night he drank it, and the next morning he was very sick. I didn't mean to kill him. I only wanted to make him sick of liquor. The next day he drank more of the brandy and was worse. I sent for Dr. Beardsley and told him that Mr. Sherman had one of his old spells. He [Nelson] continued to grow worse; other doctors were called in, but he died at 8 o'clock the following morning.

AUTHOR'S NOTES

Chapter 1

[1] *Report of the Directors of the State Prison*, 1873, 10-11.; "Gossip of the Day," *Commercial Advertiser*, February 6, 1873, 1.; "A Widow In Town," *Hartford Daily Courant*, February 4, 1873, 2.

[2] Chicago: Loyola University Study, 2002."Blue Eyes Are Increasingly Rare," *New York Times*, October 18, 2006, n.p. Since the original ethnic stock of America was Northern Europeans— English, Scottish, Irish and German— blue eyes predominated for a long time. Most "black" eyes are in fact very dark brown. Nevertheless eye color is so complex, it makes a mockery of Mendel's pea patch.

[3] "Lydia Sherman," *New York Herald*, April 22, 1872, 5.; "The Sherman Trial at New Haven," *Hartford Daily Courant*, April 17, 2011, 3.; No Title, New York Sunday Herald, May 16, 1952, 24.; No Title, New York Herald Archives, May 28, 1950, 143.

[4] "The Connecticut Borgia," *The Sun* (NY), July 6, 1871, 1.

[5] "Lydia Sherman," *The Spectator*, Vol. 46, 1873, London: John Campbell, Wellington Street, Strand.

[6] Cohen, 3-19.

[7] Ibid.

[8] Ibid.

[9] "The Poisoner," *Hartford Daily Times*, January 13, 1872, 2.

[10] "State Prison Investigation," *Hartford Daily Courant*, March 13, 1869, 2.; "The State Prison," *Hartford Daily Courant*, May 22, 1873, 2.

[11] "Lydia Sherman," *Columbian Register*, September 27, 1873, 3.; "Lydia Sherman," *Columbian Register*, January 16, 1875, 2.

[12] The first use of the term Queen Poisoner was in Erastus E. Barclay's *The Poison Fiend!* published in 1873.

[13] "Arrest and Suicide," *Hartford Daily Courant*, May 8, 1858, 3.; "The South: Acquittal of Mrs. Wharton," *Hartford Daily Courant*, January 25, 1872, 3.; "Mrs. Fair Again," *Hartford Daily Courant*, November 23, 1872, 3.

[14] Borgia refers to the Renaissance poisoner Lucrezia Borgia, whose story is in Chapter 3.

[15] "Lydia Sherman." *Commercial Advertiser*, May 28, 1873, 1.

[16] *Report of the Directors of the State Prison*, 1877, 10-11.

[17] "The Connecticut State Prison," *New York Times*, October 11, 1874, 9.; "At Large Again," *Hartford Daily Courant*, May 4, 1875, 2.; Tel. Interview with Frank Winiarski, Wethersfield Prison historian- October 21, 2011.

[18] "Mrs. Sherman's History," *The Sun* (NY), " July 8, 1871, 1.

[19] "Mrs. Sherman's Adventures," *Hartford Daily Courant*, June 7, 1877, 2.; Plans for the remodeling of the State Prison at Wethersfield, May 1870. Connecticut State Library, Hartford.; *Report of the Directors of the State Prison*, 1898, 7-8.

[20] The details of Lydia Sherman's escape from Wethersfield Prison are contained within the pages of almost every newspaper in the country. Significant details of the account given herewith were taken from the following sources: "Mrs. Sherman's Adventures," *Hartford Daily Courant*, June 7, 1877, 2.; Recapture of Lydia Sherman," *New York Times*, June 6, 1877, 1.; "Mrs. Lydia Sherman," *Hartford Daily Courant*, June 6, 1877, 2.; "The Murderess of Eight Persons: Mrs. Lydia Sherman At Large…," *New York Times*, May 31, 1877, 1.
[21] "Annual Dinner at Prison," *Columbian Register*, February 5, 1876, 2.
[22] "Recapture of Mrs. Sherman," *New York Times*, June 6, 1877, 5.
[23] "Mrs. Sherman's Adventures," *Hartford Daily Courant*, June 7, 1877, 2.
[24] Ibid.
[25] "United States District Court: Sentence of Daniel L. Hayden…," *Hartford Daily Courant*, May 28, 1875, 2.
[26] "The Murderess of Eight Persons," *New York Times*, May 31, 1877, 1.

Chapter 2

[27] "Lydia Sherman," *New York Herald*, April 22, 1872, 5.
In 1872, Lydia Sherman told her New Haven jailor, Capt. Charles Webster, that she was born "near the Town of Burlington, New Jersey." The statement was a deliberate fabrication. It is unclear why Lydia, who was front-page news across the United States as a "monster," went out of her way to spare the many generations of Danburys living in Trenton—as well as John and Elizabeth Clayton and their children in Hornerstown, but she did. Usually Lydia only worried about herself. One explanation might be Lydia's sister Ann (Danbury) Nafey of New Brunswick, New Jersey, with whom Lydia was extremely close. Ann attended Lydia's murder trial in New Haven from April 16-26, 1872, and she may have prevailed upon Lydia to dissemble on the place of her birth— among other items— in an effort to protect relatives still living in Trenton and other parts of New Jersey. The truth—as her brother, John Danbury, told a reporter during Lydia's trial—was that Lydia was born in Trenton on December 24, 1824 (New York Herald, April 22, 1872, 5). Lastly, Ann Nafey gave an interview to a reporter from *The Sun* (NY) in which she said "Our parents lived in Trenton and we were all born there" (*The Sun*, July 8, 1871, 1).
Lydia's birth year is sometimes given as 1825. This date may have gained acceptance because some people think it represents the year of Lydia's baptism, but her father, Samuel Danbury, was a Baptist and that religious sect generally did not believe in infant baptism. Thus, December 24, 1824—the birth date Lydia and her brother John gave in interviews—is probably correct.
[28] "The Huntington Militia 1792,"The Genealogical Magazine of New Jersey, January-April 1934, Vol. IX, No. 2, Whole No. 35-6, Published by The Genealogical Society of New Jersey, 33 Lombardy St., Newark, New Jersey.; Documents relating to the Colonial, Revolutionary and Post Revolutionary History of the State of New Jersey, Volume XII, 1810-1813, n.p. ; Edited by Elmer T. Hutchinson (Secretary of the New Jersey Historical Society),

MacCrellish & Quigley Co. Printers, Trenton, New Jersey, 1941, Will of Elizabeth Snook, Amwell Twp., Hunterdon Co., Dated: February 20, 1813.

[29] "Bill" covering April 22- August 25, 1813, submitted by Samuel Danbury at the settlement of the estate of Sylvester Doyle in 1814. Doyle was the owner of the Bull's Head Tavern on State Street in Trenton. Collection of the Trenton Historical Society, Trentoniana Room, Trenton, New Jersey.

[30] "Lydia Sherman," *New York Herald,* April 22, 1872, 5.; "Lydia Sherman's Crimes," *The Sun* (NY), July 8, 1871, 1.

[31] U. S. Census Records, 1840.

[32] "Bill" covering April 22- August 25, 1813, submitted by Samuel Danbury at the settlement of the estate of Sylvester Doyle in 1814. Doyle was the owner of the Bull's Head Tavern on State Street in Trenton. Collection of the Trenton Historical Society, Trentoniana Room, Trenton, New Jersey.

[33] Trenton enjoyed a storied past. Settled by Quakers in 1679, its earliest designation was "Falls by the River." By 1719, it was called "Trent towne" after William Trent one of the largest landowners in the area and perhaps the most prominent man in the early days of the city.

During the American Revolution, the city was the venue for Washington's first victory over the British. On December 26, 1776, George Washington and his army, after a treacherous crossing of the icy Delaware River, defeated three regiments of Hessian garrisoned there. Trenton even served as the young nation's capital during the months of November and December 1784.

In Samuel Danbury's youth and early adulthood, he watched much of Trenton take shape. The first statehouse was built in 1794 on West State Street, and construction concluded on Trenton's first bridge across the Delaware River in 1806. The old State Bank began operations in 1813. For the average businessman, the most desirable locations lay on the southern ends of Warren and Greene Streets, where much of the political and economic infrastructure of the city stood. The State House—and the Old City Hall when it was completed in 1837—along with many of the better hotels and taverns did an enviable business in this part of the city. Not surprisingly, the first city directory shows Samuel Danbury's butcher shop at the "foot of Warren Street."[33] As we have seen, Samuel Danbury rented a stall in the public market too, but his biggest blocks of income came from his commercial customers who owned the many different hotels and taverns in Trenton. For example, he supplied meats—veal, lamb, beef and mutton—to Sylvester Doyle's Bull's Head Tavern on State Street almost from the time he first started in business.

In Colonial times, the State of New Jersey was divided into East Jersey and West Jersey, collectively known as the Jerseys. Later, the "Division Line Run of 1743" redefined these two massive chucks of land (*See* map). Burlington was the first county created in New Jersey (1677) and included almost all of the land in West Jersey. In fact, it included the modern counties of Hunterdon, Mercer, Camden, Gloucester, and Cape May. When Hunterdon County was carved out of Burlington County in 1714, Trenton sat at the very bottom of this new county on the shores of the Delaware River. When Mercer County was created in 1838, Trenton wound up in the southwest corner of it. Until Samuel

Danbury died on July 4, 1868 at the age of seventy-eight, Trenton remained in Mercer County (as it does today).

[34] Hewitt, 19-21, 28, 43.; "Post Roads of New Jersey," Journal of the New Jersey Postal History Society, Vol. 32, No. 2, pp. 58-9. at http://njpostalhistory.org/media/archive/154-may04njph.pdf (accessed 03-14-2012)

[35] Walker et al., 370-372. Scales's Presidents and Directors of the Trenton Water Works began operation in 1804 (near the old reservoir), and managed to supply downtown Trenton until it was combined with other entrepreneurial ventures about mid-century. Note: The Fifth Ward, referred to in Walker's work, was not actually laid out until 1852. Trenton only had four wards at the time Scales's aqueduct project commenced operations. Walker uses the term "Fifth Ward" only as a quick reference to the location of Scales's farm.

[36] In the American colonies, British money was used regularly. Banks in each colony issued their own paper money, but pounds, shillings and pence continued in use. After the United States adopted the dollar as its unit of currency and accepted the gold standard, one British shilling was worth 24 US cents. Shortages of US coins caused the shilling to stay in use well into the nineteenth century.

[37] Walker et al., 339-342. The 1859 Trenton City Directory shows thirty-two butchers at a time when the city had a population of 17,200. It is reasonable to assume that in 1811, when Samuel Danbury began his shop and the city had a population of 3,800, there were probably about seven butchers.

[38] "Trenton Courts," Trenton State Gazette, January 16, 1856, 4.

[39] "Trenton Courts," Trenton State Gazette, January 17, 1856, 3.

[40] Bowlby (1973), 4-5. Sigmund Freud first gave systematic study to separation anxiety in 1926 in *Inhibitions, Symptoms and Anxiety*. Up to that time, Freud freely admitted he had "paid insufficient attention to the child's attachment to his mother . . .[and] he had paid correspondingly little to the anxiety exhibited on the separation from her."[40] However, Freud insisted on viewing everything through the prism of sexuality. The English psychoanalyst John Bowlby summed up Freud's conclusion this way, "Because 'children . . . behave from an early age as if their dependence on the people looking after them were in the nature of sexual love' and because in a separation situation the child's libido goes unsatisfied, Freud concluded that a child deals with the situation just as an adult would, namely by turning his libido into anxiety'. Four years later, this is also his explanation of the separation anxiety . . . 'It was this increased affection for his mother which turned suddenly into anxiety.'" Freud's daughter and fellow psychoanalyst Anna Freud went a step further than her father in that she studied the infants and children removed from London during World War II. For safety sake, the children of London were removed to the English countryside. Anna Freud, with help from Dorothy Burlingham, opened the Hampstead Nurseries in 1940. This gave her thousands of subjects to study, allowing her to codify the results of separation from parents and primary caregivers. In two unpretentious booklets, published in 1842 and 1844 with Dorothy Burlingham, Anna Freud offers comments that are sharp and images that are telling. Again John Bowlby capsulizes, "States of

anxiety and depression that occur during adult years, and also psychopathic conditions, can, it is held, be linked in a systematic way to the states of anxiety, despair, and detachment . . . that are so readily engendered whenever a young child is separated for long from his mother figure, whenever he expects such a separation, and when, as sometimes happens, he loses her altogether. . . .In these troubled states of early childhood, it is held, can be discerned the prototype of many a pathological condition of later years."

[41] Ibid, 6.

[42] The woman that Lydia called grandmother—Widow J. Clayton—was the mother of Lydia's Uncle John A. Clayton—his wife Elizabeth was Lydia's aunt. Lydia obviously had two grandmothers—Danbury and Ruckel. Elizabeth was Mary Ruckel's sister, and Widow Clayton was grandmother to Elizabeth's children (Lydia's cousins). Naturally, Lydia thought of this woman, Widow J. Clayton, as her grandmother too.

[43] In 1699, New Egypt was a 2,700-acre land grant to Clement Plumsted of London, a man who never visited America. "Plumsted's was the earliest known name for New Egypt.
U. S. Census Records, 1830. It is clear in browsing the 1830 and 1840 U.S. Census Records that all the residents of New Egypt (and surrounding towns) were included in Upper Freehold Township in Monmouth County. Plumstead Township was not created until 1845 when New Egypt was also incorporated. Ocean County—which New Egypt is part of today—was not created until 1850.

[44] Ellis, 633. A fulling mill took rough, homemade cloth and turned it into the flat, smooth workable fabric similar to that bought in dry good stores for use in making clothing, drapes, bedding and other household items.

[45] In an interview with a reporter (The Sun, NY, July 8, 1871, 1), Lydia's sister Ann mistakenly said that Lydia had been raised in Houtenville, New Jersey, once a village near Rahway—about ten miles from Ann Nafey's home in New Brunswick. Obviously, she was confused. Since all sources agree that Lydia was raised in the New Egypt area—near the Pine Barrens in southern New Jersey—Ann Nafey obviously meant Hornerstown (five miles north of New Egypt and considered part of that unincorporated census area) in Upper Freehold Township, Monmouth County, New Jersey. (Interestingly, Halsted Wainwright on page 24 of his *History of Monmouth County: 1664-1920*, referred to Hornerstown as Hornersville. This suggests that in the early 1800's, towns in rural New Jersey—especially on the margins of the Pine Barrens—were inchoate by nature and their names changed often.)
Lydia called her uncle "John Claygay" to protect him and his family, but the name Claygay never appears in the U.S. Census Records. After examining carefully the 1830 and 1840 U.S. Census Records, it is clear that Lydia first lived with a grandmother, Widow J. Clayton, in Hornerstown (1830 U.S. Census Records, Series M19, Roll 80, Pg. 342), and then helped out on the farm of her uncle and aunt, John A. and Elizabeth Clayton—and their children—beginning when she was seven or eight. The 1840 U.S. Census shows Widow J. Clayton (80-90 years old), living with her son, his wife and family. There were three children remaining on the Clayton farm when the

1840 U.S. Census was taken, as Lydia said. This means that Lydia removed to New Brunswick before the U.S. Census was taken in the summer of 1840. She would have been fifteen and a half years old. (1840 U.S. Census Records, Series M704, Roll 255, Pg. 206.)

Furthering the Clayton connection to Hornerstown is the proximity of John Clayton's name in the U.S. Census Records with a great many members of the Horner family—obviously descendants of Joshua Horner, who owned 150 acres plus a gristmill and a saw mill on Layaway Creek (see also Ellis, 615). Since the towns in the New Egypt area were all unincorporated, the individual town names were not mentioned. The only designation was Upper Freehold County. A great many different Horner families as well as that of John A. Clayton tilled the land covering the six miles between Imlaystown and Hornerstown.

As mentioned, Lydia made a surprising effort to protect the Clayton family. It was later retold that Lydia's brothers, John and Ellsworth, found her about 1840 living with an uncle in Camden, but facts don't support this. Since Camden County wasn't created until 1844, the only Camden was the tiny town across the Delaware River from Philadelphia. Lydia never lived there and never even mentioned it in any of her autobiographical pieces in the different newspapers. When her brother Ellsworth brought her back to New Brunswick in the spring of 1840, it was from the loving embrace of her Uncle John Clayton and his family in Hornerstown, Upper Freehold Township, Monmouth County, New Jersey.

[46] "The Poisoner," Hartford Daily Times, January 13, 1873, 2.
[47] "Confession of Lydia Sherman," New York Herald, January 13, 1873, 3.
[48] McPhee, 5. (The National Parks and Recreation Act of 1978 created the Pinelands National Reserve, which comprises 1.1 million acres—1,718 square miles—or 22% of New Jersey's total land mass.)
[49] Ibid, 63. For even something as simple as a legal marriage, a couple had to travel west of the Pinelands to Mt. Holly.
[50] Bice, 92.
[51] Rothstein, 12.
[52] Ellis, 632-35. One sideline that Dr. George Fort used to supplement his income—and simultaneously build his political career—was to collect information for the 1840 U.S. Census from 900 families in the New Egypt, Hornerstown, and Imlaystown sector of Upper Freehold Township. As Dr. Fort made house calls in the countryside, he used any spare time he had to stop at the farms en route to introduce himself and gather the necessary data. Monmouth has always been a big county, but this census work helped Dr. Fort build a good enough political base to win election to the New Jersey Constitutional Convention in 1844, an office that launched his career nicely.
[53] Starr, 32-3.
[54] Starr, 32, 42.
[55] Starr, 32.
[56] Starr, 34.
[57] "Clayton Park," at http://monmouthcountyparks.com/documents/130/clayton.pdf

(accessed 1/24/2012)

[58] "Lydia Sherman," New York Herald, April 22, 1872, 5.; "Lydia Sherman's Crimes," *The Sun* (NY), July 8, 1871, 1.

[59] Many of the Danburys, including Joseph, spelled their name differently than Samuel Danbury—the unfortunate outcome of illiteracy. The name of Joseph Danbury's firm was *Danberry & Pasco*. His brother Ellsworth spelled his name Dansburry. In an effort to give some uniformity to the family in this text, the earliest spelling—Danbury—is maintained throughout.

[60] U. S. Census Records, 1850, 1860, 1870 (Maria Danbury).

[61] "Lydia Sherman's Crimes," *The Sun* (NY), July 8, 1871, 1.; U. S. Census Records 1860, 1870.

[62] "Commutation & Commuters," *New Brunswick Times*, October 18, 1907, 2.

[63] "Court News," *Trenton State Gazette*, January 8, 1856, 2.

[64] "Lydia Sherman," *New York Herald,* April 22, 1872, 5.

[65] Wall, John P., Middlesex and New Brunswick Populations From 1737 to Present, New Brunswick Sunday Times, New Brunswick Free Public Library Collection.

[66] U.S. Census Records, 1810.; Biographical Encyclopedia, 88-9.; Public Laws of the State of New York. Albany, New York: H. C. Southwick, 1809.

[67] *Biographical Encyclopedia, 88-9.*; McManus, 165-67.

[68] Ibid, 88.

[69] In the early part of the 1800s, John Tway named his tavern Jacksonville Hotel, in honor of his political hero Andrew Jackson. For a time Lebanon was called Jacksonville, just as Lydia remembered it from the early 1840s. However, since there was already a Jacksonville in the southern part of the state, the bid to call the town Jacksonville was doomed. The Borough of Lebanon was known as Jacksonville until about mid-century, then Lebanonville and finally Lebanon.

[70] Ibid, 88-9.

[71] Ibid, 88-9.; Papers of Joseph Hawley, LOC; U.S. Census Records, 1850, 1860, 1870.

[72] "Confession of Lydia Sherman's," *New York Herald,* January 13, 1873, 3.

[73] Ibid.

[74] "Lydia Sherman," *New Brunswick Times,* May 17, 1878, 3.

[75] Ibid.

[76] "The Poisoner," *Hartford Daily Times,* January 13, 1873, 2.

Chapter 3

[77] "Confession of Lydia Sherman," *New York Herald,* January 13, 1873, 1.; "The Connecticut Murderess," *New York Herald,* November 14, 1871, 3.; In an interview with a report from the *Herald,* Ann Nafey states that Lydia married Edward Struck in 1846. (Ann Nafey was married in 1845.) Beyond that, Lydia told Capt. Charles Webster at the New Haven County jail that she was married to Edward Struck for eighteen years. Edward Struck died on May 26, 1864, which means the couple married in 1846. The State of New Jersey no longer has a record of this marriage.

[78] "Lydia Sherman," *New Brunswick Times,* May 17, 1878, 3. Carriages were almost unheard of in the United States before 1800 because the average family couldn't afford them and the roads were still so dismal that a carriage represented a poor investment indeed. Horse-drawn wagons were used on farms and in the trades, but the few fashionable carriages in America were imported from England and France. The carriage industry in America developed "almost simultaneously in many areas, with Wilmington, Newark, New Haven, Bridgeport, Philadelphia and New York among the early centers."[78] At first, a complete carriage was built in one location, but component parts producers sprouted apace. For many years, the New Haven Wheel Company was the largest maker of carriage wheels in the United States. With the common availability of separate components, it wasn't long before every town in America had a carriage maker. Still, New Haven ranked as one of the biggest carriage-making cities in the country. In 1811, a survey done by the president of Yale College showed nine carriage makers in New Haven, a number which bourgeoned to fifty-one by the outbreak of the Civil War.

[79] Ibid, 13.
[80] Ibid, 25, 21.
[81] Trow's New York City Directories, 1862, 1869.
[82] New York City Directories, 1849-1852, Doggett & Rode, 59 Liberty St., New York. Lydia's secretive ways surface with the city directories of New York. The Strucks were included in a couple of directories when they first moved to Manhattan, but then never appear again. By 1867, Lydia had left New York for good.
[83] New York (Manhattan) Wards and their Densities: 1800-1910 at http://www.demographia.com/db-nyc-ward1800.htm (accessed 09-24-2011)

As early as 1840, the population of New York had swelled to 300,000 and crime rose accordingly. Pickpockets and thieves of every description worked the docks, the horse car stops, the hotels and every other public venue of opportunity.[83] Lower Manhattan was becoming overrun with brothels, flophouses, tenements, grubby shops, and streets teeming with new immigrants looking for work. At times, the population density in the lower ten wards rose to 170,000 people per square mile. The Twelfth Ward—everything north of 86th Street—housed less than 13,000 people in the same space.

[84] Lankevich, 84-85.
[85] Lardner and Reppetto, 37.
[86] Ibid, 38.
[87] Ibid, 38.; "Greater New York," *New York Times,* May 9, 1897, 20.; "The New York of Today," *New York Times,* January 1, 1898, 4.
[88] Burrows & Wallace, 838-841.
[89] "Who Protect The City," *New York Daily Times,* August 12, 1857, 5.
[90] Haines, 184.
[91] Lardner and Reppetto, 63-4.
[92] Ibid, 97.
[93] Ibid, 65.
[94] Ibid, 50.

[95] Woolston, 17.
[96] Ibid, 21-22.
[97] Ibid, 19.
[98] Washington, 39.Ibid, 23.
[99] " Common Council; Home Department," *Spectator* (NY), May 9, 1850, 1.
[100] Haines, 204.
[101] "Manhattanville History: From Dairy Factories to University Expansion Zone," *Columbia Spectator*, March 25, 2008, n. p.
[102] Washington, 39.
[103] *Atlas of the Twelfth Ward, City of New York*, New York: E. Robinson, 1880.; "First Presbyterian Church, Manhattanville," *New York Times*, December 9, 1852, n.p.
[104] Rev. Edward Payson (Manhattan), Rev. Charles Henry Payson (Manhattan), Rev. Charles Payson Mallery (New York), Rev. Seth Payson (Rindge, NH), Rev. Edward Payson (Congregational), Rev. Edward Payson (Portland, ME), Rev Edward Payson (Chelsea, MA.), Rev. Edward Payson Terhune (Newark, NJ)— just to name a few. When describing the Payson clerics, the word *infamous* is in order for several reasons. To begin, the Paysons began as Congregationalist ministers but drifted into the Presbyterian Church as early as the end of the 1700s. The Presbyterian Church went through a disastrous schism in 1837, dividing its clerics among Old School Presbyterian (OSP) preachers and New School Presbyterian clerics. The root of this break was slavery, whereby the Old School Presbyterian ministers were allowed to keep their slaves (e.g. Rev. Frederick Thompson of Spring Hill, Tennessee), while the other branch of the church forbade slaveholding. The Civil War divided the Presbyterian Church even further and at one point a failed attempt was made at a merger with the Congregational Church in the Northwestern United States.
[105] US Census Records, 1860.
[106] TK
[107] Lardner and Reppetto, 97. The infamous "Clubber" Williams commanded the Tenderloin precinct for all but two of the years between 1876 and 1887, when a captain's official salary was $2,750. Yet in 1894, Williams acknowledged a net worth of $300,000.
[108] Ibid.
[109] Schechter , 6.
[110] "Confession of Lydia Sherman," *New York Herald*, January 13, 1873, 3.; Statistics of the United States in 1860, 11.
[111] "The Woman's Infirmary," *New York Tribune*, May 26, 1864, 6.; U. S. Census Records, 1860.
[112] Starr, 98-99.
[113] Ibid, 43.
[114] "Fast Men and City Roads," *New York Times*, -January 16, 1858, 4.
[115] The Police Among The Roughs," *New York Times*, November 5, 1863, 5.
[116] Ibid.
[117] Lardner and Reppetto, 68.
[118] "Homicide in the Thirteenth Precinct," *New York Times*, November 21, 1863, 5.

[119] Lardner and Reppetto, 21.
[120] "The Poisoner," *Hartford Daily Times,* January 13, 1873, 2.; *The Poison Fiend!,* 26.
[121] "Lydia Sherman," *New York Herald,* April 22, 1872, 5.
[122] Ibid.
[123] Ibid. Confession of Lydia Sherman," *New York Herald,* January 13, 1873, 3.
[124] Ibid.
[125] Ibid.
[126] Ibid.
[127] Ibid.
[128] "Lydia Sherman," *Hartford Daily Courant,* May 18, 1878, 1.
[129] Lydia said many times that regarding the poisonings, she never felt that she had done anything wrong. For the most part, these comments were made while she was doing time in the Connecticut Prison at Wethersfield (February 6, 1873 until her death on May 16, 1878). Note especially "Lydia Sherman," *Hartford Daily Courant,* May 18, 1878, 1.
[130] U. S. Census Records, 1860, 1870. Lydia knew she wouldn't see any policemen she knew because Harlem was in the Twelfth Precinct, while Manhattanville was in the Thirtieth.
[131] School, 88.
[132] Starr, 42.; *Current History: Monthly Magazine of the New York Times,* Vol. 16, p. 974. New York: New York Times, 1922.; Historical Statistics of the United States, Part 1, Bureau of the Census, 1875, 8. In 1860, the populations of France and the United States were 35,630,000 and 23,261,000, respectively.
[133] Rothstein, 292.; Starr, 42.
[134] "The Medical College and Medical Education in New York," *New York Times,* November 4, 1868, 4.
[135] "General News," *New York Herald,* May 26, 1864, 1.; "Commissioners of Health," *New York Herald,* May 26, 1864, 6.; "Medical News," *New York Herald,* May 26, 1864, 7.; *The Poison Fiend!,* 26.
[136] Ibid.
[137] Today that number is around 27,000. "Jefferson Medical College," at http://www.jefferson.edu/jmc/ (accessed January 13, 2012)
[138] "Jefferson Medical College," at http://www.jefferson.edu/jmc/ (accessed January 13, 2012); "Medical Schools in the U.S." *New York Daily Times,* October 5, 1852, 4.; "New York University—Medical Department," *New York Times,* October 22, 1851, 2.
[139] "Dr. Nathaniel C. Husted," *New York Times,* November 21, 1891, np.
[140] "The Poisoner," *Hartford Daily Times,* January 13, 1873, 2.
[141] "Mrs. Sherman's History," *The Sun* (NY)," July 8, 1871, 1.
[142] Vronsky, 37.
[143] Ibid, 43.
[144] TK
[145] TK
[146] Ibid.

[147] Konefes, J.L., and M.K. McGee. "Old Cemetaries, Arsenic, and Health Safety." *Water Industry News.* at http://www.waterindustry.org/arsenic-3.htm (accessed April 8, 2012).
[148] "The Influence of Geology and Land Use on Arsenic in Stream Sediments and Ground Waters in New England, USA." *Applied Geochemistry* 21 (2006): 1482-1497.; Bleiwas, D.I. *Arsenic and Old Waste.* February 22, 2000 at http://minerals.usgs.gov/minerals/mflow/d00-0195/ (accessed April 8, 2012).
[149] Bentley, R., and T.G. Chasteen. "Arsenic Curiosa and Humanity." *The Chemical Educator* 7, No. 2 (2002): 51-60.
[150] "The History of Poisons," *New York Times,* March 14, 1895, 2.
[151] Richmond, 289-98.
[152] "The Sherman Murder Trial," *Hartford Daily Courant,* April 17, 1872, 1. This particular newspaper article makes note of Lydia attire as she entered the courtroom on the first day of her murder trial in New Haven. However, throughout this text there are mentions of Lydia's taste in clothing, earrings, jewelry and assorted accoutrements.

Chapter 4

[153] "Board in Manhattanville," *New York Daily Tribune,* June 8, 1864, 2.
[154] "Confession of Lydia Sherman," *New York Herald,* January 13, 1873, 3. In hindsight, Lydia's decision to kill her children was predictable. Not only had Lydia learned as an infant that people who were in the way could be offloaded, she was also acting the way of most female sequential killers. Once again studies show that, "Historically, at least 70 percent of male sequential killers murder strangers only, while another 16 percent kill a combination of strangers with acquaintances or family. Some 8 percent of males murder acquaintances only and 3 percent family only.... This contrasts with the 34 percent of female sequentialists who kill family only and 19 percent who kill acquaintances only...."
[155] "General News," *New York Tribune,* July 4, 1864, 4.
[156] Ibid. None of the traditional research tools show a Dr. Oviatt practicing medicine in New York during the 1860s. However, Lydia often had trouble remembering names of people and places. In the early 1970s—while Lydia was living in Derby, Connecticut—the town Health Officer was Dr. George Oviatt, undoubtedly the inspiration for the mix-up. In her confession to Capt. Charles Webster at the New Haven County jail, Lydia was undoubtedly referring to the Yale-educated obstetrician, Dr. Augustus G. Elliott, who practiced in Manhattanville during the 1860s.
[157] "Confession of Lydia Sherman," *New York Herald,* January 13, 1873, 3.
[158] Ibid.; *The Poison Fiend!,* 26-7
[159] Starr, 58.
[160] "Medical Practice Act," *Hartford Courant,* April 28 1893, 9.
[161] "Confession of Lydia Sherman," *New York Herald,* January 13, 1873, 3.
[162] "Mrs. Sherman's History," *The Sun* (NY)," July 8, 1871, 1. With the post-war nursing shortage, it makes perfect sense, although this cannot be verified because hospital employment records don't go back that far

[163] "Our City Railroads," *New York Times*, December 26, 1865, 8.; "Confession of Lydia Sherman," *New York Herald*, January 13, 1873, 3.
[164] Ibid.
[165] "Confession of Lydia Sherman," *New York Herald*, January 13, 1873, 3.
[166] "Dr. Louis A. Rodenstein," *New York Times*, February 1, 1915, 9.
[167] Washington, 47.; "Dr. Louis A. Rodenstein," *New York Times*, February 1, 1915, 9.
[168] "Dr. Louis A. Rodenstein," *New York Times*, February 1, 1915, 9.
[169] "Confession of Lydia Sherman," *New York Herald*, January 13, 1873, 3.
[170] Starr, 94-5.
[171] Starr, 91.
[172] Carnegie Foundation, Bulletin Number Four, 1910, (Flexner Report).
[173] Starr, 112.
[174] "The Poison Fiend!," 27.
[175] Ibid.;
[176] Trow, 1862, 1869, 1873.
[177] Starr, 63. Again, the most significant factor tying doctors' hands was the ever-increasing supply of physicians. By the middle of the 1800s, there were 40,000 practitioners compared to the 5,000 that exited as the century began. The barriers to entry into the profession were practically nonexistent. As the number of medical schools skyrocketed—schools that offered quick degrees for a minimal investment—the total cost of a medical education remained low while the number of new practitioners increased without restriction.[177]

The first compulsory three-year grade curriculum was instituted at Harvard Medical School in 1871, when a nine-month term each year was also adopted. This reduced to school's enrollment, which forced the school to place the medical school faculty on a salaried basis—a marked change from the routine at other medical schools. "Altogether 10 medical schools—8 regular and 2 homeopathic—adopted compulsory three-year grade curricula during the 1870s and 33 medical schools—one quarter of the total—adopted a three-year grade curriculum by 1889."[177]

Another point of concern was the number of matriculating medical students who had little or no college education before medical school. Dr. Frederick Waite carefully analyzed the previous education of a large number of students who attended medical school between 1830 and 1856 by examining the alumni catalogs of all colleges of arts in New England and New York State . . . "He found 7% of the students had obtained a degree of Bachelor of Arts and another 10% had matriculated at a liberal arts college prior to attending medical college. . . . Charles W. Elliot, the president of Harvard College, carried out another study. He found that less than 10% of the medical students at Dartmouth, Bellevue hospital, Pennsylvania, Northwestern, and Michigan had BA degrees. At Harvard and Columbia the same study produced a figure of 19 percent. (The percentages were much higher in the New England schools than in those of the Midwest.)"[177]

In the years after the Civil War, the medical profession in New York could be thought of as a series of concentric circles. The nucleus of this collection of physicians was the "hospital men"—a tiny group of doctors who held half the attending positions at the hospitals. The circle just outside this nucleus was composed of members of the New York Academy of Medicine—the attendant medical society. The final ring was the County Medical Society—open to all regular physicians. At the time, there were about 800 of these physicians in greater New York. The overwhelming majority of allopaths were only allowed to join the New York County Medical Society.

While the members of New York's medical societies were trying to elevate the level of medical education, their own city was becoming the center of homeopathy in the United States. Curiously, many of the homeopaths of New York City were among the better-educated physicians in the city. "New York homeopaths, like those in Boston, considered themselves regular physicians. . . . these homeopaths rapidly developed a wide variety of homeopathic therapeutics."

Bloodletting, calomel, and other elements of heroic medical therapy were beliefs that were in the descendent in the second half of the nineteenth century. "Bonner's history of medicine in Chicago found that heroic therapy declined in the 1860s. Rosenberg study of medical practice in New York City in the 1860s found a decrease at that time in the extensive use of bloodletting. The use of emetics and cathartics declined about the same time. For instance, New York's Bellevue hospital purchased no calomel and little jalap in 1866."

[178] *The Poison Fiend!*, 27.
[179] "Confession of Lydia Sherman," *New York Herald*, January 13, 1873, 3.
[180] U.S. Census Reports, 1860, 1870.; "The Poisoner," *Hartford Daily Times*, January 13, 1873, 2. The village of Sailorsville—or Saylorsville—no longer exists. The land where the village once sat is inside Hickory Run State Park, Pennsylvania.
[181] Ibid.
[182] Rosenstone et al, Appendix A.
[183] "Confession of Lydia Sherman," *New York Herald*, January 13, 1873, 3.

Chapter 5

[184] Marriage Record of Dennis Hurlbut, 73 and Lydia Struck, 43—white "peddler" and white "tailoress," respectively—Shelton Vital Records, Shelton Town Hall, Hill St., Shelton, CT.
(When Ole Hurlbut married Lydia in November of the same year, the marriage record lists him as a peddler, so it's not entirely certain what Ole Hurlbut thought he was.)
[185] "Brief History of Shelton," at http://nynjctbotany.org/lgtofc/sheltonhistory.html (accessed 08/21/2011).
[186] Hall of Records, Town Hall, Shelton, CT. Vol. 11, 244; Vol. 11, 218; Vol. 12, 376; Vol. 12, 539,; Vol. 12, 539; Vol. 12, 824; Vol. 14, 121; Vol. 15, 457; Vol. 16, 352.
[187] Shelton Land Records, Vol. 11, p. 244, October 6, 1828; Vol. 11, p. 28; Vol. 12, p. 376, December 2, 1835; Vol. 12, p. 500, February 16, 1836; Vol. 12, p. 539, March 25, 1837; Vol. 12, p. 824, March 29, 1824; Vol. 14, p. 121, August

24, 1850; Vol. 16, p. 352, July 12, 1855; Vol. 15, p. 457, April 27, 1857, Shelton Town Hall, Hill St., Shelton, CT.
[188] Derby, DHS, 2.
[189] Hand drawn map of 1848 Derby, reissued in 1876 by the Derby Savings Bank at http://derbyhistorical.org/Maps/1848mapN.gif (Accessed November 11, 2011.)
[190] American shad, or Alosa sapidissima, meaning "most delicious," swim upstream from marine waters to spawn in the springtime. Kevin Murphy, Fly Fishing in Connecticut, Wesleyan University Press, 2012, 4.
[191] Shelton Land Records, Vol. 12, p. 500, February 15, 1836, Shelton Town Hall, Hill St., Shelton, CT.
[192] "Lydia Sherman," The Spectator, Vol. 46, 1873, London: John Campbell, 1 Wellington Street, Strand.
[193] "The Sherman Trial," New Brunswick Daily Times, April 22, 1872, n.p.
[194] where you girls were carding and source of that where you girls were carding and is able to come here lately asked to request is in the people that come election day estimate questions physically estimate questions will use a state library law from you do
[195] "Confession of Lydia Sherman," New York Herald, January 13, 1873, 3.
[196] Ibid.
[197] "The Poisoner," Hartford Daily Times, January 13, 1873, 1.
[198] Columbia University, 212.
[199] Columbia University Bulletin, 15.
[200] Ibid, 15.
[201] "The Wholesale Poisoning," Hartford Daily Courant," July 8, 1871, 1.
[202] "The Connecticut Borgia," The Sun (New York), July 6, 1871, 1.
[203] 'The Murderess, Lydia Sherman," New York Times, June 1, 1877, 8.; Probate records, including inventory of Dennis Hurlbut, Hall of Records, Hill Street, Shelton, CT.
[204] "Derby's Lucretia Borgia," Hartford Daily Courant, July 10, 1871, 1.
[205] "The Woman Monster," Hartford Daily Courant, July 4, 1871, 1.
[206] "Confession of Lydia Sherman," New York Herald, January 13, 1873, 3.
[207] Ibid.

Chapter 6

[208] Sherman, Rev. Andrew, (1904), 727-28.; Sherman, Rev. Andrew, 115, 46.
[209] Colonel Jeremiah O'Brien of Machias, Maine had a daughter named Lydia (1804-1898), but the infant was not the child of his wife Elizabeth (Fitzpatrick) O'Brien, but rather the illegitimate child of the colonel's housekeeper Thankful Whitney (1780-1864). Thankful Whitney was born in Columbia, Maine to Captain Nathan Whitney and Patience Barnard. Thankful Whitney left the child to be raised by Colonel O'Brien when she married Isaac Meader of Tamworth, New Hampshire.
Lydia Whitney's illegitimacy was hushed up for more than a century because Colonel Jeremiah O'Brien was a highly respected Revolutionary War hero. Only recently has the truth about Lydia Whitney O'Brien Sherman—bearing her

mother's surname—been brought to light. Lydia Whitney O'Brien married Aaron Simmons Sherman, the builder, of Marshfield, Massachusetts, and the couple eventually settled in Bridgewater, Massachusetts and had thirteen children. (Although just speculation, Lydia Whitney Sherman's pretentiousness may have derived from her illegitimacy.)
(This information was supplied by Richard Hall, the gr-gr-gr-grandson of Colonel Jeremiah O'Brien and his housekeeper, Thankful Whitney. Richard Hall's gr-gr-grandmother was Lydia Whitney O'Brien, and his gr-grandmother was Amelia Bartlett (Sherman) Perkins, the fourth child of Aaron Simmons Sherman and Lydia Whitney Sherman.)

[210] Sherman, Rev. Andrew, (1904), 729.; Sherman, George, 24-26.
[211] Ibid.
[212] Ibid. The children of Lydia & Aaron Sherman of Bridgewater, Massachusetts were: Horatio Nelson Sherman (b. 1824), Lydia Leavitt (b. 1825), Isaac Winslow (b. 1827), Amelie Bartlett (b. 1829), Ann Abbott (b. 1831, twin), Ebeneezer Lester (b. 1831, twin), Helen Crooker (b, 1834), Nathan Lazell (b. 1836), George Witherell (b. 1838), Jacob Perkins (b. 1840), Lucy Lovell (1842), Andrew Magoun (b. 1844), and Charles Lester (b. 1846).
[213] Ibid.; Allen, 43-45.
[214] Sherman, George, 88.
[215] Griffith, Richard W. (trans). Wareham Marriages and Intentions, 1996.; Vital Records of Wareham, Massachusetts, Town Hall, Wareham, MA.
[216] Smith, 248.
[217] "Comparing Energy Costs..." at http://nuclearfissionary.com/2010/04/02/comparing-energy-costs-of-nuclear-coal-gas-wind-and-solar/
(accessed 4/1/2012) Waterpower costs vary widely depending on the water source, the efficiency of the different components &c. However, it is generally accepted that waterpower runs 50 percent of the cost of coal power.
[218] Sherman, Rev. Andrew, (1915), 915-941.; "The Woman Monster," *Hartford Daily Courant*, July 4, 1871,1.
[219] Ibid, 916-917.
[220] U. S. Census Record, 1870.
[221] Sherman, George W., 39.
[222] Sherman, Rev. Andrew, (1915), 915-941.
[223] Murphy, (2010), 47.
[224] Sherman, Rev. Andrew, (1904), 45-46.
[225] Sherman, Rev. Andrew, (1915), 915-941.
[226] Ibid.; Connecticut Borgia," *New York World*, July 4, 1871, 3.; Derby Land Records, Vol. 39, p. 48, June 21, 1856, City Hall, Elizabeth St., Derby.
[227] "Confession of Lydia Sherman," *New York Herald*, January 13, 1873, 3.
[228] Confession of Lydia Sherman, *New York Herald*, January 13, 1873, 1.
[229] Derby Land Records, Town Hall, Elizabeth St., Derby, CT, Vol. 40, p. 452., May 12, 1859. In this transaction, for $2000, Hiram Kilbourne assumed the mortgage on "the old Hinman place," free of all encumbrances except Derby Savings Bank ($1000) and Nelson Hinman ($500).
[230] Ibid.

[231] "The Connecticut Borgia," *The Sun (NY)*, July 6, 1871, 1.
[232] Vital Records of Bridgewater, Massachusetts, Town Hall, Bridgewater, MA.
[233] "Confession of Lydia Sherman," *New York Herald*, January 13, 1873, 3.
[234] "Death of Dr. Ambrose Beardsley," *Hartford Daily Courant*, October 31, 1884, 4.
[235] Smith 293.
[236] Ibid.
[237] "Confession of Lydia Sherman," *New York Herald*, January 13, 1873, 3.
[238] "Snow Storm and Duties," *Hartford Daily Courant*, December 30, 1870, 2.;
[239] "The Woman Monster," *Hartford Daily Courant*, July 4, 1871, 1.
[240] *The Poison Fiend!*, 37.
[241] Brandy slings are brandy, water, sugar and lemon concoctions used as sedatives.
[242] Proceedings of the Connecticut Medical Society, 1880, 162; Cushing / Whitney Medical Historical Library, Yale University, New Haven, CT; Donald Lines Jacobus, *Families of Ancient New Haven* ([CD]Baltimore, Genealogical Publishing Co., Inc., 1981[originally]Rome, N.Y. and New Haven, Conn., 1922-1932), Vol. 3, 591.; Compiled by Carole Magnuson, The Barbour Collection of Connecticut Town Vital Records - Oxford 1798-1850., General Editor, Lorraine Cook White, Baltimore, Genealogical Publishing Co., Inc., 2000, 41, 42, 68.
[243] Munson, 1054.
[244] "Confession of Lydia Sherman," *New York Herald*, January 13, 1873, 3.; "Weather Reports," *Hartford Daily Courant*, December 23, 1870, 1.; "Snow Storm and Winter Duties," *Hartford Daily Courant*, December 31, 1870, 2.
[245] Temperance Societies have a long history in the United States, and they practiced under many different names. The "Grand Division Sons of Temperance was very active in the factory towns of Connectiuct after the Civil War, and operated under a "grand worthy patriarch." By the fall of 1870, there were 45 divisions in the state with a total membership in excess of 3,000 persons. (*Hartford Daily Courant*, October 28, 1870, 2.)
[246] *The Poison Fiend!*, 20.
[247] "Confession of Lydia Sherman," *New York Herald*, January 13, 1873, 3.
[248] Ibid.
[249] Rev. Andrew Sherman, (1915), 1029.; *The Poison Fiend!*, 67-8.
[250] Among Parker's contributions to medicine were the cystotomy, for the relief of chronic cystitis; a second operation for the cure of abscess of appendix veriformis; and still another procedure to treat laceration of the perineum during childbirth, cured by the severance of the coccygeal attachment of the sphincter and closure of the perineum with sutures. Lastly, he helped convert New York's Bellevue from an almshouse to a charity hospital in 1845.)[250] Charles Pinney received his M.D. in 1853 and without delay he began his medical practice in Derby. Spalding, 326.
[251] Ibid.
[252] "The Connecticut Borgia," *The Sun* (New York), July 6, 1871, 1.
[253] "Confession of Lydia Sherman," *New York Herald*, January 13, 1873, 3.
[254] Ibid.

[255] Rothstein, 285.
[256] Ibid.
[257] Youmans, 576, 693-97.
[258] *The Poison Fiend!*, 28-9.

Chapter 7

[259] "Lydia Sherman's Crimes," *The Sun* (N.Y.), July 8, 1871, 1.
[260] "The Connecticut Murderess," *New York Times,* July 4, 1871, 8.
[261] Ibid.; "The Connecticut Borgia," *The Sun* (N.Y.), July 6, 1871, 1.
[262] "The Connecticut Borgia," *The Sun* (N.Y.), July 6, 1871, 1.
[263] "The Woman Monster," *Hartford Daily Courant,"* July 4, 1871, 1.
[264] Ibid.; "The Wholesale Poisoning," *Hartford Daily Courant,* July 8, 1871, 1.
[265] "The Connecticut Murderess," *New York Times,* July 4, 1871, 8.
[266] Ibid.
[267] "The Connecticut Borgia," *The Sun* (N.Y.), July 6, 1871, 1.
[268] "Lydia Sherman's Crimes," *The Sun* (N.Y.), July 8, 1871, 1.
[269] Ibid.
[270] Ibid.
[271] *The Poison Fiend!*, 25.
[272] Ibid.
[273] Ibid.
[274] "The Great Modern Borgia," *The Sun* (N.Y.), July 4, 1871, 1.
[275] State Bar Association of Connecticut, Connecticut Bar Association (1931), The Grand Jury in Connecticut, Nahum and Schatz, 111.
[276] Ibid.
[277] *The Poison Fiend!*, 25.
[278] "The Connecticut Borgia," *The Sun* (N.Y.), July 6, 1871, 1.
[279] Ibid.
[280] "The Woman Monster," *Hartford Daily Courant,* January 4, 1871, 1.
[281] "The Connecticut Borgia," *The Sun* (N.Y.), July 6, 1871, 1.
[282] Ibid.
[283] Ibid.
[284] "Lydia Sherman's Trial," *The Sun* (NY), July 7, 1871, 1.
[285] "Nathan's Hall," at http://electronicvalley.org/derby/quiz/Pages/Gould's_Armory.htm (Accessed 12/8/2011).
[286] Ibid.
[287] "The Birmingham Borgia," *New York Herald,* July 7, 1871, 6.
[288] Connecticut Reports, Memorials of Connecticut Judges and Attorneys, Vol. 57, p. 592-595.
[289] "Lydia Sherman's Trial," *The Sun (NY),* July 7, 1871, 1.
[290] State Bar Association of Connecticut, Connecticut Bar Association (1931), The Grand Jury in Connecticut, Nahum and Schatz, 111.
[291] Ibid.
[292] "Lydia Sherman's Trial," *The Sun* (NY), July 7, 1871, 1.
[293] Ibid.

[294] Ibid.
[295] A mustard plaster is a cataplasm (soft moist mass) of mustard seed powder spread inside a protective dressing and applied to the chest or stomach to stimulate healing.
[296] Ibid.
[297] The generic name for Pepto Bismol is bismuth subsalicylate.
[298] *The Poison Fiend!*, 22, 25.
[299] Ibid.
[300] "Lydia Sherman's Trial," *The Sun* (NY), July 7, 1871, 1.
[301] Ibid.
[302] *The Poison Fiend!*, 54.
[303] Ibid.
[304] "Mrs. Sherman's Crimes," *The Sun* (NY), July 8, 1871, 1.
[305] Ibid.
[306] "The Birmingham Borgia," *New York Herald*, July 7, 1871, 6.
[307] "*Lydia Sherman's Crimes,*" *The Sun* (NY), July 8, 1871, 1.
[308] Blakesman's conversation with Lydia on the train back to Derby....TK
[309] "Lydia Sherman's Crimes," *The Sun (NY)*, July 8, 1871, 1.
[310] "Poison in Connecticut," *The Sun* (NY), July 11, 1871, 1.
[311] Ibid.
[312] Parker's Criminal Cases, 6th Vol., p. 610. Roscoe's Criminal Evidence, 93.

Chapter 8

[313] "State Items," *Hartford Daily Courant*, November 13, 1871, 4.; "The Sherman Murder Trial," *New York Herald*, November 14, 1871, 3.; "Telegraphic Items," *Hartford Daily Courant*, January 30, 1872, 3.; "State Items," *Hartford Daily Courant*, February 14, 1872, 4.
Lydia's trial was first scheduled for mid-November 1871. It was then pushed to the December docket. Later it was scheduled for the end of January, but had to be moved to Wednesday February 7, 1872. Finally, on February 21, it was announced that the trial would not begin until April. It got underway Tuesday, April 16, 1872.
[314] In Alexander Wynter Blyth's book *Poisons and their Effects* (pub. by C. Griffin, 1884), the author notes: "The analogy between the symptoms produced by arsenic and antimony is striking, and in some acute cases of tartar emetic poisoning, there is but little (if any) clinical difference. . . ."
[315] "Editorial Article 4-No Title," *Hartford Daily Courant*, April 16, 1872, 2.
[316] "The "Insanity Defence and Diminished Capacity," at http://www.law.cornell.edu/background/insane/insanity.html (accesed April 8, 2012)
[317] Rockey, Vol. 1, 125.; Osterweis, 273.; Atwater, 463.
[318] "Connecticut's Courts," at http://www.jud.state.ct.us/Publications/es201.pdf (Accessed April 8, 2012)
[319] "The Sherman Murder Trial," *Hartford Daily Courant*, April 17, 1872, 1.
[320] "The Trial of Lydia Sherman," *Boston Daily Advertiser*, April 17, 1872, 1.

[321] *The Poison Fiend!*, 30-92.; "The Sherman Trial in New Haven," *Hartford Daily Courant,* April 16-27, 1871.; The pamphlet, *The Poison Fiend!,* contains the most complete representation of what happened at Lydia Sherman's trial. By supplementing this with articles from the New Haven Register, New Haven Palladium, New York Times, New York Herald, New York Tribune, The Sun, and the Hartford Courant, a fairly concise picture of the Lydia Sherman trial emerges. The author has searched the most obvious sources for the original trial testimony, but apparently it is no longer extant.
[322] "The Sherman Trial At New Haven," *Hartford Daily Courant,* April 18, 1872, 3.
[323] Ibid.
[324] *The Poison Fiend!*, 41.
[325] Ibid.
[326] *The Poison Fiend!*, 43-4.
[327] Ibid, 43-4.
[328] Ibid, 44.
[329] Ibid, 44.
[330] Ibid, 44-5.
[331] Ibid, 46.
[332] Ibid, 46.
[333] Ibid, 46.
[334] Ibid, 49.
[335] Ibid, 49.
[336] Ibid, 49.
[337] Ibid, 49.
[338] Ibid, 51.
[339] Ibid, 52.
[340] Ibid, 53.
[341] Ibid, 54.
[342] *"The Poison Fiend!,",* 54.
[343] Ibid, 54.
[344] Ibid. 54.
[345] Ibid, 54.
[346] "The Sherman Murder Trial," *Hartford Daily Courant,* April 19, 1872, 3.
[347] Ibid, 57.
[348] Ibid, 57.
[349] Ibid, 60.
[350] Ibid, 57.
[351] *"The Poison Fiend!,",* 57.
[352] Ibid, 58.
[353] *Ibid, 59..*
[354] Ibid, 59.
[355] Ibid, 59.
[356] Ibid, 61-2.
[357] "The Sherman Murder Trial in New Haven," *Hartford Daily Courant,* April 22, 1872, 2.
[358] *The Poison Fiend!,,* 62.

[359] "The Sherman Murder Trial," *Hartford Daily Courant,* April 24, 1872, 3.
[360] Ibid.
[361] Ibid, 62, 65.
[362] Ibid, 65.
[363] Ibid. 65
[364] Ibid, 65-6.
[365] Ibid, 66.
[366] Ibid, 66-7.
[367] Ibid, 67.
[368] Ibid, 68.
[369] Ibid, 69.
[370] Ibid, 69.
[371] Ibid, 69-70.
[372] Ibid, 69-70.
[373] Ibid, 74.
[374] Ibid, 74.
[375] "The Sherman Murder Trial," *Hartford Daily Courant,* April 24, 1872, 3.
[376] No Headline, *Cincinnati Daily Enquirer,* April 28, 1872, 9. Repr of a story in the *New York Herald,* April 24, 1872, n.p.; "State Items," *Hartford Daily Courant,* April 24, 1872, 2.
[377] Ibid.
[378] Ibid.
[379] "The Sherman Murder Trial," *Hartford Daily Courant,* April 25, 1872, 3.
[380] Ibid, 77-8.
[381] Ibid, 78.
[382] "Trial of Mrs. Sherman," *New York Times,* April 25, 1872, 5.
[383] Derby Land Records, Vol. 40, p. 452, May 12, 1859. "$2000 and Hiram Kilbourne assumes mortgage on the 'old Hinman place' on the SW corner of Minerva and Fourth Streets . . .free of all encumbrances except Derby Savings Bank $1000 and Nelson Hinman $500. Since Nelson Sherman bought the place for $2050 three years before, and it now had debts against it of $3500, it's clear that Nelson Sherman and his family had plunged the property into debt, and eventually it was rescued by his employer, E.N. Shelton. At least the Shermans had a place to live, even if the Hubbards lived on the north side since 1859.
[384] *The Poison Fiend!,*, 81.
[385] Ibid, 82-3.
[386] *The Poison Fiend!,*, 83.
[387] Ibid, 83-4.
[388] Ibid, 84-4.
[389] Ibid, 85.
[390] "The Sherman Murder Trial," *Hartford Daily Courant,* April 26, 1872, 3.
[391] *The Poison Fiend!,*, 91.
[392] Ibid, 91-2.
[393] "Weather 1-No Title," *Hartford Daily Courant,* April 26, 1872, 3.
[394] "End of the Sherman Murder Trial," *Hartford Daily Courant,* April 27, 1872, 3.

[395] "Lydia Sherman: An Exciting Day," *New York Herald,* April 27, 1872, 5.
[396] Ibid.
[397] "End of the Sherman Trial," *Hartford Daily Courant,* April 27, 1872, 3.; "State Items," *Hartford Daily Courant,* May 6, 1872, 4.
[398] Trumbull, 352.; "State Convicts Women…," *Hartford Courant,* March 29, 1959, 1B.
[399] *The Poison Fiend!,*, 92.

Chapter 9

[400] *The Poison Fiend,* 92-93.
[401] Vronsky, 38.; Shurman-Kauflin, 57.
[402] "News of the State," *Hartford Daily Courant,* January 13, 1873, 4.
[403] Ibid.
[404] "The Poisoner," *Hartford Weekly Times,* January 18, 1873, 16.
[405] Ibid.
[406] Ibid.
[407] "Reported Confession by Mrs. Sherman the Derby Poisoner," *New York Times,* January 4, 1873, 1.
[408] "The Poisoner," *Hartford Weekly Times,* January 18, 1873, 16.
[409] Ibid.
[410] "Mrs. Sherman, the Female Prisoner…," *Commercial Advertiser,* February 24, 1873, 1.
[411] "The Modoc Indian Trouble," *Hartford Daily Courant,* January 2, 1873, 2.; "News of the State," *Hartford Daily Courant,* February 22, 1873, 4.
[412] "Reported Confession of Mrs. Sherman," *New York Times,* January 4, 1873, 1.
[413] "The Poisoner," *Hartford Weekly Times,* January 18, 1873, 16.; "The Jail Commission," *Hartford Daily Courant,* January 3, 1873, 2.
[414] Vronsky, 37.
[415] Phelps, 88.; Architectural drawings for changes at the Wethersfield Prison, Bryant & Rogers, Hartford:1871, Connecticut State Library, Hartford. The first ship built in Connecticut—the whaler *Tryal*—was launched from Wethersfield in 1649. In colonial times, jaunty barks and brigs offloaded goods from Europe and the West Indies onto the docks at Wethersfield and these precious cargoes were stored in warehouses on the riverbank. The principal exports from Wethersfield were "horses, rye wheat, barley . . . wool, hemp, flax, cider, tar, and pitch." Imported goods from the West Indies included sugar, cotton, wool, rum and salt.[415] A major flood in 1692 cut off this oxbow from the river and subsequently a channel was dug to reestablish a connection to the Connecticut River.
[416] "Wethersfield: Deep in Cove," *Hartford Courant,* October 9, 2011, A1.
[417] Connecticut Legislature," *Hartford Daily Courant,* July 1, 1869, 1.
[418] Murphy, *Water for Hartford,* 105-107
[419] Phelps, 88. To modernize the prison, the Hartford architectural firm of Bryant and Rogers drew plans to remodel the fifty-six foot wide cellblock section

running across the front of the prison, completing their drawings in 1870. Despite the Panic of 1873 and the ensuing Long Depression of the 1870s, the renovations to the prison were mostly completed by late1876. Unlike latter times—when there were only two entrances to the prison—the inmates were watched carefully enough to allow five separate entrances and exits without much concern.

Wethersfield Prison adhered strictly to the Auburn System made famous by the sadistic Auburn warden Elam Lynds. He believed completely in the disciplinary power of the lash, and flogged prisoners for the mildest infractions. Inmates at Auburn died regularly as the aggressive Lynds abused and over-flogged them. Religious groups intervened and eventually a bill was passed at Albany limiting the use of the *cat*—a six-stranded whip—to six blows on the naked back for even the most serious infractions. The three outstanding features of the Auburn system were striped clothing, movement in lockstep and total silence. The stripped clothing consisted of cheap, rough cotton or wool garments—depending on the season—that were gaudy and singular enough to absolutely preclude escape. The lockstep was simple enough. When they shuffled about the facility, prisoners grabbed the elbow of the man in front of them and then turned their heads to the side. In this manner, they never saw their keepers or any other prisoners. Complete silence was the real crusher though. The lack of talking completely removed the prisoners' sense of self. The denial of speech made many of the prisoners complacent and completely obedient to the warden's orders.

[420] "The Connecticut State Prison," *New York Times*, October 11, 1874, 9.
[421] "The State Prison," *Hartford Daily Courant*, May 22, 1873, 2.
[422] "State Prison Investigation," *Hartford Daily Courant*, March 13, 1869, 2.; Phelps, 91.
[423] "Editorial Article 3-No Title," *Hartford Daily Courant*, March 30, 1875, 2.
[424] Ibid.
[425] "Mrs. Sherman's Trials," *New York Times*, June 7, 1877, 5.
[426] "Mrs. Lydia Sherman," *Hartford Daily Courant*, June 6, 1877, 2.; "A Trace of Mrs. Sherman," *Hartford Daily Courant*, June 2, 1877, 1. While living in Stratford, one of Lydia's chores was to buy groceries several times a week at Fairchild's general store in the center of the village. The owner of this store, John Fairchild, could trace his roots back centuries, as the graveyards of Stratford are filled with Fairchilds—and Curtises too. One day John Fairchild asked Lydia how she would like to keep the house for a man who recently lost his wife. Dennis Hurlbut's wife Almira was a seventy-five-year-old woman who suffered from dropsy and had passed away on September 8, 1868. Since Lydia was happy working for Mrs. Curtis, she was noncommittal with Fairchild—but curious. With a little prodding, Fairchild went further. He explained that the man was elderly and had a farm near the Housatonic River in Coram, Huntington (the southern part of today's Shelton, Connecticut). Lydia agreed to give it some thought.

In all of her later statements, Lydia casts herself as a woman badly put upon by life. During moments of weakness—when she felt "downhearted and discouraged"—she resorted to arsenic administration. But when it came to the widower Dennis Hurlbut, this myth doesn't hold water. Though Hurlbut did in fact pursue her, Lydia was in it for the money. Whether arsenic entered the picture because she didn't think Hurlbut was dying quickly enough or whether Lydia planned the trajectory of his decline from the start can only be surmised. Lydia revealed that she asked Dennis Hurlbut to get some arsenic to take care of the rats around the place. Hurlbut, in turn, asked his friend Henry Northrop to pick some up for him next time he was in town. Inexplicably, Northrop's wife, Jane, objected. She explained, "If Dennis Hurlbut wanted arsenic, he could buy it himself."

This seemed intuitive beyond explanation, since Lydia hadn't killed anyone in Connecticut yet. Had information about the demise of Edward Struck—not to mention five of the couple's six children in Manhattanville—followed Lydia to the banks of the Housatonic River in southwestern Connecticut?

[427] "Social and Political," repr. of *Augusta Chronicle* item, *Hartford Daily Courant*, June 14, 1877, 2. Gen. Ben Butler was one of the true scoundrels of the American Civil War. Arrogant, conceited, cowardly, treacherous and artfully political, Butler seems to have alienated everyone he ever met, though after the war, the people of Massachusetts kept returning him to office as if he were a statesman. Will wonders never cease?

[428] "Mrs. Sherman's Adventures," *Hartford Daily Courant*, June 7, 1877, 2.

[429] Ibid.; "Mrs. Sherman's Trials," *New York Times*, June 7, 1877, 5.

[430] Ibid.

[431] *Report of the Directors of the State Prison*, 1876-77-78, 8-10.

[432] "Rhode Island Items," *Hartford Daily Courant*, June 15, 1877, 3.

[433] "Lydia Sherman: The Wickedest Woman Dead," *Hartford Daily Courant*, May 17, 1878, 2

[434] Ibid. Lydia Sherman: The Wickedest..." *Hartford Daily Courant*, May 17, 1878, 2.; "Lydia Sherman: The Last Years of Her Sickness" *Hartford Daily Courant*, May 18, 1878, 1.

[435] "Lydia Sherman: The Last Years of Her Sickness" *Hartford Daily Courant*, May 18, 1878, 1.

[436] Ibid.

[437] "Confession of Lydia Sherman," *New York Herald*, January 13, 1873, 3.

[438] Ibid.

[439] Wethersfield Vital Records, 1635-1919, Reel #4931 & Reel #4932, CSL, Hartford.

[440] "Lydia Sherman," *Hartford Daily Courant*, May 18, 1878, 1.; Today, Lydia Sherman's unmarked grave sits in the eastern shadow of the tall Veterans Memorial Monument, abutting the easternmost driveway at the cemetery.

BIBLIOGRAPHY

Atlas of the Twelfth Ward City of New York. New York: E. Robinson, 1880.

Atwater, Edward E. *History of the City of New Haven.* New York: W. W. Munsell & Co., 1887.

Beck, Henry Charlton. *Forgotten Towns of Southern New Jersey.* New Brunswick: Rutgers University Press, 1936.

Bice, Arlene S. *New Egypt and Plumsted Township.* Charlestown, SC: Arcadia Publishing, 2003.

Berkebile, Don H. (Edited by). *American Carriages, Sleighs, Sulkies and Carts.* New York: Dover Publications, 1977.

Biographical Encyclopedia of New Jersey of the Nineteenth Century. Philadelphia: Galaxy Publishing Co., 1877.

Bowlby, John. *Seperation Anxiety and Anger.* New York: Basic Books, 1973.

Burrows, Edwin G. & Wallace, Mike (1999). *Gotham: A History of New York City to 1898.* New York: Oxford University Press. 1999. pp. 838-841

Bynum, W. F. *Science and the Practice of Medicine in the Nineteenth Century.* Cambridge, UK: Cambridge University Press, 1994.

Cohen, Patricia Cline. *The Murder of Helen Jewett.* New York: Vintage, 1999.

Columbia University (compiled by). *Catalogue of Officers and Graduates of Columbia University from the Foundation of King's College in 1754.* New York: Columbia Uniersity, 1906.

Columbia University. College of Physicians and Surgeons. *Columbia University Bullitins of Information: announcement 1827/1860*. New York: Columbia Uniersity.

Conway, J. North. *The Big Policeman: The Rise and Fall of America's First, Most Ruthless, and Greatest Detective*. Guilford, CT: Lyons Press, 2010.

Ellis, Franklin. *The History of Monmouth County, New Jersey*. Philadelphia: R. T. Peck & Co., 1885.

Hafner, Arthur W. *Directory of Deceased American Physicians - 1807-1929*. Chicago: American Medical Association, 1993.

Haines, Charles Grove. *The Conflict Over the Judicial Powers in the US to 1870*. New York: Columbia University, 1909.

Hegel, Richard. *Cariages from New Haven*. New York: Archon Books, 1974.

Hewitt, Louise (comp.). *Historic Trenton*. Trenton: Smith Press, 1936.

Jones, Ann. *Women Who Kill*. New York: Holt, Rinehart & Winston. 1980.

Kingman, Bradford. *The History of North Bridgewater, Plymouth County, Massachusetts*. Published by the Bradford Kingman, 1866.

Lankevich, George L. *American Metropolis: A History of New York City*. New York: NYU Press, 1998.
Lardner, James and Reppetto, Thomas. *NYPD: A City and Its Police Force,* New York: Henry Holt & Co. 2000

Macgregor, John. *The Progress of America, from the discovery by Columbus to the year 1846*. New York: Whittaker & Co., 1847.

McPhee, John. *The Pine Barrens*. New York: Farrar, Straus & Giroux, 1967,1968.

McManus, Edgar J. *A History of Negro Slavery in New York.* Syracuse: Syracuse University Press, 1966.

Munson, Myron Andrews. *1637-1887: The Munson Record.* Printed for the Munson Association, 1896.

Murphy, Kevin. *Water For Hartford: The Story of the Hartford Water Works and the Metropolitan District Commission,* Shining Tramp Press, Wethersfield, CT., 2004 (First Wesleyan edition, 2010)

Murphy, Kevin. *Crowbar Governor: The Life and Times of Morgan Gardner Bulkeley.* Middletown, CT: Wesleyan University Press, 2011.

Nahum, Milton and Schatz, Lewis. *The Grand Jury in Connecticut.* 5 Conn. B.J. 111, 1931.

National American Society. *Americana.* American Historical Magazine, Vol. 10. University of California, 1915.

Current History. Vol. 16. New York: *New York Times, 1922..*

Novak, Robert J., Jr. (committee chairman). *Derby.* Derby, CT: Derby Historical Society, 1999.

Obituary record of the graduates of Yale University. New Haven: Yale University, 1900.

Orcutt, Samuel and Beardsley, Ambrose. *The History Of The Old Town of Derby, Connecticut, 1642-1880.* Springfield: Springfield Print Co., 1880.

Osborn, Norris Galpin. *Men of Mark in Connecticut.* Hartford: W. R. Goodspeed, 1908.

Osterweis, Rollin G. *Three Centuries of New Haven: The Tercentenary History.* New Haven: Yale University Press, 1953.

Phelps, Richard Harvey. *Newgate of Connecticut.* Hartford: American Publishing Company, 1901.

Popular Science Monthly, September 1879, Vol. 15, No. 37. New York: Bonnier Corporation, 1879.

The Poison Feind!: Life, Crimes and Conviction of Lydia Sherman . . . Philadelphia: Barclay & Co., 1873.

Report of the Directors of the State Prison, 1861-1880, Requested by the Connecticut General Assembly. New Haven: Carrington & Hotchkiss, state printers.

Richmond, Rev. J. F. *New York and Its Institutions 1609-1872. New York: E. B. Treat, 1872.*

Rockey, John L., editor. *History of New Haven County, Connecticut, Vol. 1 & Vol 2.* New York: W. W. Preston, 1892.

Rosenstone, Steven and Behr, Roy L. and Lazarus, Edward H. *Third Parties in America.* Princeton: Princeton University Press, 1996.

Rothstein, William G. *American Physicians in the Nineteenth Century: From Sects to Science.* Baltimore: Johns Hopkins University Press, 1992.

Schechter, Harold. *Fatal: The Poisonous Life of a Female Serial Killer.* New York: Pocket Books, 2007.

Sherman, Rev. Andrew. *Reminiscences of Rev. Andrew Sherman.* Americana, America Historical Magazine. Vol. 10. National American Society. University of California, 1915.

Sherman, George W. *Memorials of Lydia Whitney Sherman Who Passed On March Eighteenth, Eighteen Hundred Ninety-Eight.* Morristown, NJ: The Jerseyman Press, 1901.

Shurman-Kauflin, Deborah Dr., *The New Predator: Women Who Kill.* New York: Algora Publishing, 2000.

Smith, J. E. A. *The History of Pittsfield, Massachusetts from the year 1800 to the year 1876.* Springfield: C. W. Bowles & Co., 1876.

Smith, Mathew Hale. *Sunshine and Shadow in New York.* Hartford: J. B. Burr & Co., 1868.

School: devoted to the public school and educational interest, Vol. 7. New York: Public School News, 1895.

Simpson, Mathew, ed. *Cyclopedia of Methodism.* Chicago: Everts & Stewart. 1878.

Spalding, John Augustus, (compiled by), *Illustrated Popular Biography of Connecticut.* Hartford: Case, Lockwood & Brainard, 1891.

Spann, Edward K. *The Metropolis: New York City 1840-1857.* New York: Columbia University Press, 1981.

Smith, Chard Powers. *The Housatonic: Puritan River.* New York: Rinehart & Co., 1946

Smith, J. E. A., *The History of Pittsfield, Massachusetts From The Year 1800 To The Year 1876.* Springfield: C. W. Bryan & Co., 1876.

Starr, Paul. *The Social Transformation of American Medicine.* New York: Basic Books, 1982.

Statistics of the United States in 1860: The Eighth Census, Washington: Government Printing Office, 1866.

Stratton, Ezra M. *The World on Wheels.* New York: Benjamin Bloom, Inc. 1972.

Southwick, H. C. *Public Laws of the State of New York.* Albany, New York: 1809.

Wilson, H. (compiled by). *Trow's New York City Directory.* New York: John F. Trow, publisher.

Walker, Edwin Robert et al. A *History of Trenton: 1679-1929.* Princeton: Princeton University Press, 1929.

Washington, Erik K. *Manhattanville: Old Heart of West Harlem.* Charleston, SC: Arcadia, 2002.

Woolston, Howard Brown. *A Study of the Population of Manhattanville.* New York: AMS Press, reprinted 1968. (Columbia University Edition, 1909.)

Vronsky, Peter. *Female Serial Killers.* New York: Berkeley Books, 2007.

MAP & PHOTOGRAPHIC CREDITS

Danbury Genealogical Chart composed by the author

Chapter 1
Floor Plan of Wethersfield Prison c. 1877 – taken from the architectural drawings of Bryant and Rogers (December 1870). These Connecticut State Prison drawings are in the collection of the Connecticut State Library, Hartford, Connecticut.

Chapter 2
Map of Trenton - composed by author
Map of New Egypt area - composed by author
Rev. Van Amburgh – from *History of Hunterdon and Somerset Counties, New Jersey,* Connecticut State Library, Hartford, Connecticut

Chapter 3
Map of NYC Twelfth Ward – composed by author

Chapter 4
Dr. Louis Rodenstein – Richmond, Rev. J. F. *New York and Its Institutions 1609-1872*
Connecticut State Library, Hartford, Connecticut

Chapter 5
Map of Stratford – composed by author
Map of Coram, Huntington – composed by author
Dr. Gould Shelton – *Men of Progress,* Connecticut State Library, Hartford, Connecticut
Exemplar of Lydia's Signature – Taken from the probate records of Dennis Hurlbut, Connecticut State Library, Hartford, Connecticut

Chapter 6
Horatio Nelson Sherman – *Find A Grave,* www.findagrave.com
Map of Derby, Connecticut – composed by author
Dr. Ambrose Beardsley – from *History of Old Derby, Connecticut*
Connecticut State Library, Hartford, Connecticut

Dr. Charles Pinney – *Illustrated Popular Biography of Connecticut,* Connecticut State Library, Hartford, Connecticut
Dr. George Barker – *Popular Science Monthly,* Volume 15, September 15, 1879,
http://en.wikisource.org/wiki/Popular_Science_Monthly/Volume_15/September_1879/Biographical_Notice_of_George_F._Barker

Chapter 7
Nathan's Hall – Connecticut State Library, Hartford, Connecticut

Chapter 8
Map of New Haven, Connecticut 1872 – composed by the author
Lydia Sherman's Portrait – picture taken by Henry Cowell, April 23, 1872 - Henry Cowell's Photographic Studio, 303 Chapel St., New Haven, CT.

Chapter 9
Wethersfield Prison – drawing by the author derived from pictures at the Connecticut State Library, Hartford, Connecticut
Map of Lydia's Gravesite – composed by the author

Cover Photograph - Henry Cowell, April 23, 1872 - Henry Cowell's Photographic Studio, 303 Chapel St., New Haven, CT.

ACKNOWLEDGEMENTS

When an author chooses to write about an illiterate family, whose patriarch was born in 1790, the feasibility of the task is always in doubt. No letters or diaries exist, and information about the family survives only in census reports, public records and local newspapers. So said, Lydia Sherman's story was compelling enough to sustain me.

Of particular concern was Lydia's early life where the seeds of her sociopathy originated. Based on this, I am deeply grateful to all of the many librarians and workers at historical societies who brought forth all of the local records that I so badly needed.

In New Jersey, this includes reference librarian Kathleen O'Brien at the New Jersey State Library in Trenton, librarians Kathleen Medich and Hsien-min Chen at the New Brunswick Free Public Library.

Among the many historical societies, a tip of the hat goes out to Barbara Price of the Gloucester County Historical Society, Maureen O'Connor Leach and Kate McGuire at the Trenton Historical Society, and Dianne DiBeranda of the Camden County Historical Society.

With regard to New Jersey's municipal officials, gratitude goes out to Timothy Taylor, Burlington County Clerk in Mt. Holly, and Lainie Ramirez, Registrar of Vital Statistics in New Brunswick, New Jersey.

New Jersey Church Officials who were willing to help include

Mary L. Mild of the First Baptist Church of Trenton, who spent many hours combing through ancient church burial records in an effort to locate Samuel Danbury's grave.

Information on the controversial cleric Robert Van Amburgh came from many sources including Pastor Stephen Yon of the High Bridge Reformed Church near Lebanon, New Jersey.

At Rutgers University, my gratitude goes out to Michael Joseph and Catherine "Katie" Carey for their efforts in unearthing old records on Lydia's marriage and early married life; Also, a special note of appreciation goes to Mike Siegel at Rutgers who works so hard to maintain the Rutgers mapmaker website on the Internet.

In New Jersey, it should also be made clear that I could never have pieced together the Danbury genealogy with the generous help of Betty Nelson of California, whose grandmother was a Danbury of Trenton. Even at this late date, we have some differences of opinion regarding Samuel Danbury's two wives, but the vast majority of the genealogy meets with the approval of both of us.

Lydia's life in New York and Connecticut was laboriously pieced together with the help of many different librarians and members of historical societies. Included in this group, great thanks goes to Mike Vanderheijden at the Yale University Law Library. He was good enough to send me a PDF of the original pamphlet *The Poison Fiend*, published in 1873. This recounting of Lydia's arsenical poisonings and New Haven trial by the Philadelphia entrepreneur Erastus Elmer Barclay was my introduction to the most intimate details of Lydia's life and crimes. In a different spot on the Yale campus, a big dollop of thanks goes to George Moore at the Cushing / Whitney Medical History Library for locating the educational details of a number of doctors in this story.

Also in New Haven, an expression of gratitude goes to reference librarian Allison Botelho of the New Haven Public Library for information of the same sort.

For all of their help with the medical aspects of Lydia's story, I am deeply indebted to my Internist John Papandrea M.D. of West Hartford, CT, Pediatrician Kevin Joseph Murphy M.D. of Brockton, MA and retired Cardiac Thoracic Surgeon Bob Ikard M.D. of Nashville, TN. Bob Ikard was also good enough to read the final manuscript and make important suggestions.

Dave Kelly of Wethersfield has been the sexton of the Ancient Burying Ground in Wethersfield for decades. It was through him that some of the finer points of Lydia's imprisonment and burial in 1878 came to my attention. Many thanks.

Frank Winiarski—formerly of Wethersfield—probably knows more about the old Wethersfield Prison than anyone in Connecticut and he was very helpful in making sense of Lydia's years behind bars and her burial in the Ancient Burying Ground.

Many historical and genealogical contributions were made by the able staff of the Connecticut Historical Society—Judith Ellen Johnson, Diana McCain, Barbara Austen, Nancy Finlay, Cindy Harbeson, Sierra Dixon, Susan P. Schoelwer, Jill Davis Adams, Sharon Steinberg and Richard C. Malley. For their help, I will always be indebted.

Also at the Connecticut State Library—in the History and Genealogical Department—I want to thank Dick Roberts, Mel Smith, Carol Ganz, Carolyn Picciano, Jeannie Sherman, Bonnie Linck, Steve Rice, Kristi Finnan and Kevin Johnson.

A special word of gratitude goes to the Connecticut State Librarian Kendall F. Wiggin and Curator David Corrigan of the Museum of Connecticut History at the Connecticut State Library for the help they have extended to me in my writing career.

This, I'm afraid, is only a representative collection of the people who contributed to *Lydia Sherman: American Borgia*. For those I may have inadvertently failed to mention by name, rest assured that this book would never have come together without your help. You have my thanks.

INDEX

Albany Medical College, 132
Aldrich-Mees lines, 66
American Institute of Homeopathy, 80
American Medical Association, 80, 130
Ancient Burying Ground, 12, 211
Annandale, New Jersey, 40
arsenic
    properties, 66
    history, 67-70
    tests for, 66-68, 133
Augusta Chronicle, 206
Baker, Scott, 137, 156
Barclay, Erastus Elmer, 204
Barker, Dr. George, 131-139, 153-155, 163, 173-192
Barnum, P.T., 126
Beardsley, Dr. Ambrose, 98, 116-121, 128-137, 147-157, 168-170, 172-175, 184-186, 190, 220
Bennett, James Gordon, 14, 52
Berkshire Medical Institute, 117-118
Birmingham (Derby)
    History, 105
    Cemetery, 137, 156
Blackman, Selah, 96, 100, 137-138, 156
Blackwell's Island, 70
Blakeman, Sheriff Henry, 135-143, 156, 158-161
Bloomingdale Insane Asylum, 56, 70
Borgia, 17

Borgia, Lucrezia, 69

Bowlby, John, 28-29

Brewster & Company, 43

Bridgewater, Massachusetts, 104-105, 115, 217

Burlington, New Jersey, 25, 116, 139

Bushnell Park, 13

Butler, John, 44-45, 57

Church, Dr. Samuel, 97

Civil War, 51, 54, 60, 64, 68, 79, 83, 84, 109-112, 137, 146, 204

Clayton, John, 12, 30, 213

Clayton, Paul (Clayton Park), 35

Clayton, Widow J., 25, 29

Cochran, James, 85

Colt Patent Fire-Arms, 22

Colt, Samuel, 109

Columbia College of Physicians and Surgeons, 69, 73, 97

Connecticut State Prison, (Wethersfield prison), 13, 17-18, 131, 197, 200-202, 209

Coram, 87-102, 111-114, 136-137, 169

Coram Cemetery, 100, 137

Cowell, Henry, 185-186

Curtis, James Langdon, 85-86

Curtis, Maria Fairweather, 85-90, 129

Danbury & Pasco, 36

Danbury clan, 11

Danbury, Ellsworth, 35-36, 41, 167

 Mary (wife), 35

Danbury, John, 36, 40, 114, 167, 193

Danbury, Joseph, 36-37, 167, 170, 193

255

Danbury, Samuel, 24-28, 43
  birth, 24
  butcher, 24
  market stall, 25-27
  marriages, 24-25
Danbury, Mary (Ruckel), 24
Danbury, Mary (Rockhill), 24-25
Day, Benjamin, 14
Domestic Medicine, 35
Dorsey, Henry, 19
Downes, William, 180
Dutton, Dr. Thomas, 120-121, 152
Edmonds, Jacob, 41
Elliott, Dr. Augustus, 73-76
Fair, Laura, 16
Fairchild, John, 87-89
Faraday, Michael, 66
FBI, 11, 195
First Church, Wethersfield, 12, 202
Fleet, Dr. Francis, 80-81
Flexner Report, 81-82
Ford, William, 179
Fordham, New York, 39
Fort, Dr. George, 33-34
Foster, Pros. Atty. Eleazer, 145, 156, 163, 166, 169, 177, 184-185, 188-192
Fowler's Solution, 69
Gardner, Atty. Samuel, 142, 146, 156, 166, 174, 186, 190-194
Gilbert, Abijah, 135-139, 146, 148

Glatman, Harvey Murray, 11
grave disinterment, 137-138
Green, Rev. William, 203
Hall, Henry, 82, 85
Hartford & Wethersfield Horse Railroad, 22
Hartford Courant, 13
Harvard Medical College, 128, 130,
Hayden, Dan, 22
Herbert, D.A. Charles, 140
Hewes, Warden E.B., 17, 19, 207-211
Hewes, Josephine, 23
High Bridge, New Jersey, 39
Hornerstown, 28-34, 205
Howe, Dr. John, 104-105
Hubbard, Lewis, 150, 175, 187-189
Hubbard, Mary, 119, 123, 127-129, 150, 187, 189
Hurlbut, Dennis, 87-113, 122, 136-142, 154-171, 181, 189, 194-195
    Almira (wife), 87, 90, 92, 100
    cider, 95-96
    death of, 98
    first meets Lydia, 89
    proposes marriage, 90
    shows Lydia farm, 90
    shad fishing, 93-94
    will, 95
Jackson, Dr. George, 60-73
Jacksonville, N.J. (*see* Lebanon)
Jewell, Gov. Marshall, 140
Jewett, Helen (Dorcas Doyen), 15

Jones, Mary, 110-122, 131, 144-145, 148, 153, 157-158, 183-184

Lafarge, Charles, 68-69

Lafarge, Madame, 68-69

Lebanon, New Jersey, 38

Lonely Hearts Killer, 11

King, Governor John A., 46

Marsh, James, 66-68

Maxon, John, 84-85

Mellor, Joseph, 66

Methodist Church, 32, 35, 41, 106, 110, 210-211

Middletown Hospital, 18

Minor, George, 20

Mitchell, U.S. Marshal (Detective) John, 139-141

Mitchell, Dr. John, 53-54

Morton, Rev. William, 90

Murphy, Dr. Robert D., 212

Nafey, Ann, 18, 36, 76, 138-140, 167, 170, 193, 205

Nafey, John, 167, 193

Nathan's Hall, 136, 144-145, 155, 160

New Brunswick, New Jersey, 16, 29, 35-43, 114, 138-140, 158, 167, 205

New Brunswick Theological Seminary, 37-38

New Egypt area, 12, 29, 33

New Haven County jail, 11, 16, 162, 170, 186, 193-197

New Haven Superior Court, 9, 16, 164

New Jersey Express Company, 37

New York

    Bronx (Goatsville), 47-48

    Castle Garden, 45

    Draft Riots, 47, 54

    First Presbyterian Church, 51, 64

    Five-Points, 45, 47

    Harlem, 48-49, 51, 59-60, 76-77

    Manhattan (water) Co., 45

    Manhattanville, 48-83

    Metropolitan Police, 47-84

    Municipal Police, 46-47

    Tenderloin, 47

New Haven Palladium, 198-202

New York Herald, 14, 15, 52-53, 195

New York Times, 23, 62-63, 99, 208

New York World, 143

Oliver, Chief Charles, 138-140

Orfila, John Bonaventure, 68

Owens, William, 41

Paris Green, 68, 171

Park Church, Hartford, 13

Park, Judge John, 164, 170, 190, 192-193

Parker, Dr. Willard, 129-130

Payson, Rev. Edward, 51, 77, 80, 82

Peck, George, 139, 155, 159, 176, 179, 182, 186

Perkins, Mrs. Amelia, 105, 109

Physicians (nineteenth century)

    autopsies, dislike of, 64

    branches of medicine, 53-54

    burial permits, 64

    code of ethics, 81-83

    education, 61-64

    livelihood, 33-35, 54, 60, 82-83

licensing, 74-75

Pine Barrens, 12, 30, 32

Pinney, Dr. Charles, 98, 116, 128-138, 149-154, 172-174, 183

Pinney, Dr. Royal Watson, 129

Platt, Justice Seabury, 135-162

Poison Fiend!, The, 194, 204

Primitive Physic, 35

Queen Poisoner, 11, 139

Randolph, Governor Theodore, (N.J.), 140

Ressler, Robert, 11

Robinson, Richard, 15

Rodenstein, Dr. Louis, 76-82

Roxbury, Connecticut, 92

Rutgers (Queens College), 37-38

saleratus, 95-96

Sanford, Judge David, 11, 13, 164-196

San Quentin, 11

Scheele, Carl, 68

Schwackhamer, Conrad, 52

Schieffelin, Jacob, 49

Sears, Mrs. Ellery, 205, 209

Shelton, Dr. Gould, 98, 130-138, 154, 173-174, 180, 187

Shelton Tack and Nail, 93, 105, 107, 109, 124

Sherman, Aaron Simmons, 103-105, 109

Sherman, Rev. Andrew, 104, 109-110, 122, 145, 181

Sherman, George, 122-123, 145, 180-182, 186

Sherman, Horatio Nelson
  Wife (1), Mary Snow Jones Sherman, 105-109
    death of, 110

Children:
- Nelson, Jr. (Nellie), 105, 116-157, 172-175
- Mary Clarabel, 109
- Ada (Addie), 109-158, 169, 174, 183
- Ann Perkins, 109
- Nathaniel Nye (Nattie), 109-131, 139, 148, 157, 175, 183, 189, 191
- Frank Henry (Frankie), 109-137, 148-149, 153-158, 169,
- autopsy on Nelson, 130
- birth, 102
- buys Minerva St. house, 110
- death of, 129
- New Haven spree, 124-125
- parentage, 102-103
- patents, 109
- salary, 109, 112

Wife (2), Lydia Danbury Struck Hurlbut Sherman

Sherman, Lydia Danbury

Children:
- Lydia, 44, 74-79
- John Wesley, 45,
- George Whitfield, 45, 75-76
- Ann Eliza, 46, 76-77
- Josephine, 46, 52
- Martha Ann, 46, 74-75
- Edward W., 46, 75

and her father, 28-29

confession, 11-12, 194-203, 213-218 (Appendix A)

domestic service, 37-40

death of, 210

looks, 13-14

lying, 41

meets Dennis Hurlbut, 89

meets Edward Struck, 42

meets H. N. Sherman, 111

nursing work, 76

origin of psychosis, 28-30, 38-41

poisoned by cider, 96-98

prison escape, 13-24, 205-208

Sherman, Lydia Whitney O'Brien

illegitimate birth, 103

trial testimony, 174-176

visiting in Derby, 109, 130

wedding party, 105

Shurman-Kauflin, Dr. Deborah, 196

Springfield, Massachusetts, 22, 205

St. James Episcopal Church, 106, 110, 119, 122, 131, 188

Struck, Cornelius, 43-71

Struck, Edward, 12, 43-71, 83

Sun, The (N.Y.), 14, 141, 142

Tammany Hall, 45

Taylor, George & Henry, 112, 118

Thomas, William, 93, 98, 101, 111

Thompson, Gertrude, 74, 78, 85

Thompson, William, 75, 80

Torrance, Atty. David, 146, 166, 184

Townsend, Rosina, 15

Trenton, New Jersey, 12-23

Trinity Cemetery, 12, 64, 75-78, 82

Tweed, William Marcy, 45

Union Station, Hartford, 13, 22

Union Station, New Haven, 13, 115

University of Pennsylvania, 33, 78

Valley Railroad, 22

Van Amburgh, Rev. Robert, 37-40

Margaret (wife), 37

Waldron, Detective Frederic, 206

Waterhouse, Sarah, 13-23, 203-209

Watrous, Atty. George, 142-149, 162, 166-196

Wakelee, Gideon, 96, 100-101, 137-138, 156

Webster, Warden Charles, 12, 162, 186, 195-201

Webster, Jennette, 12, 162, 195-201

Wesley, John, 35

witches, 194

Wood, Mayor Fernando, 46

Wooding, Rev. Mr. George, 209-212

Wooster, Col. William, 135-160, 166, 184, 190-191

Yale Medical College, 121, 130-132, 153, 173

Yorkville, 43

Made in the USA
Charleston, SC
03 March 2013